Death, Immortality, and Meaning in Life

FUNDAMENTALS OF PHILOSOPHY SERIES
Series Editors
John Martin Fischer, University of California, Riverside
John Perry, Stanford University

Death, Immortality, and Meaning in Life

JOHN MARTIN FISCHER

New York   Oxford
OXFORD UNIVERSITY PRESS

Oxford University Press is a department of the University of Oxford.
It furthers the University's objective of excellence in research, scholarship,
and education by publishing worldwide. Oxford is a registered trade mark of
Oxford University Press in the UK and certain other countries.

Published in the United States of America by Oxford University Press
198 Madison Avenue, New York, NY 10016, United States of America.

For titles covered by Section 112 of the US Higher Education
Opportunity Act, please visit www.oup.com/us/he for the latest
information about pricing and alternate formats.

Library of Congress Cataloging-in-Publication Data

Names: Fischer, John Martin, 1952- author.
Title: Death, immorality, and meaning in life / John Martin Fischer.
Description: Oxford ; New York : Oxford University Press, [2020] | Includes
   bibliographic references and index.
Identifiers: LCCN 2018061775 (print) | LCCN 2018053162 (ebook) |
   ISBN 9780190921149 (pbk.) | ISBN 9780190921156 (eBook)
Subjects: LCSH: Death. | Immortality (Philosophy) | Near-death experiences.
Classification: LCC BD444 .F57 2020 (ebook) | LCC BD444 (print) |
   DDC 128/.5—dc23
LC record available at https://lccn.loc.gov/2018061775

9 8 7 6 5 4 3 2 1
Printed by Sheridan Books, Inc., United States of America

CONTENTS

....

ACKNOWLEDGMENTS

This book would never have been written without two very generous grants from the John Templeton Foundation: "The Science, Theology, and Philosophy of Immortality" ("The Immortality Project") and "Immortality and Meaningfulness in Life." The views presented here are not necessarily those of the foundation. I am deeply grateful for this support, and for all the encouragement and assistance provided by Michael Murray, John Churchill, and Alex Arnold of the Templeton Foundation.

I thank the Immortality Project Team at UC Riverside for everything they did to make it a success: Benjamin Mitchell-Yellin, Jason Gray, Heinrik Hellwig, and Jayne Gales. Their contributions—both intellectual and administrative—were tremendous.

Many people have given detailed and helpful comments on drafts of some or all of the chapters: David Beglin, Michael Cholbi, Rebecca Copenhaver, Mary Ann Cutter, Taylor Cyr, Neil Feit, Cody Gilmore, Pierre Keller, Aaron Harper, David Hershenov, Andrew Law, Steven Luper, Todd May, Ayoob Shahmoradi, and Mark Wrathall. I am very thankful to all of them. I am particularly grateful to John Perry, Aaron Preston, and Travis Timmerman for especially detailed comments. I am indebted to James Baillie for helpful conversations about the book, as well as comments. Michael Cholbi has provided welcome guidance about resources and literature related to the issues treated in this book.

Robert Miller of Oxford University Press has supported this project, as well as the series in which it appears (*Fundamentals of Philosophy*), from the beginning. I am also grateful to Sydney Keen of OUP for her assistance in the production of the book.

For thirty-five years I discussed these issues, especially the question of why death is bad, with Anthony L. Brueckner. We had many conversations on this and related topics while we were in the philosophy department at Yale University, and we published a series of articles on these issues. I always learned from him and, at the same time, had fun. In a review in *The New Yorker* of a recent novel by Bill Clinton and James Patterson, the reviewer wrote, "Writing, like dying, is one of those things that should be done alone or not at all." Wrong on both counts!

The love of my wife, Tina, and two children, Ari and Zoe, continues to inspire me and fill me with awe and gratitude.

One sunny afternoon, when he wasn't feeling well, Jobs sat in the garden behind his house and reflected on death. He talked about his experiences in India almost four decades earlier, his study of Buddhism, and his views on reincarnation and spiritual transcendence. "I'm about fifty-fifty in believing in God," he said. "For most of my life, I've felt that there must be more to our existence than meets the eye."

He admitted that, as he faced death, he might be overestimating the odds out of a desire to believe in an afterlife. "I like to think that something survives after you die," he said. "It's strange to think that you accumulate all this experience, and maybe a little wisdom, and it just goes away. So I really want to believe that something survives, that maybe your consciousness endures."

He fell silent for a very long time. "But on the other hand, perhaps it's like an on-off switch," he said. "Click! And you're gone."

Then he paused again and smiled slightly. "Maybe that's why I never liked to put on-off switches on Apple devices."

—WALTER ISAACSON, *Steve Jobs*

Death, Immortality, and Meaning in Life

....

CHAPTER 1

Meaning in Life

In my writings I advocated, what to me was the only truth, that it was necessary to live in such a way as to derive the greatest comfort for oneself and one's family.

Thus I proceeded to live, but five years ago something very strange began to happen with me: I was overcome by minutes at first of perplexity and then of an arrest of life, as though I did not know how to live or what to do, and I lost myself and was dejected. But time passed and I continued to live as before. Then those minutes of perplexity were repeated oftener and oftener. . . . These arrests of life found their expression in ever the same questions: "Why? Well, and then?"

—LEO TOLSTOY,
My Confession (Chapter Two)

....

Introduction

What is the meaning of life? Many people think of philosophers as being preoccupied with this question (when they are not worrying about an unnoticed tree falling in the forest!). The question is both enticing and off-putting. Despite the importance for human beings of figuring out "what it's all about," the question might seem presumptuous, or at least a waste of time. Who could ever identify—in an uncontroversial or even very plausible way—the meaning of life? Why think there is one "meaning" of all human life? What features make our lives more (or less) meaningful? Who's to say?

Here's a story related by Robert Nozick:

A person travels for many days to the Himalayas to seek the word of an Indian holy man meditating in an isolated cave. Tired from his

journey, but eager and expectant that his quest is about to reach ful-
fillment, he asks the sage, "What is the meaning of life?" After a long
pause, the sage opens his eyes and says, "Life is a fountain." "What
do you mean, life is a fountain?" barks the questioner. "I have just
traveled thousands of miles to hear your words, and all you have to tell
me is that? That's ridiculous." The sage then looks up from the floor of
the cave and says, "You mean it's not a fountain?" In a variant of the
story, he replies, "So it's not a fountain."[1]

A deference to "authority" figures does not seem called for in trying to
figure out the meaning of life. No one—no guru—has privileged access
to the meaning of life. Any answer to the question of the meaning of life
borders on the trite. And what exactly are we asking about?

The question of the meaning of life seems to be a question about the
point or purpose of human life in general. Although this is a relatively
clear question, answering it is not so simple, especially if one doesn't
assume the existence of a god who created us with certain intentions. If
God created us, He could have given us a purpose, and the meaning of
life could then be fulfilling our purpose. (We'll return to this idea later.)
But if we do not believe in God, how could we specify the purpose of
human life in general?

To avoid these problems, many philosophers have sidestepped the
question of the meaning of life. Instead, they have tackled a related,
but at least a bit less mysterious and daunting, issue: meaning *in* life or
meaningfulness in life. When people ask about the meaning *of* life, they
are not typically wondering about the purpose of human life in general.
Rather, they are asking about meaning (or meaningfulness) *in* human
life. What makes an individual's life meaningful? What features make a
human life more (or less) meaningful?[2]

Before we try out some ideas about meaning in life, we should
"locate" this kind of meaning in relation to other important goals
we have: happiness and morality. We certainly want to be happy. But

---

1. Robert Nozick, *Philosophical Explanations* (Cambridge, MA: Harvard University
Press [Belknap], 1981): 157.

2. For this way of characterizing the distinction between "meaning of life" and
"meaning in life," see Susan Wolf, "The Meanings of Lives," in John Perry, Michael
Bratman, and John Martin Fischer, eds., *Introduction to Philosophy: Classical and
Contemporary Readings*, 4th ed. (New York: Oxford University Press, 2007): 62–74. The
essay also appears in all subsequent issues of Perry/Bratman/Fischer.

meaningfulness is not the same as happiness, although we would expect a connection between them. If one's life is meaningful, then probably the individual would be happy. But we can certainly imagine people with meaningful lives—scientists, artists, poets, philosophers, and so on—who struggle in their fields and are thus not very happy (if they are happy at all). Or we can consider people whose careers are deeply engaging and meaningful, but whose personal lives are troubled and who are thus not very happy. The recent suicides of the enormously successful fashion designer Kate Spade and the famous chef and television personality Anthony Bourdain illustrate this point.

We can also imagine a very happy individual whose happiness comes from what we would consider trivial or superficial activities—maybe a life devoted to crossword puzzles, Sudoku, or counting the bulbs in the banks of lights at Dodger Stadium. We shouldn't be elitist, and perhaps these lives are *to some degree* meaningful. But meaning in life is *not* the same as happiness. One can have a very happy life that is only somewhat meaningful, and a very meaningful life that is not very happy.

Additionally, a meaningful life need not be a *moral* life. Presumably a mafia boss could have a meaningful life that is highly immoral. Tyrants such as Stalin or Hitler had meaningful lives, even though they were morally awful. Here I am relying on intuitive judgments about meaning in life; we will explore more carefully candidates for meaning-conferring features soon. Stalin seemed to have a meaningful life: he had a circle of associates and friends, a family, left a big "mark" on history, affected many people, and so forth. Meaningful, but morally monstrous: he ordered the murder of millions of innocent people. Same with Hitler.

Similarly, a moral life could fail to meet intuitive ideas about meaningfulness in life. The devotee of Sudoku could be kind, courteous, and respectful of others' rights and feelings, but his morality does not make up for the triviality of his life's activities. The Dodger Stadium bulb counter might be the nicest guy in the world, helping downtown LA's many homeless people (when not counting light-bulbs). Morality is *not* the same thing as meaning in life. Morality, meaning, and happiness may often go together; but they can pull apart, and they are distinct concepts.

We have a pretty good grasp of the concepts of morality and happiness, even if we disagree on what specifically makes someone moral or happy. We don't have such an understanding of the idea of meaning in life (or meaningfulness in life). So far we have said it is a value or goal—something that generates reasons for action—that is different from happiness and morality. It is not just a value; it is a "final" value, in the sense that we do not value or seek it in part because it will lead to (or be part of) something else. Rather, we seek it for itself. Meaningfulness is a final good; some might use the term "intrinsic" good or value.

We also think of meaningfulness as "important" or "deep." It is not a superficial or trivial kind of value. Some argue that the reasons for action that come from meaning in life are not subordinate to the reasons of happiness or even morality. Thus, we can understand how someone who pursues a meaningful life is not necessarily irrational in doing so, even while sacrificing (to some extent) happiness or morality. As Susan Wolf puts it:

> Recognizing that meaning is something desirable in life . . . means recognizing that there is more to life than either of these categories [happiness or morality], even taken together, suggests. This means, among other things, that it need not be irrational to choose to spend one's time doing something that neither maximizes one's own good nor is morally best.[3]

Another feature of meaningfulness in life is that it admits of degrees—it is not all or nothing. This is similar to happiness (and perhaps also to morality). Some human lives are more meaningful than others, and some elements add more meaning than others. So we can think of meaning in life as an important, deep, final good or value that is not the same as happiness or morality, and that admits of degrees.[4] Even this characterization is not fully adequate, but we will get a clearer picture of meaning in life when we canvass suggestions for what gives life meaning. For now our sketch of the account of meaning is enough to grasp the relevant notion and to discuss more of its features, and its relationship to other concepts (such as death and immortality).

---

3. Susan Wolf, *Meaning in Life and Why It Matters* (Princeton, NJ: Princeton University Press, 2010): 49.

4. Thaddeus Metz, "The Meaning of Life," in the *Stanford Encyclopedia of Philosophy*. Also, see his very comprehensive and helpful treatment in *Meaning in Life* (Oxford: Oxford University Press, 2013).

Meaning in Life

What makes a life meaningful? We can start by noting some necessary conditions of a meaningful life; whatever else is part of a meaningful life, these features must be present. First, a meaningful life is not just a matter of pleasant internal states—pleasures or other experiences. It is in part a matter of how we are *connected* to the external world.

To illustrate this point, let's return to Robert Nozick and consider his famous "experience machine":

> Suppose there were an experience machine that would give you any experience you desired. Superduper neurophysiologists could stimulate your brain so that you would think and feel you were writing a great novel, or making a friend, or reading an interesting book. All the time you would be floating in a tank, with electrodes attached to your brain. Should you plug into this machine for life, preprogramming your life's experiences? If you are worried about missing out on desirable experiences, we can suppose that business enterprises have researched thoroughly the lives of many others. You can pick and choose from their library or smorgasbord of such experiences, selecting your life's experiences for, say, the next two years. After two years have passed, you will have ten minutes or ten hours out of the tank, to select the experiences of your *next* two years. Of course, while in the tank you won't know that you're there; you'll think it's all actually happening.[5]

This and many other examples show that we don't just care about our internal states (experiences), but also about how we are connected with external reality. We don't want to be fundamentally mistaken about reality, living in our own bubbles (pleasant or engaging as they may be). Pleasant experiences (at least *some*) are surely part of a meaningful life, but, just as surely, they are not the *only* feature of a meaningful life. We care about having *true* beliefs about important matters. It is hard to see how an individual who is mistaken about all (or most) of the central features of his life (as he experiences it) could have a meaningful life.

We can be wrong about *some* things, and maybe this is even a good thing! We might think that our romantic partner believes we are a bit better-looking, or more interesting, than he or she actually does!

---

5. Robert Nozick, *Anarchy, State, and Utopia* (New York: Basic Books, 1974): 42–43.

(Research shows that happy people tend to have unduly optimistic beliefs about such matters, and that depressed people tend to be right.) But we would be deeply disturbed if we were deluded about the fidelity and love of our partner, the respect of our friends and colleagues, and so forth. As Nozick writes, no one would want a life connected to the experience machine for long stretches; nor would we want it for our children. We don't want just to *seem* to see a beautiful sunset or a majestic mountain at dawn; we care about *actually* seeing them. We don't just want to *seem* to have a loving family; we care about *actually* having one.

So being significantly deluded or out of touch with reality threatens (or eliminates) meaningfulness. We don't want to be "in our own worlds." Further, we don't want to be puppets. In the film *Stranger Than Fiction*, the protagonist (played by Will Ferrell) is a character in a novel, and all of his actions are controlled ("written") by the author (not him). His story is not really his own; he is just playing a part in a narrative written by someone else. If we discovered we were relevantly similar to Will Ferrell in this film, we would *not* think our lives (thus far) were meaningful. We would be mere puppets.

In order for our lives to be meaningful, we need to write our own stories. We cannot be under the control of others, or nature. It is only by having free will that we are capable of writing *our own* stories—our own narratives. Exactly how to understand free will (in the sense required for writing our own story and thus having a meaningful life) is controversial. Intuitively, being manipulated or controlled by someone else would rule out free will. Similarly, being causally determined (by external factors and the laws of nature) would at least *appear* to threaten free will. There are, however, disagreements about these issues. We need not solve—or even address—them here. For our purposes it suffices to note that a meaningful life requires free will (understood in an intuitive sense, even if we can't fully analyze it).[6]

The reason why we wouldn't want to be hooked up (involuntarily and for our whole lives) to the experience machine is that we want actually to *live our lives*, to be active in our engagement with life's challenges and joys. We don't just want a rich set of experiences—we want to be connected to reality in the way we think we are. We don't just want to

---

6. For a helpful introduction to these issues, see Robert Kane's contribution to the series (*Fundamentals of Philosophy*) in which the book you are currently reading is published: *A Contemporary Introduction to Free Will* (New York: Oxford University Press, 2005).

"behave"; we want to *act freely*. We express our active powers by writing our stories through free will.

The thought that meaning in life is not compatible with passivity is captured in this passage from Susan Wolf:

> For me the idea of a meaningless life is most clearly and effectively embodied in the image of a person who spends day after day, or night after night, in front of a television set, drinking beer and watching situation comedies. Not that I have anything against television or beer. Still the image, understood as an image of a person whose life is lived in hazy passivity, a life lived at a not unpleasant level of consciousness, but unconnected to anyone or anything, going nowhere, achieving nothing—is, I submit, as strong an image of a meaningless life as there can be. Call this case The Blob.[7]

We have begun by sketching two constraints on a meaningful life: the individual must not be significantly deluded (detached from reality), and he must not be a puppet. Meaningfulness requires active and robust engagement with reality; the Blob is relatively isolated and passive, and thus his life gets a low meaningfulness score. It is "going nowhere."[8]

An individual capable of living a meaningful life must be able to write her own story. Indeed, I suggest that the "meaning" of an individual's life (as opposed to human life in general) just *is* her story. Even if one were to accept this, there would still be the question: What elements of our stories make them more *meaningful* (or make them describe more meaningful lives)? For a human being who is in touch with reality and writes her story via free will, what makes her life more meaningful? The content of the individual's story (her narrative) is the meaning of her life, but what makes this content depict a more meaningful life?

Wolf's sketch of the Blob suggests some elements of the content of lives that many would judge meaningful. A meaningful life is not excessively repetitive or totally (or largely) passive. It involves connections with others—at least some deep connections. These are typically with our family and close friends, but they can also be with colleagues and

---

7. Wolf, "The Meanings of Lives," 839.

8. The 1988 horror film *The Blob*, a remake of the 1958 cult classic with the same name, depicted a more active blob, who (which?) threatens the citizens of (fictional) Arborville, California. Two teenagers try to protect their homes from what is described as "a gelatinous alien life-form that engulfs everything it touches." One review called it "an unnecessary, if gooey, remake." *Beware the Blob* is the 1972 sequel.

associates. A meaningful life involves engagement with activities that are directed toward accomplishments.[9] Some have thought that meaning is enhanced by "leaving a mark" on the world—a lasting product of one's efforts, such as a book or a building or a song or a poem or . . . Sometimes people hold that a meaningful life requires being in touch with something "greater than oneself." Note that these features are simply ideas about meaning-conferring features that are often put forth, but I do not claim that they (or any subset of them) capture the ultimate truth about meaning in life. We should simply keep them in mind as we explore meaningfulness further.[10]

A Religious Approach

One of the most influential ideas about meaning-conferring elements in life refers to God's purpose for human beings. On this view, a meaningful life is fulfilling God's purpose for us. In an influential book, the minister Rick Warren touts the "purpose-driven life."[11] Fulfilling a purpose is important in life; we often flounder and feel that our lives have lost meaning when we have no purpose (perhaps because of retirement or one's children leaving home or various sorts of life changes).

Note that our lives would not get meaning from fulfilling *any old purpose*, even one set by a "higher" or more powerful being. Suppose that superintelligent and powerful extraterrestrials colonized Earth and deemed it the purpose of human life to be eaten (at a "ripe" old age) by them. Or they thought of our purpose as being their toys or playthings, and so forth. Fulfilling these purposes would not make our lives meaningful.[12]

Rick Warren's idea is that meaningfulness comes from fulfilling *God's* purpose for us. This purpose is set by a *perfect* being, and such a being would not specify absurd purposes, such as being eaten or

---

9. For an interesting discussion and some *caveats*, see Kieran Setiya, *Midlife* (Princeton, NJ: Princeton University Press, 2017).

10. For more suggestions, see Nozick, *Philosophical Explanations*, 571–600. Also see Metz, *Meaning in Life*.

11. Rick Warren, *The Purpose Driven Life: What on Earth Am I Here For?* (Grand Rapids, MI: Zondervan, 2013 [expanded version; originally published in 2002]). Of course, Warren is not the only person to have advocated a purpose-driven life, and specifically from the religious perspective, but his book has been influential among contemporary Christians (and the general public)

12. See Nozick, *Philosophical Explorations*, 586.

being playthings. Also, this crystallizes the idea of being in contact with something greater than oneself: God and His purpose for us. Warren's approach combines two powerful elements: the importance of having purposes, and the value of a relationship with God. A problem with this view is that it presupposes the existence of God. Many will not accept this sort of religious view, and thus will not find the view about meaning in human life compelling.

Another problem, even for those who accept the religious perspective, is to figure out what God's purpose for you really is. Warren formulates these purposes very broadly. The most pertinent to our discussion here is to "find your mission" (as specified by God). But how do you do this? Is it the same for each human being? If so, then presumably this purpose would have to be specified so broadly that it would be of dubious value in guiding us. Or is it different for each person? If so, how would you know what it is? And if God were to know in advance what your mission or purpose is, how could you have free will in setting your own goals? Don't we presuppose that our path in life is not fixed in advance and known by an all-knowing and all-powerful being?

It will be prudent to explore conceptions of meaning in human life that do not require a belief in a perfect being. In the end, some might retain the view that meaning in life is fulfilling God's purpose for us, but even someone who is inclined toward this view will benefit from considering other ideas.[13] Clearly, those who do not accept classical monotheism will need to look elsewhere for meaning in life.

A Secular Approach: Our Projects

Perhaps we shouldn't look to purposes that come from outside us, even from "higher" beings. As free creatures, we can give ourselves our own purposes—we can set goals for ourselves and undertake projects. Surely the meaningfulness of our lives is bound up with certain (typically) long-term goals we care especially about: our projects. We can distinguish between two important kinds of assessment of projects: "subjective" and "objective." Both play an important role in evaluating meaningfulness in human life.

---

13. For a nice development of the religious approach, see Stewart Goetz, *The Purpose of Life: A Theistic Perspective* (New York: Continuum, 2012). I have also pointed to other religious literature on meaning in life in "Suggestions for Further Reading" at the end of this chapter.

The Subjective Part: Passion. First, the subjective aspect. Sometimes we are relatively indifferent to an activity. We are compelled to do it, or have an obligation to do it, but we don't really care about it in any significant way. Unless we are very depressed, we get excited about other activities. We are passionate about these projects—we really care about them. When we are asking for guidance in enhancing meaning in our lives, or we are attending a college graduation, we are often told, "Find your passion." Whatever exactly this means, the projects about which we are passionate help to give meaning to our lives.

Let's pause briefly to consider the slogan, "Find your passion." It seems perfectly clear, until one thinks about it. Rebecca Copenhaver reflects:

> Let's begin with the imperative portion of this phrase, "Find," in Find Your Passion. It suggests that this is something you can set out to do, something you can put on a To Do List. Wednesday: do laundry, find passion. This is only a little bit funny, though, because I have students in my office every year who have been seriously misled by this piece of advice. Consciously or unconsciously, many students are under the impression that first you find your passion, then you pursue it. But this gets things exactly the wrong way round. You don't find a passion by setting out—in advance—to find it, and then learn it. Passion finds you, you don't find it. And it finds you only after a lot of hard work, most of which you will not be passionate about.[14]

When finding your passion, it is not as though you mentally survey all your interests and somehow identify the one that is "your passion." Why suppose there is just one? And how would you identify it? (This problem is parallel to the challenge of figuring out your "mission" discussed earlier. "Find your passion!" is like "Find your purpose!" or "Find your mission!") You could imagine thinking about all your desires for activities and grading them based on their *intensity*; the most intense desire points to one's passion. But this presupposes that one's passion is already "out there," or perhaps "in here," ready to be identified or "discovered"—an implausible picture of how this all works.

A more accurate way to think about finding your passion is that you "try things on for size." You are intrigued by certain activities, and try

---

14. Rebecca Copenhaver, Convocation Address, "Find Your Passion," Lewis & Clark College, August 29, 2013.

them. Perhaps you are further intrigued, and you explore more. New avenues open up, new activities, new relationships. It may be that you decide to go in a very different direction from your original path. Or it may be that these early "experiments" in life do indeed direct you toward your passion on a straight line. The important point is that your passion is not already determinate—just waiting to be "found," like a colorful Easter egg. In a way, you *create* your passion; you don't discover it. It is a bit like an arranged marriage. As Copenhaver goes on to say, "Passion is not the *cause* of work, it's the *effect* of it. The work comes first. It always does."[15]

A scientist may be passionate about finding a cure to a terrible disease, or discovering "cleaner" forms of energy, or finding life on other planets, or . . . An individual may be passionate about pursuing social justice, helping to save our beautiful planet, running marathons, developing her chess game, deepening a relationship, and so on. A religious person might be passionate about prayer, helping the poor, enlightening others in a way that elevates them, and so forth. Among other things that give richness to her life, an atheist might care deeply about exposing the hypocrisy of some religious people, and the truth that there is no God (in her view). These—and so many other—projects can be compelling and help to "define" a person. They give life a specific meaning and make it meaningful.

It is hard to imagine a meaningful life without passion and engagement in projects one cares about. These projects need not be "grand," such as figuring out the origins of the universe or saving the planet. They can involve loving one's family and being supportive of friends, reading books by one's favorite author, following politics, enjoying mystery novels, watching films, rooting for one's hometown sports teams, or watching the sun rise over the mountains every morning. Active engagement in activities one cares about is central to living a meaningful life.

Reflect on an individual forced to become a physician because that's what her parents wanted for her. She might deem her work worthwhile, and she might do a good job. Still, she is bored and alienated, feeling that she is not expressing something important about herself.

---

15. Paul A. O'Keefe, Carol S. Dweck, and Gregory M. Walton argue that there is evidence in their empirical studies that "Find your passion!" is not a psychologically helpful motto. Better: "Develop your passion!": "Implicit Theories of Interest: Finding Your Passion or Developing It?" *Psychological Science*, first published September 6, 2018 (online).

I know attorneys who do not question the value of their work, but have no passion for it. Perhaps they feel that they are just cogs in the legal machine, and that another individual could do the job as well as they could. There are undoubtedly many physicians (and lawyers and others) who love their work, but one can see that there are some who have to find passion (some might say "meaning") elsewhere.

We need passion and happiness in our lives. Otherwise we will surely feel a kind of emptiness. We will feel that something important is missing. A life without love and caring—about people and activities—is flat and sterile. The point is not (simply) that one would be unhappy; rather, life would lack meaning, or at least an important part of meaning.

Passion is the subjective element of meaningfulness. But is that all there is? One could be passionate about an activity that most people would consider trivial or silly; engagement with these projects seems weird or bizarre. Weirdness or bizarreness doesn't necessarily rule out meaning in life, but triviality would seem to. At least, passionate engagement with a trivial or silly project would not add much to the meaning in one's life (the meaningfulness of one's life), even if it did make one happy.

Recall our bulb-counting Dodger fan. And what if someone were enthusiastically committed to counting the blades of grass in his front lawn?[16] Of course, the exact number changes over time, but let's suppose it is a smallish lawn. This project, no matter how passionate one is, does not confer much meaning. Would it be a meaningful life if that is *all* you did, or all you really cared about? Perhaps our grass counter is happy (as long as we think of "happy" as, roughly, "contented"), but we would resist the notion that his life is (very) meaningful. Susan Wolf also considers "more bizarre cases," such as a "man who lives to make handwritten copies of the text of *War and Peace*, or a woman whose world revolves around her love for her pet goldfish."[17] Are these meaningful lives, even if (say) the goldfish lives a long life (for a goldfish)? I doubt that even the most ardent animal lover would answer, "Yes."

The Intersection of Subjective and Objective. A (more) meaningful life then would seem to involve *both* a subjective and objective component of value, suitably interlocked. Meaning in life comes from passion for a

16. John Rawls, *A Theory of Justice* (Cambridge, MA: Harvard University Press [Belknap], 1971): 432.

17. Wolf, *Meaning in Life and Why It Matters*, 16.

project that is objectively valuable, at least to some degree. Susan Wolf defends this view:

> ... meaningfulness in life [comes] from loving something (or a number of things) worthy of love, and being able to engage with it (or them) in some positive way. As I have put it on other occasions, meaning in life consists in and arises from actively engaging in projects of worth. [footnote omitted] On this conception, meaning in life arises when subjective attraction meets objective attractiveness, and one is able to do something about it or with it.[18]

Wolf's view obviously requires some "objective" notion of attractiveness (value) of a project. This will render the view implausible to many. Perhaps, as Wolf suggests, the worry can be diminished by pointing out that the view need not imply "objective" standards of attractiveness in any *strong* (and implausible) sense. Objectivity here can be understood as "consensus of the relevant community"—objectivity as intersubjectivity. This idea of consensus remains both vague and difficult to apply, but it should be clear enough to be helpful.

A similar idea of consensus must be employed in other areas of philosophy, most notably ethics. In specifying goodness of an individual and rightness of action, it seems that we must invoke consensus; similarly, in specifying objective attractiveness (as it relates to meaning in life), it is hard to see how to avoid an invocation of social consensus. Wolf's proposal, then, is (roughly): meaningfulness (in a given social context) comes from the intersection of subjective attraction and objective attractiveness, where objectivity is given by the social consensus.

In rejecting the idea that subjective attraction is all there is to meaning, the view might seem to be elitist in an objectionable way. But I do not think that this is necessarily so. It may be that some will *interpret* or *specify* the social consensus in a way that is elitist, but this does not imply that the *proper* interpretation is elitist.

Even so, what counts as objectively attractive will not only differ across social groups, but it will be a matter of controversy within a group. Recall the Blob. Although many people would give it a relatively low meaningfulness score, *why* exactly is drinking beer and watching sitcoms not objectively attractive? How is the Blob different from the PBS Yuppie—the

---

18. Wolf, *Meaning in Life and Why It Matters*, 26.

individual who drinks a glass of Chardonnay and watches *Masterpiece Theatre?*[19] It can seem elitist in an objectionable way to judge the Yuppie's life (significantly) more meaningful than the Blob's. And why exactly are the activities of doing crossword puzzles and Sudokus less objectively attractive than (say) perfecting one's chess game or even working out the solution to a philosophical puzzle?[20] These questions raise difficult issues, not unlike those that arise in ethics (in specifying the right action in conflict situations), and I will have more to say about them in the section on nihilism. Nevertheless, I think that we can make these distinctions in a reasonable fashion, relative to our social consensus. More important, there *do* seem to be at least some clear cases in which the activity is not objectively attractive: counting blades of grass, sands on a beach, books in a library, transcribing *War and Peace*, and so forth.

Susan Wolf elaborates on the need to engage in objectively attractive activities (as part of a meaningful life):

> [Why does objective attractiveness matter to us?] At least part of the answer, I believe, has to do with a need, or at least an interest or concern, to see one's life as valuable in a way that can be recognized from a point of view other than one's own.[21]

This idea provides a naturalistic interpretation of the idea that meaning in human life consists in part in being in contact with, or engaged with,

---

19. "PBS" is short for Public Broadcasting System, which shows the BBC (British Broadcasting Corporation) program, *Masterpiece Theatre*.

20. Patrick Creadon's 2006 film, *Wordplay*, depicts the world of devoted (some would say "obsessed") aficionados of crossword puzzles. Here and elsewhere (including an episode of the HBO series *Real Sports with Bryant Gumbel*), the *New York Times* (and National Public Radio) "puzzle master" Will Shortz is highlighted. Crossword puzzles can be complex, difficult, and deeply engaging—unlike, for example, tic-tac-toe. It would be hard to make a case for the objective attractiveness of tic-tac-toe, but why exactly not crossword puzzles? It may take a rather quirky person to become enthralled by them, but objective attractiveness does not imply *universal* subjective attraction, or even anything close, in order to generate meaning.

In her book *Natural Causes*, Barbara Ehrenreich reports that some tout Sudoku as a way of training the mind: Barbara Ehrenreich, *Natural Causes* (New York: Hatchett Book Group, 2015). And there is a community of jigsaw puzzle fanatics depicted in the film *Puzzle*.

Of course, I have pointed to communities of passion for these activities, which doesn't in itself show that they are *objectively* attractive. But these groups at least raise the possibility of their objective attractiveness, and how they differ from (say) philosophical conundrums.

21. Wolf, *Meaning in Life and Why It Matters*, 27.

something "larger than oneself." This of course has nothing to do with physical size. (Otherwise, Sisyphus would meet this criterion by rolling the [large] rock up the hill.) Wolf's suggestion is that we understand the notion as being engaged in a project whose value can be recognized by others.

Wolf writes:

> If we are engaged in projects of independent value—fighting injustice, preserving a historic building, writing a poem—then presumably others will be able to appreciate what we are doing, too. . . . This makes us at least notionally part of a community. . . . The scorned artist or lonely inventor, the scientist whose research no one seems to approve, may be sustained by the thought that her work is good, and that the day may come when others will understand and value it.[22]

As philosophers from Aristotle to the present have emphasized, we are by our nature social creatures. One important aspect of this is that we don't want to be alone in our pursuit of value. We have a deep need to have our own judgments about meaningfulness validated from the perspective(s) of others.

Presumably the items in the standard list of meaningful activities—such as making a mark through one's own free actions, being in contact with something larger (or greater) than oneself, having rewarding relationships of love, friendship, and solidarity with colleagues, and so forth—will pass Wolf's test of loving what is worthy of love. That is, Wolf's view would have it that these activities (by and large) are located at the intersection of subjective attraction and objective attractiveness.

Grant that meaning is enhanced by activities that come from the intersection between passion and objective value. We still want to know how many such activities are required, and whether the activities are "weighted" as more or less meaningful. Perhaps the view is that meaningfulness is *enhanced* by activities that flow from the intersection. So, when this sort of activity is *added* to others, it increases the meaningfulness of the life. Also, maybe just one such activity renders a life minimally meaningful, but this is unclear; it might be that there has to be a suitable mix of them. The problems of getting a firmer grasp of the relevant kind of objectivity, and also specifying the set of activities required for a meaningful life, are challenges for Wolf's view.

---

22. Wolf, *Meaning in Life and Why It Matters*, 30.

Nihilism

Zooming In, Zooming Out, and Zooming In Between. Let's take "nihilism" to be the doctrine that there is no meaning in life. (This is nihilism about meaning; there can also be nihilism about morality, or about value of any sort.) Some philosophers are nihilists, and they are motivated by various arguments. One path to nihilism holds that there are simply no objective standards for attractiveness (in the sense relevant to meaning). Simply deferring to a social consensus is not appealing. After all, the views that go into the consensus can be produced by all sorts of contingent factors: culture, religion, history, upbringing, economic and social class, and so forth. If our pasts had been different, as they could have been, our views would be different. Further, it is just unclear that there is *any* consensus about various activities, and all of this suggests that we should call into question all judgments of relative meaningfulness. Is *Downton Abbey* (PBS) objectively better than *All in the Family* (network sitcom)? How would we establish this? A democratic vote or "poll" probably would favor *All in the Family*. Is chess or philosophy to be ranked higher than crossword puzzles on the meaning scale? How would we ever justify this?

These are difficult questions, which I'll put aside here so that we can move forward. But I will note that they would have to be answered in a comprehensive defense of meaningfulness in human life. Also, nihilists often deploy "zoom-out" arguments. One such argument asks us to zoom out *temporally*, and to recognize that our lives will be over at some point (unless we achieve immortality in the future). I can see that my life will be over, and at some point I will be forgotten. It can seem that this renders our lives meaningless, and that I can recognize this even now.

But why skip to the end? If you are reading a very good novel, you could wreck the experience by skipping to the end. So why do it? You could skip to the end of the television series you are "binge-watching," but why do it? It would spoil the experience. Similarly, why should the viewpoint from the end of our lives be decisive? The pleasurable experience of eating a delicious meal will be over, but we have reason to enjoy eating the meal now. The joy of raising young children to adulthood will be over, but this is not a reason not to do it. Similarly, life will be over, but this is no reason to suppose that we cannot find joy and meaning along the way. The temporal zoom-out argument is unconvincing.

Making this point, Thomas Nagel writes:

> It is often remarked that nothing we do now will matter in a million years. But if that is true, then by the same token, nothing that will be the case in a million years matters now. In particular, it does not matter now that in a million years nothing we do now will matter.[23]

Some nihilists use the spatial zoom-out argument (or perhaps an "abstraction zoom-out argument"). They point out that if we abstract away from the details of our lives and consider them from a distance, we will find that meaning is drained from them; our lives would be no different from the life of Sisyphus rolling the rock up the hill, only to have it roll down, and then rolling it up again, and so forth. We get up, go to work, engage in some relaxing or recreational activities, take care of our family, and go to sleep. We do it the next day, and the next, and so forth—like Sisyphus. Richard Taylor puts this point nicely:

> We toil after goals, most of them—indeed every single one of them—of transitory significance and, having gained one of them, we immediately set forth for the next, as if that one had never been, with the next one being essentially more of the same. Look at a busy street any day, and observe the throng going hither and thither. To what? Some office or shop, where the same things will be done today as were done yesterday, and are done now so they may be repeated tomorrow.
>   ... The two pictures—of Sisyphus and of our own lives, if we look at them from a distance, as it were—are in outline the same and convey to the mind the same image.[24]

Taylor also points out that the lives of nonhuman animals, such as migratory birds, spawning fish, and the glow-worms in the caves in New Zealand, are cyclical, pointless, and without objective meaning. About the glow-worms, Taylor writes:

> ... there are caves in New Zealand, deep and dark, whose floors are quiet pools and whose walls and ceilings are covered with soft light. As you gaze in wonder in the stillness of these caves it seems that

---

23. Thomas Nagel, "The Absurd," originally published in 2003 and reprinted in David Benatar, ed., *Life, Death, and Meaning* (Lanham, MD: Rowman and Littlefield, 2004): 29–40; the quotation is on p. 30.

24. Richard Taylor, "The Meaning of Life," originally published in 2000 and reprinted in David Benatar, ed., *Life, Death, and Meaning* (Lanham, MD: Rowman and Littlefield, 2004): 19–28; the quotation is on pp. 24 and 25.

the Creator has reproduced there in microcosm the heavens themselves. . . . As you look more closely, however, the scene is explained.
Each dot of light identifies an ugly worm, whose luminous tail is
meant to attract insects from the surrounding darkness. As from
time to time one of these insects draws near it becomes entangled
in a sticky thread lowered by the worm, and is eaten. This goes on
month after month . . . until what? What great thing awaits all this
long and repetitious effort and makes it worthwhile? Really nothing.
The larva just transforms itself finally to a tiny winged adult that lacks
even mouth parts and are devoured by the cannibalist worms, often
without having ventured into the day, the only point to their existence having now been fulfilled. This has been going on for millions of
years, and to no end other than that the same meaningless cycle may
continue for another millions of years. . . . And we are part of that life.
    . . . All living things present essentially the same spectacle.[25]

From a distance our lives are indeed similar, exhibiting cyclical
patterns of everyday life. But if we want to understand meaning, why look
at our lives from a great distance? We live our lives from a perspective
located in the here and now. Why shouldn't this "lived" perspective be the
one that specifies meaning in our lives? Why not zoom in for meaning?

From far away I couldn't distinguish a Rolex from a Timex. (I might
even have problems from close up, but put this to the side—and don't tell
my wife!) From a great distance I couldn't distinguish a diamond ring from
a ring in a Cracker Jacks box. But a Rolex is not a Timex, and a diamond
ring is not a little treasure to be found in a candy-covered-popcorn box.
The distant perspective blurs important distinctions and leaves out crucial
details. Same with meaning in life. From the perspective that matters, we
are not like migratory birds, the New Zealand glow-worms, or Sisyphus.

---

25. Taylor, "The Meaning of Life," 25–26.
In an article on New Zealand in *Lonely Planet* (Summer 2018), the author writes:

> Stubbs [the guide] leads the way down into the Ruakuri Cave, the midday
> sun vanishing behind the snap of a trapdoor. As we squeeze through narrow
> gaps into a cavernous obsidian-black hangar, our eyes adjust to the darkness.
> And then they appear: thousands of underground stars lighting up the vaulted
> gallery like a lattice of subterranean sky.
>   Stubbs shines a torch on the glowworms, which were known first to the
> Maori as "titiwai," water stars. The larvae glow to attract prey that might become
> entangled in hanging threads of mucus-covered silk. "These little fellas are just like
> me," he says, "not pretty when the lights are on, but beautiful when it's dark." (67)

Zooming out makes it impossible to see the rich texture of our lives, including its *particularity*. Kate Bowler writes:

> ... there is nothing generic about human life. ... There is no life *in general*. Each day has been a collection of trivial details—little intimacies and jokes and screw-ups and realizations. My problems can't be solved by ... formulas ... God may be universal, but I am not. I am Toban's wife and Zach's mom and Karen and Gerry's daughter. I am here now, bolted in time and place, to the busy sounds of a blond boy in dinosaur pajamas crashing into every piece of furniture.[26]

A perspective "in between" the zoom-out and zoom-in viewpoints is available. This might be called the "stepping-back" perspective. This is a less extreme way of achieving a more "objective" perspective. One of our capacities, as rational creatures, is the ability to reflect on our own preferences, values, and projects with an eye to evaluating and perhaps changing them. In stepping back, we can form preferences about our preferences. Many philosophers think that the stepping-back perspective is necessary for autonomy and moral responsibility. They think that our capacity to evaluate and change our own motives and ethical principles gives us freedom and responsibility, and renders human beings unique.[27]

---

26. Kate Bowler, *Everything Happens for a Reason and Other Lies I Have Loved* (New York: Random House, 2018): 124–125

In a famous passage from *The Death of Ivan Ilyich*, Leo Tolstoy wrote:

> The syllogism he had learnt from Kiesewetter's Logic: "Caius is a man, men are mortal, therefore Caius is mortal," had always seemed to him correct as applied to Caius, but certainly not as applied to himself. That Caius—man in the abstract—was mortal, was perfectly correct, but he was not Caius, not an abstract man, but a creature quite, quite separate from all others. He had been little Vanya, with a mamma and papa, afterwards with Katenka and with all the joys, griefs, and delights of childhood, boyhood, and youth. What did Caius know of the smell of that striped leather ball Vanya had been so proud of? Had Caius kissed his mother's hand like that, and did the silk of her dress rustle so for Caius? Had he rioted like that at school when the pastry was bad? Had Caius been in love like that? Could Caius preside at a session as he did? "Caius really was mortal and it was right for him to die; but for me, little Vanya, Ivan Ilyich, with all my thoughts and emotions, it's altogether a different matter. It cannot be that I would die. That would be too terrible." Such was his feeling. (Chapter VI)

27. For a discussion of these views, especially those of Harry Frankfurt and Gary Watson, see Kane, *A Contemporary Introduction to Free Will*, 93–106. It is interesting that the very capacity that makes us persons with free will and the capacity to lead meaningful lives can also lead to absurdity. Thomas Nagel holds that the intractable clash between these perspectives makes our lives absurd: "The Absurd."

Stepping back in this way is totally compatible with objective attractiveness and meaning; some might even argue that this capacity is *necessary* for meaning in life (especially insofar as freedom is required for meaning—the freedom to write our own story). Meaning does not disappear from the zoom-in and stepping-back points of view, and these are our perspectives in living our lives (and reflecting on them). When we zoom out, life may not seem worth living. But this is because we have lost the *proper* perspective.[28]

Beware! Return of the Blob. Note also that repetitiveness and the lack of a finished product do not in themselves imply the lack of meaning in an individual's life. The PBS Yuppie's life is just as repetitive as the Blob's. A Zen monk lives a repetitive life, doing the same chores, chanting the same mantras, and so forth. Every day is the same, in the same way that every day is the same for Sisyphus. The Yuppie and the Monk may have nothing to show for it—no tangible accomplishment. Enlightenment is an accomplishment, but not tangible. The Yuppie and the Monk lead meaningful lives, repetitive as they may be. It is an interesting question what distinguishes them from the Blob.

Is the problem that the Blob's attention is blurred somewhat by beer drinking? But what about the Yuppie's pleasant buzz from Chardonnay? (We can imagine that they both imbibe the same amount of alcohol.) Would it make a difference if the Blob were drinking a locally brewed, hand-crafted beer? Perhaps the worry about the Blob is that it lives a largely passive life. Earlier I claimed that we tend to consider being active, and not largely passive, a feature that confers meaningfulness. But it is not clear that the Blob is more passive than the Yuppie and the Monk; we can imagine that they all distribute their energies between their "sitting" and other activities equally. Their bodies move in roughly the same way, with the same amount of sitting. And surely a paraplegic's life is not less meaningful for being less physically active.

---

28. The famous opening line of Camus's *The Myth of Sisyphus* is, "There is but one truly serious philosophical question and that is suicide." Albert Camus, "The Myth of Sisyphus," in *The Myth of Sisyphus and Other Essays* (New York: Alfred A. Knopf, 1955 [essay originally published in 1944]). He supposedly said that, when we wake up every morning to horrifying news about the world, we find ourselves asking whether to kill ourselves or have a cup of coffee.

I'll take the coffee!

Is the Blob's *mind* less active? In the passage in which Susan Wolf introduces the Blob (quoted earlier), she refers disparagingly to its "hazy passivity." But why exactly is the Blob less mentally active than (say) the PBS Yuppie? Surely the Blob thinks about the sitcom he is watching, in the same way that the Yuppie thinks about *Downton Abbey*. They both enjoy the programs and relax (with the aid of their respective alcoholic drinks), and they both may be engaged in the shows in a similar way. They both seek not just entertainment, but they also get insights into our human lives.

We might wonder why exactly we privilege being active over being passive. There are traditions in other cultures (including Eastern cultures and philosophies) that give priority to silent stillness. They prize a kind of "mindfulness" that involves taking in everything and appreciating it profoundly. Here the idea is to be in tune with one's environment and one's self, and this attunement can be entirely passive. It might be a beautiful connection with nature, unmediated by the complications coming from our minds. Who is to say that active projects contribute more to meaning? Why is *doing* more important than *being*?[29]

These (and other) questions show that once we scratch below the surface, our ordinary intuitive judgments about relative levels of meaning in life are difficult to explain and justify. I do not mean to claim that we cannot, upon reflection, make and justify these kinds of

---

29. See, just to begin (and there is a huge literature that is relevant), Ram Dass, *Be Here Now* (San Cristobal, NM: Lama Foundation, 1971); Eckhart Tolle, *The Power of Now: A Guide to Spiritual Enlightenment* (Vancouver, B.C.: Namaste Publishing, 2004); Jack Kornfield, *Meditation for Beginners* (Mumbai: Jaico Publishing House, 2010), and more recently, Robert Wright, *Why Buddhism Is True: The Science and Philosophy of Meditation and Enlightenment* (New York: Simon & Schuster, 2017). For further discussion, see Kieran Setiya, *Midlife: A Philosophical Guide* (Princeton, NJ: Princeton University Press, 2018); and Brian O'Connor, *Idleness: A Philosophical Essay* (Princeton, NJ: Princeton University Press, 2018). Setiya, following Aristotle, distinguishes activities with a purpose ("telic" activities) and activities that do not aim at some outside goal or purpose ("atelic" activities). Setiya encourages us to adopt some atelic activities, which are rewarding in themselves and not because they lead to some accomplishment. These activities can help to impart meaning to our lives and stave off depression.

Aristotle distinguished between an *energeia* (activity) and a *kinesis* (process). An *energeia* is "complete in itself," whereas a *kinesis* points to an external or "resultant" product. The "tense test" distinguishes the two notions: "I am walking" entails "I have walked." In this sense "I am walking" is complete in itself. In contrast, "I am walking to the store" does not entail "I have walked to the store." *Energeia* are valuable, when they are valuable, just in themselves, as "atelic" activities.

judgments, and, specifically, I do not wish to suggest that we cannot plausibly distinguish the Blob from the PBS watcher or the Zen monk. I am simply pointing out that the issues are more complex and difficult than we might initially have thought.[30] This is not unlike the situation in other areas of philosophy, especially ethics. Despite the incompleteness in our views about the meaningfulness of specific activities and ways of life, and the justification of these views, we can proceed based on a general consensus, within our culture, about a range of clear cases.

Conclusion

Former United States Senator John McCain was asked what he did to keep his mind active during his five and a half years of captivity (and torture) in a North Vietnamese prison (often called the "Hanoi Hilton"). He replied, "I spent a lot of time thinking about the meaning of life." Even if human life in general has no meaning—and thus there is no "meaning of life"—we can say that an individual life has a meaning. This is the content of his story.

We can also identify factors that make a life more (or less) meaningful, relative to our social consensus. The consensus will at least track relatively "clear" cases, such as Martin Luther King (on the positive side) or a grass-blade counter (on the negative). Judgments about meaningfulness may not be worse off than those about "goodness" or "rightness" as regards their authority, so we need not despair. It may be that in these contexts (ethics and meaning in life) the best we can do is rely on social consensus, incomplete and problematic as this may be.

---

30. It might be that the Blob drinks to *anesthetize* himself, and he does not engage actively with the sitcom. In contrast, perhaps the Yuppie's Chardonnay *enhances* his active engagement with the television program. In this version, there is indeed a difference with respect to activity. Similarly, some forms of meditation involve the *active* focusing of the mind (with the hope that this will lead to greater focus and "being present" in life). At a deeper level, then, it might be that the value of being active, rather than passive, can indeed be invoked to distinguish the Blob, on the one hand, from the others. Also relevant is the "extent" of the activity; *some* "trash TV," sofa sprawling, and beer drinking is fine— but Wolf's Blob, like Sisyphus, is portrayed as engaging in the relevant activities all or most of the time. Similarly, *some* plugging into Nozick's experience machine is fine, but, as Nozick pointed out, a plugged-in life would not be meaningful insofar as it would not be *active*. I have greatly benefitted from discussions with James Baille about these issues.

We have considered a plausible account of meaningfulness in life, presented by Susan Wolf: meaningfulness is at the intersection between subjective attraction and objective attractiveness. As she puts it, meaning comes from loving what is worthy of love. You have to have passion for a fitting object of passion. Various particular factors have been identified in evaluating the meaningfulness of life: lack of repetition, social connection, love, friendship, leaving a (relatively) permanent mark, accomplishing something tangible, linking to something "greater than oneself," fulfilling God's purpose, being active rather than passive, and so forth. Perhaps these factors would be endorsed by our social consensus, by and large, although we can raise questions about any of them (even within our own cultural perspective). We can understand these factors (among others) as helping to specify objective attractiveness.

Only a being who can act freely, and is in contact with reality (in a suitable way), can live a meaningful life. Such a being writes his or her story through free will. The more the story takes place at the intersection between subjective and objective value, the more meaningful it is.

We typically think—it is part of our social consensus—that it is particularly bad when a being with the capacity to lead a meaningful life dies. Perhaps it is a bad thing when any sentient creature dies, but it is even worse—possibly a tragedy—when someone with this capacity dies. If you were in a position in which you couldn't save both creatures, it would certainly be better to save a healthy human being, rather than (say) a cat (much as my wife and I love cats). One natural way of explaining this is because it would be a worse thing if the human being died than the cat. The human being is capable of living a meaningful life, whereas the cat is not. More would be lost if the human being were to die. This is of course controversial, but it is shared widely within our culture. Later I will suggest a plausible explanation of this view.

Allow me to emphasize that none of this implies that the cat's life is not important to the cat, or that *nothing* of value is lost when a cat dies. Very importantly, the claim about the lack of a capacity to lead a meaningful life does *not* imply that it is permissible to treat animals cruelly or even cause any significant pain (especially, unnecessary pain). It is indeed worse when a human dies than when a cow or a pig dies; something more is lost. Again: this in no way entails or lends a shred of credibility to the notion that we may cause needless pain to other sentient creatures. I should note that our actual practices, including "factory farming," often do cause unnecessary suffering to animals.

We think about meaning in life for various purposes. As we noted earlier, we have reason to pursue meaningful activities, where this sort of reason is not necessarily a moral reason, or a reason of happiness. It *matters* to us to live meaningful lives, and we want to understand what such a life would look like. We are by our very natures "meaning-seeking creatures." As such, we naturally wonder "what it's all about." But there is also a connection between meaning in life and the badness of death. The death of a creature capable of living a meaningful life is bad in a special way.[31] It is plausible that only human beings—only creatures with the capacity to lead a meaningful life—have the *right* to life; the right to life guards something particularly precious.

This leads us to think about death, and to consider exactly how it can be bad for a human being. If the death of a human being is particularly bad—possibly a tragedy—then it must be a bad thing *for the individual*. (It is not just, or even primarily, the effects of death on others that make it bad, when it is bad.) But death can seem like a mystery. What is it? If it is nothingness or an experiential blank, how could it be bad for the individual who dies? Even though death stops our lives, and takes away the capacity to live a meaningful life, it (the state of being dead, rather than dying) does not involve pain and suffering (on a secular approach). So why is death bad?

Plan of the Book

Before we dive in head first, I'll sketch the plan of the book. In Chapter One we have distinguished the meaning of life from meaning in life (or meaningfulness in life). We have canvassed some main approaches to specifying meaning in life, and we have claimed that the death of an individual capable of living a meaningful life can be especially bad. In Chapter Two we'll consider proposals for a definition of death, and we'll also begin to consider some challenges (originating with the Greek philosopher Epicurus) to the common-sense view that death can be a bad thing for the individual who dies. The three main Epicurean challenges are as follows: How can death be a bad thing for an individual, without

---

31. For an important defense of this claim, see Ruth Cigman, "Death, Misfortune, and Species Inequality," *Philosophy and Public Affairs* 10 (1981): 47–64.

involving any negative experiences for her? When is death bad, if it is bad? And if prenatal nonexistence was not bad, how can death (posthumous nonexistence) be bad? (This the famous "Mirror Image" Argument, put forward by Lucretius, a Roman follower of the Greek philosopher Epicurus.) The next two chapters will explore these questions.

In Chapter Three we will explore whether anything that does not involve negative experiences can be bad for an individual. After all, on the secular view, death (the state of being dead) does not involve negative experiences—or any experiences at all. In Chapter Four we will try to figure out the time of the harm of death (if it is indeed a harm). Also in this chapter we will grapple with what many think is the most fascinating and difficult problem pertaining to death: Lucretius's Mirror Image Argument.

The death of a creature capable of a meaningful live can be significantly bad, or so we think. But if we think so, we need to address these puzzles. In Chapters Three and Four, we will look carefully at whether death can be bad for the individual who dies, and we will also consider the relationship between the value status of death (whether or not it is bad) and attitudes such as fear and dread. If death can be bad, is it appropriate to fear it? To what extent?

Let's suppose that death can indeed be a bad thing for a human being. Would it then be desirable to live forever? Many of us naturally think it would be great to be immortal—why not? In Chapter Five we'll distinguish different conceptions of immortality and begin to consider both optimism and skepticism about the desirability of immortality. In Chapter Six we will set out a framework (following Bernard Williams) for evaluating immortality. This framework requires that a worthwhile immortal life be recognizably human, *my* life, and not tedious. In this and the following chapter we will consider various objections to the idea that immortality could meet these conditions.

In Chapter Six we will evaluate the contention that an immortal life would not be recognizably human. Would we be able to "relate to" a life in which there are no boundaries, no stages, and no story with an ending? The climax and denouement of a story are crucial, but an immortal life doesn't have these elements. So how could immortal lives be stories, or have stories? Do all human lives have to be associated with a narrative?

In Chapter Seven we will consider additional objections. Would an immortal person still be me? How could it be me if in a thousand years the individual in question—the allegedly "future me"—has no memories of me now and has significantly different values? Would an immortal life continue to engage me, or would it necessarily become boring? How could I stay interested in life after thousands of years? These are the identity and boredom objections.

Near-death experiences (NDEs) are often interpreted as a portal to immortality in a heavenly realm. This claim will be the topic of Chapters Eight and Nine. In Chapter Eight we'll consider some of the main arguments for a supernaturalistic interpretation of NDEs (according to which we use nonphysical minds to grasp a heavenly realm). For example, how can we be conscious, and acquire verifiable information, during a time at which our physical brains are "offline"? How can blind individuals have visual NDEs? Why are NDEs throughout the world (and history) very similar? It seems that the best explanation is supernaturalism, and we will subject this view to scrutiny. *Must* NDEs be interpreted "supernaturalistically"? Is it possible to interpret NDEs— their nature and significance—in a naturalistic way? In Chapter Nine we'll identify the stories NDEs tell, and we will ask whether they are *necessarily* supernatural.

In Chapter Ten we will evaluate contemporary treatment of the elderly and dying, in light of our reflections on meaning in life, the badness of death, and the attractions of immortality. We will show how NDEs point to improvements in our societal practices of treating older populations and dying people.

These are fascinating and deep issues. So get ready to take the plunge!

Annotated Suggestions for Further Reading

The existentialist philosophers, including Søren Kierkegaard, Albert Camus, and Jean-Paul Sartre explored these issues at great length: Albert Camus, "The Myth of Sisyphus," in *The Myth of Sisyphus and Other Essays* (New York: Alfred A. Knopf, 1955 [originally published in 1944]); and *The Stranger* (New York: Alfred A. Knopf, 1998 [originally published in 1942]): Jean-Paul Sartre, *Nausea* (London: Penguin Books, 2000 [originally published in 1938]); and Søren Kierkegaard, *Either/Or* (London: Penguin Books, 1993 [originally published in 1843]); *Fear and Trembling* (London: Penguin Books, 1986 [originally published in 1843]); *The Concept of Dread [Anxiety]* (Macon, GA: Mercer University Press, 1985 [originally published in 1844]); and *The Sickness Unto Death* (Princeton, NJ: Princeton

University Press, 1980 [originally published in 1849]). For a helpful general introduction to existentialism, see Paul Roubiczek, *Existentialism: For and Against* (Cambridge: Cambridge University Press, 1964).

Some useful collections: Oswald Hanfling, ed., *Life and Meaning: A Reader* (Oxford: Blackwell, 1987); E. D. Klemke and Steven M. Cahn, eds., *The Meaning of Life: A Reader*, 4th ed. (New York: Oxford University Press, 2017); and David Benatar, *Life, Death, and Meaning: Key Philosophical Readings on the Big Questions*, 3rd ed. (Langham, MD: Rowman and Littlefield, 2016). Also very helpful: Joshua Seachris, ed., *Exploring the Meaning of Life: An Anthology and Guide* (Malden, MA: Wiley-Blackwell, 2012).

Thomas Nagel's *What Does It All Mean?* (New York: Oxford University Press, 1987) is an introductory treatment of some of the issues relating to death and meaningfulness, as well as other fundamental questions. Nagel offers more advanced treatments of these issues in *Mortal Questions* (New York: Cambridge University Press, 1979); and *The View from Nowhere* (New York: Oxford University Press, 1986). Robert Nozick's *Philosophical Explanations* (Cambridge, MA: Harvard University Press, 1981) contains an in-depth analysis of meaning in life.

Susan Wolf explores the meaning of life and meaning in life in *Meaning in Life and Why It Matters* (Princeton, NJ: Princeton University Press, 2010). This book includes Wolf's important Tanner Lectures on Human Values and helpful commentaries by John Koethe, Robert Adams, Nomy Arpaly, and Jonathan Haidt. There is an illuminating defense of a subjective view in Cheshire Calhoun, *Doing Valuable Time: The Present, the Future, and Meaningful Living* (New York: Oxford University Press, 2018).

Thaddeus Metz summarizes many of the central debates about the meaning of life in his contribution to the online *Stanford Encyclopedia of Philosophy*, and he presents a more comprehensive discussion, with his own original views, in *Meaning in Life* (Oxford: Oxford University Press, 2013). He explores various ways to explain our intuitions about meaningfulness by reference to a deeper, underlying idea, and he offers his own suggestion. Keiran Setiya offers insights about meaning in life in *Midlife: A Philosophical Guide* (Princeton, NJ: Princeton University Press, 2017). He points out that we should not just credit accomplishment-oriented activities.

For religious approaches to the meaning of life, see (in addition to the volume referred to earlier, Joshua Seachris, ed., *Exploring the Meaning of Life: An Anthology and Guide*); Joshua Seachris, ed., *God and Meaning: New Essays* (New York: Bloomsbury, 2016); and Stewart Goetz, *The Purpose of Life: A Theistic Perspective* (New York: Continuum, 2012).

David Benatar argues for nihilism in *The Human Predicament: A Candid Guide to Life's Biggest Questions* (New York: Oxford University Press, 2017); and *Better Never to Have Been: The Harm of Coming into Existence* (Oxford: Oxford University Press, 2006). For a rather more optimistic view, see Iddo Landau, *Finding Meaning in an Imperfect World* (New York: Oxford University Press, 2017).

In a fascinating and original book, Samuel Scheffler argues that our lives would lack meaning (and, in particular, subjective passion), if we were to become convinced that the human species would go out of existence shortly after we die: Samuel Scheffler, *Death and the Afterlife*, Niko Kolodny, ed. (New York: Oxford University Press, 2013). On Scheffler's view, meaning requires a true belief in the afterlife *of the species*—the continuation of the species after I die.

Christine Korsgaard presents a fascinating defense of a more robust view of animal rights than I have argued for in this chapter: *Fellow Creatures: Our Obligations to the other Animals* (Oxford: Oxford University Press, 2018).

Mark H. Bernstein offers another way of getting to the same conclusion about animal rights in: *The Moral Equality of Humans and Animals* (London: Palgrave-MacMillan, 2015).

Just for fun: the film *Monty Python's The Meaning of Life*.

CHAPTER 2

The Meaning of Death

Nothing can be of such great benefit to you, in your quest for moderation in all things, than to frequently contemplate the brevity of one's life span, and its uncertainty. Whatever you undertake, cast your eyes on death.

—SENECA,
Epistle 114

....

Introduction

What is death, and what happens to us after we die? Some think that much of our lives and many of our social and religious institutions are devoted to managing our fear of death. This view even has a name: "terror management theory."[1] Throughout human history we have been fascinated and troubled by death. But alongside the natural tendency to fear—or at least be troubled by—death is the idea that, since it is an experiential blank (without even a subject of experiences), death (as opposed to the process of dying) cannot be bad for the individual who dies.

---

1. Ernest Becker, an anthropologist, is the "father" of terror management theory (TMT): *The Denial of Death* (New York: Free Press, 1973). Contemporary proponents of TMT include Sheldon Solomon, Jeff Greenberg, and Tom Pyszczynski, whose recent book is *The Worm at the Core: On the Role of Death in Life* (New York: Random House, 2015).

The idea that much of civilization stems from our fear of death is, of course, not a new idea. It has been discussed especially by the French existentialists, although its roots can be traced back (in modern philosophy) to Schopenhauer, Kierkegaard, and Nietzsche. For works in which existentialists discuss meaning in life, see "Suggestions for Further Reading," Chapter One. The work of the contemporary proponents of terror management theory can be thought of as (in part, at least) an adaptation and application of the insights of these philosophers.

Dying can be painful, but how can the *status of being dead* be bad for the individual who dies? It is interesting to think about this question on either a secular assumption that death is an experiential blank or a religious assumption of an afterlife. Although I will generally adopt the secular perspective in this book, we will also touch on the issues from a religious standpoint.

Many of us think that death can definitely be a bad thing for the individual who dies, even though being dead may be an experiential blank. This, I think, is the "commonsense view" about death's badness. But it is, on its surface, puzzling.

In this chapter we will explore some definitions of death and adopt one as a working hypothesis for our purposes. (We have to know what we're talking about!) Then we will lay out the main arguments (stemming from Epicurus) for the comforting view that death cannot be bad for the individual who dies. These are challenges to the commonsense view (that, at least sometimes, death can be a bad thing for the individual who dies). Further, the arguments challenge the idea that death is to be dreaded or feared (at all). Having laid out these worries, we will address them in more detail in the next two chapters. In Chapter Three we will look carefully at the first challenge—that nothing can be bad for an individual without involving any negative experiences for that individual. In Chapter Four we will consider the second two challenges (about death and time).

The Definition of Death

Most of us think, without much reflection, that death *can* be a bad thing for the individual who dies. Perhaps it is not always bad for an individual to die. For example, if a person is in terrible, unrelenting pain, or is impaired so significantly that she cannot live at least a minimally acceptable continuation of her life, then, arguably, her death (now rather than later) would not be a bad thing for her. Here we are distinguishing "death" from "dying." Dying is the last part of living—a process that can (although does not necessarily) involve considerable pain and suffering. There is no puzzle about how pain and suffering can be bad, so it is not puzzling how dying can be bad for the individual who dies. There is an existing subject of the harm. But we might wonder how death itself (the *status* of being dead) could be a bad thing for the individual who dies.

It is clear how the death of one person can be a bad thing for others—those who love or care about her or depend on her. After all, these people will suffer in various ways because of the death of the individual, and, again, there is no puzzle about how suffering can be bad. But death does seem at least sometimes a bad thing *for the individual who dies.* Indeed, it is thought to be one of the worst things, if not the worst, that can happen to you. Is this widespread view correct, and, if so, how can it be explained?

In order to answer this question, we'll need to come up with a working definition of death. We will assume in this chapter that death does not include any part of life. As such, it might not involve pain or suffering (depending on views about the afterlife, to which we shall return), and yet we still might think that death, so conceived, could be a bad thing for an individual. In thinking about death in this way, we are either construing it as a "transition" between the last part of life and the first part of being dead or as the state of being dead. (This transition does not include any part of living; thus, we distinguish dying from death, even when death is construed as a transition.) Sometimes we'll be using "death" to refer to the transition, and sometimes we'll be referring to the status, but the proper interpretation should be clear from the context.

It is not straightforward to give a definition of death that applies to humans and other organisms and is not "circular."[2] (I will explain the problem of circularity later.) It might be that we'll have to settle for an account of "human death," but we'll start by trying to give a general definition of death.

Death as the Cessation of Life. Suppose we say that death is the cessation of life. Right off the bat we might wonder whether this is circular. Do we have a good grasp of "life" that does not rely on a prior conception of death? If not, the definition of death would indeed be circular. For instance, if we thought of life as the continued functioning of an organism that is not yet dead, this would obviously not work! So the definition of death as the cessation of life assumes that we understand life in a way that does not presuppose what we want to figure out: death.

Probably the best way to understand life, in this context, involves an organism's biological functioning; the specific form of biological functioning will depend on the kind of organism. At a basic level, an organism must function to allow it to get nutrition and to eliminate waste; that is, the organism must engage in metabolism. In a human

---

2. Fred Feldman, *Confrontations with the Reaper: A Philosophical Study of the Nature and Value of Death* (New York: Oxford University Press, 1992).

being, life requires that the heart beats to circulate the blood and that the brain functions to direct metabolism, cell repair, and so forth. Note that we are not assuming that the brain must continue functioning in a way that would support consciousness; we do not want to rule it out that an individual can be alive without the capacity for consciousness. Here the brain would support the biological life processes, but not consciousness. (Whether such an individual would be a *person* [with the full range of moral rights], as opposed to a live human being, is a different question.)

It is not crucial, for our purposes, to specify how long the heart may stop compatibly with life or the exact neurophysiological functioning of the brain required for life (and how long this can stop consistent with life continuing). It is enough to start with the proposal that death is the cessation of life, where life involves the heart's beating and the brain's functioning in certain ways. The heart can stop beating for a few minutes, and the individual can be resuscitated—she hasn't died. Again: the *exact* amount of time the heart can stop consistent with continued life is difficult to specify, but unnecessary here. (In a legal context, we would have to be more precise.) In the end, we might have to remain a bit vague about exactly *which* "life processes" must continue and what (temporary) interruptions are consistent with the continuation of life processes.

The cessation of life is then a plausible first stab (sorry!) at a definition of death. If this weren't a philosophy book, we could probably leave it here, but in philosophy we want to press on our initial views in light of potential problems, in order to get at the essence of a concept (such as death). This analytical process can involve considering unusual or even hypothetical examples. Philosophy is not like politics: we *do* answer hypothetical questions! This is because philosophy seeks the truth, and not just superficial agreement. We want to understand death in depth, but we also want to have something simple and clear we can work with. We'll aim at that.

Consider the phenomenon of suspended animation.[3] The most common form of suspended animation is freezing. In biology labs microorganisms are grown in a culture, and then the whole thing is frozen. Whatever biological functions are required for life cease. Subsequently, when needed, the microorganisms are allowed to thaw out, and they will "return to life." It seems that they have ceased living temporarily

---

3. For helpful discussion of this problem, and those I consider later, see Feldman, *Confrontations with the Reaper*, 60–71.

and then resumed their lives (without having died). But on the definition of death we are considering, the microorganisms would have died when they are frozen, since this counts as a cessation of life.

Earlier I claimed that the temporary cessation of the heartbeat of a human being (for a short time) is compatible with the life processes continuing. That is, I have claimed that in those cases the relevant life processes continue. How is this different from the frozen microorganism (in which, I contend, the relevant processes have ceased)? Earlier I was discussing cases in which the heart stops beating for a *short* time and then restarts. During this time, the crucial life processes directed by the brain are *still going on*. Given these two facts, I think that the temporary cessation of the heartbeat is different from the situation of the frozen microorganisms. *All* of their life processes cease for a *substantial* amount of time. (Later we will consider human beings whose hearts and brains stop functioning for substantial amounts of time [hours] but are resuscitated via modern medical techniques.) Again: you might think that these microorganisms have not died, but, on the "cessation of life" account, they would have died.

There are many examples of the use of freezing to preserve microorganisms. It is also an important step in certain reproductive techniques. Further, it might be possible in the future to "cryogenically preserve" a human being and thaw him out at some (much) later time, thus causing him to resume his life. We cannot successfully do this now, or it is at least very doubtful that we can, despite the fact that some wealthy people have already taken the first step of being cryogenically preserved. It is certainly not *incoherent* to imagine that we will be able to do this in the future. If so, this would show the inadequacy of our proposed definition of death, at least if we think that the frozen individuals (the very same individuals) come back to life when they thaw out. The cryogenically preserved individual has ceased living (in the sense of the relevant biological functioning), and yet arguably he has not died.[4] The cases of freezing microorganisms and the cryogenic preservation of persons are challenges for the notion that death is the cessation of life.

---

4. Cody Gilmore has argued that the frozen are neither dead nor alive. They are not dead because they still have the capacity to start up life processes. They are not alive as they no longer metabolize: Cody Gilmore, "When Do Things Die?," in Ben Bradley, Fred Feldman, and Jens Johansson, eds., *The Oxford Handbook of Philosophy of Death* (New York: Oxford University Press, 2013): 5–59.

Death as the **Permanent Cessation** *of Life.* What if we were to say that death is the *permanent* cessation of life?[5] This would have the correct result in the cases of suspended animation, because the frozen organisms have not *permanently (irreversibly)* ceased to exist and function in the right ways. So, on this proposal, they have not yet died.

Ideally, we would like a definition of death that could be accepted by proponents of both secular and religious views. They disagree on *what happens* during the time of our status as dead, but they should be able to accept the same *definition* of death; otherwise they would not be disagreeing about the same thing. How does the "permanent cessation of life" proposal fare from a religious viewpoint? We have been understanding "life" to imply that certain biological processes take place. So we could say that death is the permanent cessation of these specific processes. The proposed definition could not be accepted by a person who holds that we continue to live (perhaps in heaven or hell) after these processes have permanently ceased. On this religious view, we have *not* (really) died when our body permanently stops functioning in the relevant ways.

Note that the previous suggestion for a definition of death (the mere *cessation* of life processes, not necessarily the *permanent* cessation of these processes) has the same sort of problem for someone who accepts the view that we continue to live in heaven or hell. Again: on this view, we have *not* (really) died when our bodies stop functioning in the indicated ways. From a certain religious perspective, we continue to live, no matter what is happening to our body.

Is it a problem for the proposal that death is the permanent cessation of certain biological processes that it is incompatible with some religious views? Perhaps we will just want to reject those religious views, but it would be better to have a definition of death that doesn't rule out these views from the start. Again: we want to come up with a definition of death that could be accepted by both proponents of secular and certain religious views.

Perhaps a proponent of the religious view will distinguish "bodily death" from "death." Bodily death would be the permanent cessation of the relevant biological functions of *this body*. Let's put aside the notions

---

5. By "permanent," I mean "irreversible." That is, the notion of permanence is not just that the individual *is* never brought back to life, but that he *cannot* be. I owe this point to David Hershenov.

that God could resurrect the individual's particular body, and that this body would still engage in the specified biological processes in heaven. Bodily death then would correspond to the ordinary notion of death (in which a dead person is no longer married, no longer has to pay his credit card bills and mortgage [although his estate may], and so forth).

When a religious person (who holds that we continue to live in heaven or hell) claims that death can be bad for the individual who dies, we can interpret her to be claiming that *bodily death* can be bad. It can be bad insofar as there is an individual who still lives and has bad experiences in hell; this is not puzzling, since the subject of the harm continues to exist.

Certain Buddhists and Hindus believe in reincarnation. Here we can say that the individual dies in the sense of bodily death. She continues to exist and, indeed, to live in that *she* (the very same person) "acquires" a new body. It is characteristic of the religious framework that bodily death is not death itself. Christians hold that Jesus was resurrected: he died and then came back to life. That is, he suffered bodily death but not death itself. Bodily death would be the permanent cessation of the biological processes in Jesus's body, although he continues to exist and then acquires a different body.

It would still be desirable to know what would count as death itself, and not merely bodily death; how else could we evaluate the claim that we have eternal life? So the proponent of the religious views we have discussed will still need to come up with an account of death itself. More specifically, if you believe that we do not *really* die when our body permanently stops functioning, it is important to understand *real* death—death itself. This is a challenge, then, for the religious views (as well as secular approaches).

Quite apart from worries about the afterlife, problems emerge for the proposed definition of death as the permanent cessation of life. This is because, as Jay Rosenberg originally pointed out, there appear to be ways of ceasing to be alive that do not count as death.[6] Consider, for instance, this example discussed by Feldman:

> . . . [Rosenberg] describes the case of an amoeba, Alvin. He tells us that Alvin was a fat and healthy amoeba. According to the story, Alvin was so fat and healthy that at precisely midnight on Tuesday night/Wednesday

---

6. Jay Rosenberg, *Thinking Clearly about Death* (Englewood Cliffs, NJ: Prentice-Hall, 1983): 96ff. Feldman agrees with Rosenberg: Feldman, *Confrontations with the Reaper*, 66–71.

morning, Alvin underwent fission and became two amoebas. According to Rosenberg, Alvin no longer existed on Wednesday. Apparently, Alvin was "replaced" by his two descendants, Amos and Ambrose. Rosenberg claims that Alvin's example shows that "there are other ways for a life to come to an end besides death."[7]

It seems that Alvin has permanently gone out of existence and that he is no longer alive, although he did not die.[8] Thus, cases of fission are cases of permanent cessation of life in which the individual has not died. Cases of fusion are similar in this respect; the two entities (let's say, living organisms) that fuse go out of existence permanently as individual entities, but they do not die. Thus, death cannot be defined as the permanent cessation of life, especially insofar as we want a *general* definition of death, and not just one that applies to human beings. (Note that the problems of "deathless exits from life" also apply to the "cessation of life" proposal, and not just the "permanent cessation of life" suggestion.)

We could adjust the definition to say that death is the permanent cessation of life, except in a case of fission or fusion. But adding such ad hoc qualifications never is a good idea, and it does not solve the problem here. Consider, for example, the process of metamorphosis.[9] When a caterpillar becomes a butterfly, the caterpillar ceases to be alive, and yet it does not die.[10] This seems to me to be another example of a permanent exit from life that is not a death.

OK, one more try. Suppose we said:

> An individual dies if and only if it permanently ceases living, and it does not become at least one other living being.

We might dub this a "stingy" ceasing to live; it is stingy because the organism does not give life to any other being, kind of like your rich aunt who leaves you no money in her will.

This "stingy" account would appear to solve the problems of fission, fusion, and metamorphosis. It is a promising definition of death. Let's just simplify and work with the idea that death is the permanent

---

7. Feldman, *Confrontations with the Reaper*, 66.

8. This is admittedly controversial. Some hold that Alvin has indeed died. Our ordinary intuitions about death do not apply straightforwardly (or perhaps at all) here.

9. Feldman, *Confrontations with the Reaper*, 66.

10. Again some will hold that the caterpillar has indeed died, and ordinary intuitions about death do not obviously yield a resolution of this disagreement.

cessation of life, where we can take this formula as shorthand for a more nuanced definition of the sort just proposed. For our purposes the simpler formulation will do.

The Problem of Modern Resuscitation. This simple account is attractive, but it too has problems. Sam Parnia, MD, has argued that we ought to adopt the account of the death of a human being we originally considered: an individual dies if and only if he ceases living. He points out that resuscitation science has made tremendous progress, and we are now able to resuscitate people whose hearts and brains have stopped functioning for hours. This is truly remarkable. Parnia holds that they have died and come back to life.[11] (This would be incoherent, if death were the *permanent* cessation of life.) On this view, near-death experiences (which we will discuss in Chapters Eight and Nine) would be more accurately called "actual-death experiences." Johnny Hallyday, the French rock and pop singer (sometimes called "The French Elvis"), shows that he agrees with Parnia, having said: "I died, but I didn't like it, so I came back."[12]

The definition of death as the permanent cessation of life thus has problems if one thinks that in cases of resuscitation the individual has died and later comes back to life. It also implies that resurrection is by definition impossible—a problematic view from some religious points of view. Parnia's approach would at least have the virtue of making resurrection *logically possible.*

Whereas we could adopt Parnia's conceptual framework, I am not sure that it is correct. That is, it is not at all clear that we really *should* say that resuscitated people have died and then come back to life. This might just be a "manner of speaking," or a colorful way of highlighting a point—that the individual was in dire straits and almost died.[13] Note, also, that Parnia's way of speaking would implausibly imply that cases of

---

11. Sam Parnia, MD, *What Happens When We Die* (Carlsbad, CA: Hay House, 2008), and Sam Parnia, MD, with Josh Young, *Erasing Death: The Science That Is Rewriting the Boundaries Between Life and Death* (New York: Harper House, 2013). There are also remarkable stories of medical "miracles" in Joshua D. Mezrich, MD, *When Death Becomes Life: Notes from a Transplant Surgeon* (New York: HarperCollins, 2019).

12. In 2009 he was diagnosed with colon cancer and had surgery. Due to damage related to this surgery, doctors at Cedars-Sinai Medical Center in Los Angeles induced a temporary coma to repair the damage. He died (again?) in 2017.

13. I am also not sure that literal resurrection is logically possible.

suspended animation are really cases of death; after all, they involve the cessation of life. But it seems that individuals preserved in this way have not (yet) died. This was one reason why we switched to a definition in terms of the *permanent* cessation of life.

So the situation is this. Parnia says that the resuscitated individuals (whose hearts and brains have stopped functioning for hours) have literally died and then come back to life (and some have *actual*-death experiences). An alternative view is that they come *close* to dying (and some have *near*-death experiences), but do not actually die. I doubt that there is a fact of the matter as to which terminology we should adopt. Both ways of speaking capture part of what many people find correct. For the sake of sticking with a more traditional way of speaking, I will assume that death is the *permanent* cessation of life. Nothing substantive hangs on adopting this assumption, rather than Parnia's, with respect to our discussions in this book.

The philosophical issues are about whether the state of being dead for (at least) an extended period can be bad for the individual. The interesting questions about the badness of death are *not* about a period of unconsciousness (with no heartbeat or brain functioning) for an hour or two. So, even if we were to agree with Parnia and call this relatively short period "being dead," we would not focus on this short state of being dead, when we reflect on the philosophical questions. We would just put these "deaths" aside and ask the philosophical questions about longer periods of being dead. Why would *this* sort of death be bad for the individual who dies? Or we could ask, "Why would the permanent status of being dead be bad for the individual who dies?

Epicurean Skepticism about Death's Badness

We'll stick with the simple idea that the death of a human being takes place when this individual permanently stops living, that is, when the core biological processes permanently cease. The view that death can be a bad thing for the individual who dies is widespread, even among those who take it that death is an experiential blank. But it is also puzzling. So it should not be surprising that there is a long tradition of skepticism about death's badness. The Greek post-Aristotelian philosopher Epicurus and his followers, including the Roman philosopher Lucretius, inspired much of this skepticism, which continues to have strong proponents in contemporary philosophy.

Epicurus famously wrote that when the person is, death is not; and when death is, the person is not. Here is the passage from Epicurus's *Letter to Menoeceus*:

> So death, the most terrifying of ills, is nothing to us, since so long as we exist, death is not with us; but when death comes, then we do not exist. It does not then concern either the living or the dead, since for the former it is not, and the latter are no more.[14]

Although Epicurus here writes that death is "the most terrifying of ills," he has already written that good and evil imply sentience. We can interpret Epicurus as discussing death as *purportedly* the most terrifying of ills (or "evils"). This passage nicely captures part of the skeptic's views; death would seem to be a misfortune without a subject. Following Thomas Nagel, in his classic article, "Death," we might distinguish three basic problems for the commonsense view: the problem of how an experiential blank can be bad, the problem of the time of the badness of death, and the challenge to explain how death is different from prenatal nonexistence.[15] How can we deem death a bad thing for the individual who dies, on the assumption that the individual has gone out of existence?[16]

We typically think that misfortunes or ills involve negative experiences. How can an experiential blank be bad for someone? Second, at what time does the harm of death (if it is a harm) take place? We can usually attach times to harms. So, for example, pain is bad for one at the time one has it and at any future time at which one's having had the pain has a negative effect on one's experiences. But when does the harm of death (the status of being dead) take place? This is not the question of when death takes place, but, rather, when the *harm* or *badness* of death takes place. In general, we can distinguish the time of a harmful event from the time of the badness of that event; the badness of a sprained ankle continues to occur long after the time of the sprain.

---

14. Epicurus, *Letter to Menoeceus* (trans. C. Bailey), in Whitney J. Oates, ed., *The Stoic and Epicurean Philosophers: The Complete Extant Writings of Epicurus, Epictetus, Lucretius, Marcus Aurelius* (New York: Random House, 1940): 30–31.

15. Thomas Nagel, "Death," in Nagel, *Mortal Questions* (Cambridge: Cambridge University Press, 1979): 1–10; reprinted in John Martin Fischer, ed., *The Metaphysics of Death* (Stanford, CA: Stanford University Press, 1993): 61–69.

16. I will use "ill," "harm," "misfortune," and "bad thing" interchangeably, although there are certainly contexts in which it is important to draw distinctions between these notions.

Epicurus's dictum comes into play here: when death is, the person is not, so if the harm of death is thought to take place when the individual is dead, then it is a harm without an existing subject. And if the harm of death is thought to take place while the individual is still alive, then the harm of death will take place even before death occurs. Either option is perplexing.

The third challenge is about our judgments and attitudes toward past and future nonexistence. How do we distinguish our thoughts and attitudes about the time after we die from the time before we are born? If prenatal nonexistence was not bad, how could death be bad? In order to understand this challenge, we will have to consider the "deprivation theory" of death's badness.

How can a mere experiential blank be a bad thing for an individual? The standard response is the "deprivation theory" of death's badness. On this view, death is a bad thing for an individual insofar as it deprives her of what would have been on balance a desirable continuation of her life. The deprivation theory of death's badness is promising insofar as it points toward the possibility that something (a mere deprivation) could be bad for an individual, *without* including any pain or "negative experiences." It provides at least the first step toward an answer to the first challenge to the commonsense view stated earlier: how can death be bad without involving any unpleasant experiences?

The deprivation theory is an appealing answer to the question of why death is bad (when it is bad). Christopher Hitchens captures the flavor of the deprivation view:

> It will happen to all of us, that at some point you get tapped on the shoulder and told, not just that the party's over, but slightly worse: the party's going on—but you have to leave. And it's going on without you.[17]

---

17. Christopher Hitchens, in a debate with Sam Harris, Rabbi David Wolpe, and Rabbi Bradley Shavit Arte, in Los Angeles, California, February 15, 2011: https://archive.org/details/AfterlifeDebateWChristopherHitchensSamHarrisRabbiDavidWolpeAnd

Death, then, would be the ultimate cause of FOMO—fear of missing out. Of course, there are limitations to this metaphor for the deprivation theory of death's badness. When you know that the party is going on without you, this is frustrating. You are still around to have these feelings, even though you are not still at the party. This gives rise to FOMO. In contrast, you are not still around to have any feelings after your death.

But accepting the deprivation theory of death's badness, attractive as it is, leads right into a trap set by Lucretius. His fascinating and important argument presents problems for the deprivation theory. Here is the passage from his *De Rerum Naturum*:

> Look back again to see how the unending expanse of past time, before we are born, has been nothing to us. For Nature holds this forth to us as a mirror image of the time to come after our death. Is there anything terrible there, does anything seem gloomy? Is it not more peaceful than any sleep?[18]

The argument can be interpreted as follows. We do not consider the fact that we were born when we were actually born, rather than earlier, a bad thing for us or something to be lamented. And yet our "late birth" deprives us of what might well have been, on balance, good, in the same way (or a similar way) that our "early death" does. On the deprivation theory, it seems that the fact that we will die when we actually do, rather than later, should be considered as just like the fact that we were born when we actually were, rather than earlier. As Lucretius put it, the two facts are "mirror images" of each other, and thus should be treated in the same way. Since we don't look at our late birth as a misfortune or harm for us, we should not consider our early deaths a misfortune or harm for us—or something to be feared.

So there are at least three basic problems for the commonsense view that death can be a bad thing for an individual, on the secular assumption. How can something that contains no unpleasant experiences be bad for an individual? When does the badness of death occur? And if we don't consider our late birth a bad thing for us, why consider our early death a bad thing for us? We will explore all of these questions in Chapters Three and Four.

More on Epicureanism

The Epicurean Diagnosis of Our Death Anxiety. Epicureanism about death offers an alternative to the commonsense view that death is bad, even though it is an experiential blank. The Epicurean view is attractive in various ways, and it is more nuanced than it might at first appear.

---

18. Lucretius, *De Rerum Naturum*, 3.

The Epicureans seek to relieve us of anxieties that are based on what they take to be confused views about various things, not just death.[19] As human beings, our lives can be difficult, and we often have anxiety. Any reduction in our worries, especially profound anxieties, is to be welcomed. When considering death, Epicureanism asks us to think carefully about the fact that we won't exist when death occurs. They contend that if we do so, we will see that death cannot be a bad thing for us and that it is nothing to be feared.[20]

Epicureans offer various diagnoses of our tendency to think of death as a bad thing for the individual who dies and to be disturbed by it. They contend that, when we picture ourselves as dead, we tend to think (implicitly or subconsciously) of ourselves as still existing and experiencing misfortunes. We might picture ourselves in a coffin and imagine the claustrophobia and terror this would involve (given that we are still conscious). We might imagine ourselves decaying and moldering in our graves, perhaps being gnawed by rats or other animals. If we suppose—illicitly—that somehow we are still "there" and conscious, we would be imagining ourselves suffering greatly. A particularly poignant example of this kind of thinking is Harold Pinter's sentiment about his wife, Antonia Fraser, "I shall miss you so much when I'm dead."[21]

Consider also this passage from Tom Stoppard's play, *Rosencrantz and Guildenstern Are Dead*:

> ROS: Do you ever think of yourself as actually *dead*, lying in a box with a lid on it?
>
> GUIL: No.
>
> ROS: Nor do I, really . . . It's silly to be depressed by it. I mean one thinks of it like being *alive* in a box, one keeps forgetting to take into account the fact that one is *dead* . . . which

---

19. Martha Nussbaum, *The Therapy of Desire: Theory and Practice in Hellenistic Ethics* (Princeton, NJ: Princeton University Press, 1994).

20. Irving Yalom, a psychotherapist, has adopted this Epicurean view in helping his patients come to terms with death: Irving D. Yalom, *Staring at the Sun: Overcoming the Terror of Death* (San Francisco, CA: Jossey-Bass [Wiley imprint], 2009).

21. See Antonia Fraser, *Must You Go? My Life with Harold Pinter* (New York: Nan A. Talese/Doubleday, 2010).

should make all the difference . . . shouldn't it? I mean, you'd never know you were in a box, would you? It would be just like being asleep in a box. Not that I'd like to sleep in a box, mind you, not without any air—you'd wake up dead, for a start, and then where would you be? Apart from in a box. That's the bit I don't like, frankly. That's why I don't think of it . . . Because you'd be helpless, wouldn't you? Stuffed in a box like that, I mean you'd be in there forever. Even taking into account the fact that you're dead, it isn't a pleasant thought. *Especially* if you're dead, really . . . ask yourself, if I asked you straight off—I'm going to stuff you in this box now, would you rather be alive or dead? Naturally, you'd prefer to be alive. Life in a box is better than no life at all. I expect. You'd have a chance at least. You could lie there thinking—well, at least I'm not dead! In a minute someone's going to bang on the lid and tell me to come out . . . "Hey you, whatsyername! Come out of there!"[22]

But the Epicureans point out that it is a mistake (one is tempted to say a "grave" mistake!) to imagine your bodily situation after death and to import yourself as a conscious being into the situation. After all, when death is, the person is not.[23] Insofar as one's negative attitudes toward one's death are based on such thoughts, it is helpful to show how they are confused.

A Problem for Epicureanism. One might think that Epicureanism is obviously inadequate because it seems to entail that an individual would have no self-regarding reason to avoid a threat to his life. (Of course, one's death can be bad for others who care or depend on one, but the worry here is that a hermit would not have any reason to avoid such dangers.) This would seem to presuppose that we would have no self-regarding reason to want to continue to live. These apparent results of the Epicurean view that "death is nothing to us" are implausible. If

---

22. Tom Stoppard, *Rosencrantz and Guildenstern Are Dead* (New York: Grove Press, 1967): 70–71.

23. In the HBO television series *Game of Thrones*, one of the characters says, "A man has the choice between a moment of cowardice or spending the rest of his life dead."

they were indeed results of the view, then the Epicurean would have purchased immunity from death anxiety at the cost of very unattractive implications.[24]

We can make the worry vivid by considering a hypothetical case. Suppose a hermit—with no one (not even family) who cares about him or depends on him—is walking along a train track and sees a train coming very fast. He believes that if he doesn't step off the track, he will be killed instantly (and painlessly) by the train. Of course, this is a wild supposition for which no one in the real world could have decisive evidence, but I ask you to "go with" the example to explore the relevant point about Epicureanism. It would seem that such an individual would have no reason to step off the track, on the Epicurean view. After all, death is nothing to him and thus it is not a bad thing that he would die.

If Epicureanism contends that the hermit should be completely indifferent to his own death, and that he has no reason to continue to live, then it would seem to imply (implausibly) that he has no reason to step off the track to avoid the oncoming train. Now if you say that in the real world the hermit could not know that he would not be subject to terrible pain in the process of being run over by a train, I would reply that it is awkward to think that *this* is the reason why the hermit should step off the track. It seems that there should be a more basic reason, which would obtain even in the hypothetical case in which the hermit *could* somehow know that he would not experience pain, if he were run over by the train.

The Epicurean will insist that there is indeed a reason for the hermit to prefer continued life, insofar as his life will have some suitable amount of pleasure. The Epicurean, of course, argues that death is nothing to us and is not a bad thing for us. But it does not follow from this that one couldn't or shouldn't prefer to go on living. For the Epicurean, although death is not a bad thing for the individual who dies, continued life may well be a good thing, and thus one could prefer continuing to live to

---

24. For helpful discussion of these issues, see Steven Luper-Foy, "Annihilation," *Philosophical Quarterly* 37 (1987): 233–252; reprinted in Fischer, ed., *The Metaphysics of Death*, 269–290; and Stephen Rosenbaum, "Epicurus and Annihilation," *Philosophical Quarterly* 39 (1989): 81–90; reprinted in Fischer, ed., *The Metaphysics of Death*, 293–304.

dying.[25] The Epicurean adopts hedonism as an account of what is intrinsically good for an individual. If the hermit believes that his continued life would have at least an acceptable amount of pleasure, he has reason to want to continue to live and to step off the tracks.

Some have criticized Epicureanism because they have thought that the Epicurean must say that a hermit has no reason not to commit suicide.[26] After all, the Epicurean does not believe that the hermit's death is a bad thing for him. But, again, the Epicurean may hold that the hermit has good reason to reject suicide. The hermit may well prefer continued life to death, because he deems pleasure good. This is completely compatible with the hermit's thinking that death would not be a bad thing for him. The Epicurean might put it this way: "Although death is not bad, life is better than nothing."[27]

You might wonder: if life is good, then isn't death worse? Isn't it bad to end up with the worse alternative? An Epicurean would reply that if life is good, then it is indeed better than death. So if one has a choice between a good life and death, it makes sense to choose life. But it is in general *not* true that if *A* is better than *B*, then *B* is bad. It is better to be given a million dollars than half a million, but getting a half-million dollars is not too shabby! Certainly, if I know that in the future I will get a half-million dollars in a situation in which it would be possible (and better) to get a million, this would not be a reason for *dread* or *fear*.

Since the Epicurean argues that death cannot be a bad thing for the individual who dies, he also believes that it is not rational or appropriate to *fear* or *dread* one's future death. But this does not imply that one should be totally indifferent to one's death in the future. One might, after all, prefer that it take place later than it actually will, and when

---

25. For nice developments of this sort of response on behalf of the Epicurean, see Rosenbaum, "Epicurus and Annihilation" and David Hershenov, "A More Palatable Epicureanism," *American Philosophical Quarterly* 44, no. 2 (2007): 171–180.

26. There is a useful discussion of this issue and defense of Epicureanism in James Warren, *Facing Death: Epicurus and His Critics* (Oxford: Clarendon Press, 2006): 161–212. Warren also considers the question of whether an Epicurean has reason to have a will (specifying a distribution of his assets after death).

27. Although the logic of Epicureanism does not require it, or entail that we have no reason not to commit suicide, Epicurus's follower, Lucretius, did in fact commit suicide.

death is near, one might prefer to continue living. Again: for the Epicurean, although death cannot be a bad thing, living well is a good thing and worth pursuing.

Is it coherent to suppose that death can thwart a preference to continue to live, but still not be a bad thing for the individual who dies? You might think that whenever something thwarts a preference, it is a bad thing for the individual. But this doesn't seem to be true, since one could prefer something that would in fact be bad for oneself; thwarting this preference would not be bad for one. It is just not clear what the relationship is between an individual's preferences and his good.

Given that there are apparent difficulties with the commonsense view (as put forward by the Epicureans and crystallized by Nagel), and the Epicurean position is more nuanced than some have supposed (and not *obviously* subject to counterexamples), it will be helpful to consider more carefully the problems for the commonsense view raised by the Epicureans. It is a widespread and compelling view that death can indeed be a very significant misfortune—a very bad thing—for the individual who dies. Some think of it, in Epicurus's phrase, as "the most terrifying of ills." It is thus worth trying to figure out whether this view can be maintained.

Conclusion

Death is the permanent cessation of living, where living involves specific biological processes: the heart's beating to pump blood, and the brain's functioning in a way that can regulate and control metabolism, cell repair, and so forth. This is not a fully adequate definition, as it is vague, and there are applications that are controversial. But this account of death at least helps us to pick out the target concept. We can work with it.

We tend to think that death can be a bad thing—even a terrible thing—for the individual who dies. But there are problems associated with this view, especially on the assumption that there is no afterlife. How can death be bad, if it does not involve any negative experiences? When is death bad? Since death is the mirror image of prenatal nonexistence, which we do not think of as bad, how can we consistently deem our future deaths bad?

These are significant challenges. Epicurus and his followers find these problems insuperable and conclude that death cannot be a bad thing for the individual who dies. Epicureanism offers a coherent and apparently viable alternative to the view that death can be bad for the individual who dies, an alternative that offers considerable comfort and consolation. It would help us to manage our terror of death.

We don't, however, want to accept a position just because we would welcome its truth; this would be wishful thinking. The commonsense view that death, construed as an experiential blank, can be a misfortune for the individual who dies is widespread and resilient. It makes sense, then, to think carefully about the challenges for this view. If the challenges can be met, then we should not be too quick to fall into the comforting arms of Epicureanism, despite its appeal. But we will see that we needn't fall into despair either.

Annotated Suggestions for Further Reading

The works by Thomas Nagel referred to in the "Suggestions for Further Reading" for Chapter One are again important.

Shelly Kagan's *Death* (New Haven, CT: Yale University Press, 2012) is a lively discussion of death, immortality, and related issues. It is based on his lectures in a course at Yale University, which were videotaped as part of the Open Yale Courses project. These lectures are available online at oyc.yale .edu/philosophy/death.

Two helpful and accessible books on the topics discussed in this chapter and the rest of the book are Todd May, *Death* (Stocksfield Hall, UK: Acumen, 2009) and Christopher Belshaw, *10 Good Questions about Life and Death* (Malden, MA: Wiley/Blackwell, 2005).

Some collections are as follows: John Martin Fischer, ed., *The Metaphysics of Death* (Stanford, CA: Stanford University Press, 1993 [this anthology contains an extended introductory essay]); Ben Bradley, Fred Feldman, and Jens Johansson, *The Oxford Handbook of Philosophy of Death* (New York: Oxford University Press, 2013); Steven Luper, ed., *The Cambridge Companion to Life and Death* (New York: Cambridge University Press, 2014); and James Stacey Taylor, ed., *The Metaphysics and Ethics of Death: New Essays* (New York: Oxford University Press, 2013). Steven Luper's contribution to the online *Stanford Encyclopedia of Philosophy*, "Death," contains a very helpful overview and bibliography.

A more advanced systematic treatment of death and related issues, with a particular emphasis on the definition of death, is Fred Feldman, *Confrontations with the Reaper: A Philosophical Study of the Nature and Value of Death* (New York: Oxford University Press, 2012).

When Jahi McMath, a young woman in Oakland, California, was declared dead by the hospital, her parents disagreed. For a detailed discussion of this difficult and emotionally charged case, see the article, "What Does It Mean to Die?" that appeared in *The New Yorker:* https://www.newyorker.com/magazine/2018/02/05/what-does-it-mean-to-die.

CHAPTER 3

Bads without Negative Experiences?

If a murderer is asked whether he has harmed his victim, he might well reply, "Harmed him? Hell no: I killed him outright!" . . . The death of a victim, it would seem, is not a . . . "harmed condition" . . . [I]t is no condition at all, but rather his total extinction.

—Joel Feinberg,
Harm to Others

....

Introduction

It certainly seems as though death can be a bad thing for the individual who dies. Further, there are (roughly) two views of death: religious and secular. It is clear how death can be bad for an individual, on some religious views: one can end up in hell. You're still there, and you are the subject of unimaginable horrors. But it is not so clear how death can be bad for an individual, on the secular view. After all, as the Epicureans point out, on this view the individual has gone out of existence by the time death takes place. You're not there at all.

The Epicurean holds that something can be a bad thing or harm for an individual at a time only if that individual exists at that time. You have to be there to be the subject of the misfortune. Why should we agree? An important reason stems from the view that something can be bad for an individual only if it is connected in some way with negative or unpleasant *experiences* of the individual. In order for an individual to have negative or unpleasant experiences at a time, he must exist (in some form or other) at that time. How can something be bad for an individual if the individual has no negative experiences—no pain or suffering—as a result of the thing in question? And how could someone have any negative experiences if he does not exist? Of course, you could have anxiety or fear (unpleasant experiences) about the *prospect* of your death; but this is different from having anxiety or fear as a *result* of your death.

Two Experience Requirements

The first way of connecting experience with badness posits a "strong" or "tight" connection between badness and negative experiences. On this view, something can be a bad thing or harm for an individual at a time only if the individual experiences something "negative" (such as pain, suffering, frustration, and so forth) at that time or later. On the secular view, the strong experience requirement entails that death cannot be bad for the individual who dies. An "actual experience" requirement would vindicate Epicureanism about death.

But various philosophers have argued that we should not connect badness with negative experience so tightly. These philosophers have presented examples in which it seems that a person is harmed by something but never experiences anything negative as a result. This passage from Robert Nozick helps to get us started in thinking about the possibility of harm without negative experience:

> Imagine we read the biography of a man who *felt* happy, took pride in his work, family, life, etc. But we also read that his children, secretly, despised him; his wife, secretly, scorned him having innumerable affairs; his work was a subject of ridicule among all others, who kept their opinion from him; *every* source of satisfaction in this man's life was built upon a falsehood, a deception. Do you, in reading about this man's life, think, "What a wonderful life. I wish I, or my children, could lead it?" . . .
> . . . This man lived a lie, though not one that he told.[1]

Nozick's point is that something can be a misfortune for a person even if she never suffers as a result. We can similarly imagine that your privacy is violated, even though you never discover this fact. Perhaps you are the subject of secret surveillance by the government. This would seem to be a bad thing for you, although you may not suffer as a result; after all, you never find out about it.

---

1. Robert Nozick, "On the Randian Argument," *The Personalist* 52 (1971): 282–304; reprinted in Jeffrey Paul, ed., *Reading Nozick* (Totowa, NJ: Rowman and Littlefield, 1981): 206–231; the quotation is from p. 221.

Consider also an important example offered by Thomas Nagel, the "Betrayal Case."[2] (This example is similar to the one offered by Nozick.) Imagine that a group of people whom you thought of as friends—who present themselves as friends—despise you, although you do not realize this. They get together regularly—maybe weekly—and criticize you behind your back. Perhaps they accuse you of plagiarism, cheating on your income taxes, lying to your romantic partner or spouse, and so forth. We assume that you never find out about these meetings or otherwise experience anything unpleasant or negative as a result of them. It seems to many that a bad thing has happened to you here, although you do not actually have any negative experiences as a result of the betrayals.

To clarify, the assumption is not just that you never find out about the meetings and thus never experience disappointment and distress based directly on the betrayals. You do not experience *anything* negative as a result of anyone's behavior caused by the betrayals: the betrayals neither cause you to have negative experiences directly nor *indirectly* (say, by eliminating opportunities you otherwise would have had).

Now it is pretty obvious that what these acquaintances of yours are doing at these "get-togethers" is morally wrong. The Epicureans and the proponents of the commonsense view (that death can be bad without involving unpleasant experiences) agree on this point. Indisputably, your so-called friends act badly. The disagreement comes when the proponent of the commonsense view goes a step farther and says that *you* have been wronged and harmed by these people. The claim is that these people have not just done something wrong, but that they have harmed you. The example at least appears to show that you can be harmed—a bad thing can happen to you—although you experience nothing negative as a result of it (directly or indirectly). It challenges a tight connection between harm and experience.

This example is controversial. Some Epicureans will simply dig in their heels here and say that you are *not* harmed in this case. Perhaps they will deny that you have been betrayed at all; or they might say that, although the typical betrayal causes negative experiences and is bad, this "atypical" betrayal is not a bad thing for you, since you experience nothing

---

2. Thomas Nagel, "Death," in Nagel, *Mortal Questions* (Cambridge: Cambridge University Press, 1979): 1–10; reprinted in John Martin Fischer, ed., *The Metaphysics of Death* (Stanford, CA: Stanford University Press 1993): 61–69. The case is presented on pp. 64–65 of the reprinted paper.

negative as a result of the betrayal. On this view, what you don't know, and doesn't show up in any way in your experiences, doesn't harm you. But many think that you have indeed been betrayed and harmed in this case.

Other Epicureans will accept this claim (that you have indeed been harmed in the Betrayal Case). These Epicureans must reject the close connection between harm and negative experiences—"the strong experience requirement." But they still insist on a connection, even if looser, between badness and negative experience. They contend that you are harmed in the Betrayal Case because you *could have* found out about the betrayals or otherwise have had negative experiences as a result of them. The betrayals are *risky*; they set up the risk of negative experiences, and thus the betrayals harm you. These Epicureans accept a second experience requirement, which posits a connection between harm and the *possibility* of negative experiences; we can call this the "weak experience requirement."

Since you *can* have negative experiences as a result of the betrayals, this sort of Epicurean can agree with the intuition (shared by many) that you are harmed in the Betrayal Case. Further, this version of the experience requirement, as with the stronger version, would provide reason to accept the basic idea of Epicureanism: you have to exist, in order to be harmed. A nonexistent individual doesn't even have the *capacity* for negative experience.

Evaluation of the Weak Experience Requirement

A Counterexample. The weak existence requirement is plausible. It has the correct result in the Betrayal Case—that you have indeed been harmed, since you could have had negative experiences as a result of the betrayals. It is congenial to Epicureanism.

But consider what might be called the "Shielded Betrayal Case." Here we add an "experience shield"—an agent, White, who can prevent you from ever finding out about the clandestine meetings and experiencing anything negative as a result of these unfortunate gatherings. White is poised and ready to intervene, in case you are about to find out (or have a negative experience related to the meetings). So, for example, if someone were to attempt to telephone you to tell you about the meetings, White could prevent her from making the connection by severing the telephone line or causing the cell phone to malfunction or temporarily paralyzing the person, or whatever. And if someone were to try to email you or text you the information, White could destroy your computer and cell phone, or invalidate your service contracts. And so forth. We can imagine that White definitely can shield you from unpleasant experiences; she *cannot* be foiled in shielding you.

White not only has the power to prevent you from having any negative experiences stemming from the meetings, but she intends to use it if (but only if) necessary. She is committed to using her resources and technology to prevent you from having any negative experiences as a result of the meetings, but she will not intervene at all if there is no need to (that is, if no one is trying to get in touch with you, and there is no impending possibility of your having negative experiences as a result of the meetings).[3] White is an "experience shield." An experience shield is like an antiballistic missile system (ABM). It lies dormant unless it senses a threatening missile, but then it swings into action. An experience shield, such as White, is like an ABM where the threats that are intercepted are not missiles, but pieces of information: missives, not missiles!

Now we explicitly add to the description of the case that White does *not* intervene, and everything goes exactly as it does in the original Betrayal Case. The meetings take place with just the same scurrilous verbal attacks as in the original case. It seems to me that you are harmed—a bad thing has happened to you—in the original case, the Betrayal Case. And I think that if so, you are similarly harmed in the Shielded Betrayal Case. After all, everything that actually happens—that actually takes place in the behavior of the participants in the meetings—is exactly the same in both cases, and it would seem, intuitively, that harm or badness to you depends solely on the actual behavior that is putatively harmful in the cases. How could the mere fact that an experience shield, such as White, exists, but is not triggered and thus plays no role, make a difference to your status in the cases? The Epicurean who grants that you are harmed in the (original) Betrayal Case and thus adopts the weak requirement must accept a highly unpalatable result: it is possible that in two cases the behavior and causal consequences of putatively harming factors are *exactly the same*, and yet in one case the "target" is harmed, whereas in the other the target is not harmed.

---

3. The astute reader will recognize the similarity of this case to the famous "Frankfurt-style Cases" (FSCs), in which it appears that an agent is morally responsible for his action, although he could not have done otherwise. In the FSCs, the "counterfactual intervener" Black plays the parallel role to White in the Shielded Betrayal Case: Harry Frankfurt, "Alternate Possibilities and Moral Responsibility," *Journal of Philosophy* 66 (1969): 829–839.

If you are indeed harmed in the Shielded Betrayal Case, as I believe, then we have a case in which an individual is harmed, although it is not possible for him to have negative experiences as a result of the behavior in question. This then would be a counterexample even to the weak experience requirement. There is not even a loose connection between misfortune and experience.

An Epicurean Reply in Support of the Weak Experience Requirement. Some Epicureans will not give up! They contend that we do *not* have a counterexample to the claim of a loose fit between negative experience and badness, because you are *not* harmed in the Shielded Betrayal Case. Their intuitive judgment about the case is that you are not harmed precisely because there is no way that you can find out about the behavior of the people at the meetings or otherwise have negative experiences as a result of this behavior. Here the idea is not just that what you don't know can't harm you; it is that what you *can't* know can't harm you. They are more confident of the weak experience requirement than of an initial intuition that you are harmed in the Shielded Betrayal Case.

Of course, we don't yet have an *argument* for the Epicurean claim here—just an intuitive judgment about the case. Many would contend that we don't need an argument; their intuition about the case is firm. This might be all the Epicurean can say, but it might also be all she needs to say. It just seems clear to anyone inclined toward the Epicurean view about death that you are not harmed in either the original Betrayal case or Shielded Betrayal.

But it always helps to have an argument, and I shall now sketch an argument that has been offered by a contemporary Epicurean. This argument offers examples in which an agent who cannot have the relevant negative experiences does *not* appear to be harmed, and this seems to be precisely *because* the individual cannot have negative experiences. The challenge then is to distinguish these cases from the Shielded Betrayal Case.[4]

This version of Epicureanism starts with the uncontroversial observation that betrayals are *typically* risky. They are in this respect like (say) incautious firings of guns.[5] Incautious firings of guns impose harms on victims by exposing them to the risk of injury or death. Suppose,

---

4. David Suits, "Why Death Is Not Bad for the One Who Died," *American Philosophical Quarterly* 38 (2001): 69–84.

5. Suits, "Why Death Is Not Bad for the One Who Died," 77.

however, that in the case of the incautious firing of a gun, we add features to the situation that guarantee that no one will be injured or killed (à la the Shielded Betrayal Case). We assume that precautions are in place that *ensure* that no one will be adversely affected by the incautious firing of the gun. Now the Epicurean holds that no harm to anyone has taken place, because no risk has been imposed. We should not transfer our intuitions about typical cases to atypical cases.

Similarly, drunk driving is typically wrong and risky. But if barriers are in place that make it absolutely impossible for a pedestrian who is walking in the neighborhood to be affected in any way by a particular instance of drunk driving, it does not seem that the pedestrian is harmed. After all, what is typically risky behavior (drunk driving) is not in fact risky in this situation, and thus there is no harm to the pedestrian. Of course, as in the case of incautious firings of guns, the drunk driver is behaving recklessly, and thus he is blameworthy for *that*. But whom does he harm?

In the incautious gun-firing case and the drunk-driving case, where even the possibility of negative experiences is ruled out, there is no harm. It might seem to be precisely *because* of the impossibility of negative experiences that there is no harm to the passersby. If this is right, then how can you be harmed in the Shielded Betrayal Case? In this case, as in the other two, even the *possibility* of negative experiences is ruled out. If we extrapolate from the gun-firing case and the drunk-driving case, it would seem that the Shielded Betrayal Case is no counterexample to the weak experience requirement. If we think carefully about the gun-firing and drunk-driving cases, perhaps we are forced to adjust our original intuition about the Shielded Betrayal Case and conclude that there is no harm in this case.

A Response to this Epicurean Argument. The folks who favor the commonsense view don't give up easily either! The most promising way to answer this sort of defense of Epicureanism relies on a *normative* (or ethical) theory of interests. Human beings have interests—relatively long-term "stakes" in things. We have interests in having enough food, adequate shelter, good healthcare, clean air and water, and so forth. We have interests in freedom of speech and religion. I think it is normatively plausible that we have an interest in our reputation not being falsely besmirched. We certainly prefer that others think well of us, and that they do not falsely besmirch our reputations. But it is not just that we prefer these things; it seems that we have an *interest* in our reputations not being falsely besmirched in slanderous or libelous ways.

In general, a harm is a setback of an interest.[6] We have interests in not experiencing pain or suffering, and that is why it is often harmful to cause others pain and suffering. Similarly, we have interests in not being subject to the *risk* of pain and suffering. But these "experiential" interests are not the only ones we have. It seems to me that, on any plausible normative theory, we have an interest in not having our reputations falsely besmirched. Thus, it seems to me that in the Shielded Betrayal Case you are harmed: your interest in not having your reputation falsely besmirched is set back.

In contrast, I do not think that, on any plausible normative theory of interests, we have an interest in other people not driving drunk or incautiously firing guns, where they are guaranteed by the circumstances not to cause injury or death as a result of this behavior. We have an interest in not having risks of certain sorts imposed on us. So, in general, we do have an interest in others not firing guns incautiously or driving drunk; that is, we have an interest in others not behaving in these ways *in typical situations*, where risks would be imposed. But I don't think it is plausible that we have interests in others not incautiously firing guns or driving drunk in *all* circumstances.

This is why the passersby are not harmed in the cases under discussion, although you *are* harmed in the Shielded Betrayal Case. They are all cases in which it is impossible for the individual in question to have negative experiences as a result of the purportedly harmful behavior, but *this* fact is not the explanation of the lack of harm in the gun-firing and drunk-driving cases. In these cases no interest of yours is set back—that's the explanation of the absence of harm in these cases. In contrast, you are harmed in Shielded Betrayal Case, because an interest of yours is set back, even though you cannot experience anything negative as a result of the betrayals.

I believe that this approach is promising for meeting the challenge of distinguishing the Shielded Betrayal Case from the other two cases. The analysis would show that the Shielded Betrayal Case would indeed indicate the falsity of the requirement of a weak connection between harm and negative experience. But how do we know that there is an interest at stake in the Shielded Betrayal Case (an interest in our reputations), but not in

---

6. Joel Feinberg defends this account of harm at length in his classic four-volume work, *The Moral Limits of the Criminal Law*. The four volumes were published by Oxford University Press, New York, from 1984 to 1988.

the cases of drunk driving and incautious firing of guns? I think this asymmetry in interests is plausible from a normative perspective, but it will be controversial. An Epicurean will be unsatisfied with this explanation of the alleged difference between the cases. Can we come up with an example (or set of examples) that more strongly supports the commonsense view that death can be bad for the individual who dies? That is, can we come up with a more convincing example in which an individual is harmed by something, even though she cannot experience anything negative as a result?

A Different Response to the Epicurean: The Stroke Case. Suppose that, as a result of an injury or stroke (which, themselves, are not painful), an intelligent, active, and thriving adult, in the prime of his life is reduced to the mental condition of a contented infant.[7] Imagine, further, that all of the individual's needs can be met by a caregiver, and that he is free from pain, suffering, or any worries. We build into the case the assumption that this individual will be cared for all of his life. Let's call this the Stroke Case.

The individual appears to be harmed by the catastrophic stroke, but he does not and *cannot* experience anything negative as a result. I here assume that the individual after the stroke is the same person (in the relevant sense) as the individual before, and it seems to me that this individual suffers a great misfortune, even though he is unaware of it and does not (and cannot) suffer from it. (Note that the assumption of sameness of the person is not a controversial issue in the Shielded Betrayal Case and related cases, and thus it is helpful to have them available for serious consideration, despite their relative complexity.)

The Stroke Case and similar cases (one can be incapacitated in various ways, such as accidents, falls, and so forth) successfully impugn the weak experience requirement and thus break the stalemate about the Shielded Betrayal Case (and its relationship to the other cases). The Incapacitation Cases (as we might call them) are situations in which an individual is harmed, and yet he *cannot* have a negative experience as a result of the allegedly harmful events. His very capacity for such an experience is removed.

We can extrapolate this lesson to death. Death might be a bad thing for an individual, even though she cannot have any negative experiences (or, indeed, any experiences at all) when dead. A bad thing can happen

---

7. This example is in Nagel, "Death," reprinted in Fischer, ed., *The Metaphysics of Death.* The case is presented on pp. 65–66 of the reprinted paper.

to us, even though it robs us of the capacity to experience bad things. Death is like this: it deprives us of the very capacity to have experiences.

In the Stroke Case it is plausible that the individual who is harmed still exists, and in the case of death the individual goes out of existence. When death is, the person is not. So this is a difference between the Stroke Case and death, and this might call into question the extrapolation from the Stroke Case to death. But I do not think that this difference *makes a difference*. It doesn't matter that death eliminates the capacity to experience anything negative by annihilating the individual. A stroke and death are just different *routes* to the relevant property: the lack of the capacity to have a negative experience as a result of the purportedly harmful activity.

Recapitulation. Let's take stock. We started with the strong experience requirement, on which it is necessary *actually* to have negative experiences, in order to be harmed by something. The Betrayal Case calls this into question, so we switched to the weak experience requirement, which states that you are harmed only if you *can* have a negative experience as a result of the thing in question. The Epicurean defends the weak experience requirement, but the Shielded Betrayal Case challenges this.

The point of Shielded Betrayal is that a bad thing can happen to someone enveloped in a bubble—an experience-free zone. If this is so, then death might be bad for the individual who dies, even though death is a bubble of nonexistence: a permanent experience-free zone. We have seen, however, that it is not straightforward to distinguish Shielded Betrayal from other cases (involving drunk driving and incautious firings of guns in bubbles—in "risk-free zones"). In these cases we do *not* think that the individual has been harmed. How are these cases different from Shielded Betrayal? I have suggested that the distinction can be made in terms of interests: there is an interest in your reputation, but there is no interest in someone's not firing a gun in a context in which you cannot be struck by the gun.

To avoid controversy about precisely what interests people have, we could just invoke the Stroke Case. This is simple, without any of the complications of the cases discussed earlier, and it seems to be a clear case in which a bad thing has happened to an individual who cannot have any negative experiences as a result (assuming that the same individual exists after the stroke). If Shielded Betrayal is not convincing to you, or the arguments about it are too complicated, just stick with the

Stroke Case—a relatively simple and clear counterexample to the weak experience requirement. For all that has been said, death might well be a bad thing for the individual who dies. (Sleep well, reader!)

Badness and Fear

Return to the view that death can be bad for the individual who dies without involving any negative experiences. Does it follow from death's badness that it is appropriate or rational to *fear* death? No. There is room for the proponent of the view to deny that death's badness implies that it is appropriate or rational to *fear* death. These are two analytically separate issues.[8]

We might apply many of the insights of the Epicurean about the supposed badness of death to the issue of whether we should *fear* death. Indeed, the issue of what *attitude* is appropriate toward death is arguably the main thrust of the Epicurean view; the Epicurean is primarily concerned to relieve our anxieties about death and to help us to achieve a kind of tranquility about death. (Recall that Epicurus described death as thought to be "the most *terrifying* of ills" [my italics].) Perhaps it is true that what one can't know can still harm one. But it does seem that one shouldn't *fear* something that won't—and cannot—involve any negative experiences for oneself.[9]

Think of it this way. On the secular view, death would be like being under general anesthesia—forever. I have had general anesthesia while undergoing surgery. When I awakened, I realized that I had not had any unpleasant experiences (or any experiences at all) during the time of the surgery. (Let's assume that I was not given a drug that caused me to forget whatever experiences I had.) Now I can imagine that I never awaken. Would it be rational to *fear* this condition in the future? It could be a *bad thing* for me that I never awaken—it could deprive me of

---

8. Kai Draper argues that Epicurus would concede that death is a "comparative bad" insofar as it deprives the individual of a good continuation of life. But he claims that his main contention is that death is not an "absolute bad" and thus should not be feared or dreaded: "Epicurus on the Value of Death," in James Stacey Taylor, ed., *The Metaphysics and Ethics of Death* (New York: Oxford University Press, 2013): 71–79.

9. Draper, "Epicurus on the Value of Death." One might resist this contention by pointing out that someone can fear what will happen to people one loves and cares about after one's death. I owe this point to David Beglin. An Epicurean might reply that one can be *concerned* about what will happen to these people and deem it important that they fare well; but they will claim that *fear* is inappropriate here.

what otherwise would be a good continuation of life. But I don't think I should *fear* this sort of scenario. It wasn't unpleasant at all to be under general anesthesia, which I can imagine continuing forever. The value status of death (its badness, for example) is a different matter from the appropriateness of certain attitudes toward death (including fear of it). The Epicurean contends that fear would be inappropriate when directed toward nothingness, as opposed to pain.

We just don't know what awaits us after we die.[10] Apart from the possibility of an unpleasant afterlife, I think that nothingness *itself* can seem frightening, despite the Epicureans' attempts to damp down our anxieties. Julian Barnes writes:

> I find this in my diary, written twenty and more years ago:
> People say of death, "There's nothing to be frightened of." They say it quickly, casually. Now let's say it again, slowly, with re-emphasis. "There's NOTHING to be frightened of." . . . The word that is most true, most exact, most filled with meaning, is the word "nothing."[11]

Nothingness can be frightening. We don't just fear being around and suffering. We fear not being around at all, losing our viewpoint on the world entirely. It definitely helps to know that you won't be suffering, but if this is because you won't exist at all, the comfort might seem cold (or, at best, partial).

No matter what awaits us after we die, at least *some* fear seems justified. Human beings find it hard to eliminate the fear of death. Perhaps it is a mistake to fear death, but if so, it is a mistake that is hard to shake. The inescapable fact about death (on the secular view) is that our point of view will vanish, and this in itself is frightening.

In P.D. James's mystery novel *Death of an Expert Witness*, the forensic pathologist, Dr. Lorrimer, tells his assistant:

> "You'll be getting exhibits from your first murder case this morning. Don't let them worry you, Brenda. There's only one death we need to be frightened of, and that's our own."[12]

---

10. In *The Tragedy of Hamlet*, Act III, Scene I, Shakespeare refers to death as a place from which no one has returned (and described it), calling death ". . . the undiscovered country, from whose bourn [n]o traveller returns . . ."

11. Julian Barnes, *Nothing To Be Frightened Of* (New York: Alfred A. Knopf, 2008): 99.

12. P.D. James, *Death of an Expert Witness* (New York: Warner Books, 1977).

Conclusion

We have considered an important challenge to the commonsense view that death can be a harm or bad thing for the individual who dies. How can one deny the existence of an afterlife and still believe that death can be a bad thing for the individual who dies? If all misfortunes involve negative experiences, and death contains no experiences, why is death bad?

Some interesting examples appear to show that there are misfortunes (other than death) that don't even contain the *possibility* of negative experiences (for the individual who is purportedly harmed). They (and especially the Incapacitation Cases, such as Stroke) go a long way toward showing that death can be bad for the individual who dies—even if it does not involve even the possibility of negative experiences.

Even though the argumentation in parts of this chapter can seem intricate, we can boil things down to a simple disagreement. Those inclined toward the Epicurean view are likely to judge that in such cases as Betrayal and Shielded Betrayal you are not harmed. Those are their considered intuitive judgments about the cases, which are consistent with maintaining some sort of necessary connection between harm and negative experience. This supports their core belief that death cannot be bad for the individual who dies. In contrast, the critic of Epicureanism will judge that you are indeed harmed in these (and related) cases, and thus the connection between harm and negative experience, in any form, is broken. This opens the door to the view that death may well be bad for the individual who dies.

Given that the prospect of a permanent lack of consciousness can be frightening, it seems to be appropriate to fear death at least to *some* degree. It is not easy to entirely expunge our fear of death. I won't be there at all! Nevertheless, the Epicureans may help us to recognize that we should not fear death *as much* as we might, if we don't reflect carefully on the nature of death. They contend that if we think about the fact that we will not suffer, our fear of death will diminish. Epicureanism then might point us to a less neurotic and unhealthy fear of death, even if we still deem it a bad thing and fear it to some degree.

You might think of two extremes: the Epicurean denial of the rationality of *any* fear of death, and a crippling fear of death. Perhaps the

Epicurean point can be "softened," while still acknowledging that death is scary. I think death can indeed be bad for the deceased, and that it is rational to fear death at least to *some* degree. But I do not think there is any reason to *dread* death, to focus on it obsessively, or to fear it so much that it gets in the way of flourishing. We will never exist again, but it is not as though we will be *tortured* forever. The Epicureans have a point, although not the one they especially cherish.

Annotated Suggestions for Further Reading

Joel Feinberg gives a comprehensive analysis and discussion of harm as a setback of an interest in his four-volume work, *The Moral Limits of the Criminal Law* (New York: Oxford University Press, 1984–1988).

For sympathetic treatments of Epicureanism, together with important historical and textual analyses, see Martha Nussbaum, *The Therapy of Desire: Theory and Practice in Hellenistic Ethics* (Princeton, NJ: Princeton University Press, 1994); James Warren, *Facing Death: Epicurus and His Critics* (Oxford: Clarendon Press, 2006); and Phillip Mitsis, *Epicurus' Ethical Theory: The Pleasures of Invulnerability* (Ithaca, NY: Cornell University Press, 1988). A helpful resource is James Warren, ed., *The Cambridge Companion to Epicureanism* (Cambridge: Cambridge University Press, 2006).

A seminal treatment of Epicureanism is Thomas Nagel, "Death," in Nagel, *Mortal Questions* (Cambridge: Cambridge University Press, 1979): 1–10; reprinted in John Martin Fischer, ed., *The Metaphysics of Death* (Stanford, CA: Stanford University Press, 1993): 61–69. Nagel elaborates in Thomas Nagel, *The View from Nowhere* (New York: Oxford University Press, 1986, revised edition, 1989).

For some additional critical reflections on Epicureanism, see Steven Luper, *Invulnerability: On Securing Happiness* (Chicago: Open Court, 1996); Fred Feldman, *Confrontations with the Reaper: A Philosophical Study of the Nature and Value of Death* (New York: Oxford University Press, 2012), especially pp. 127–142; and John Martin Fischer, *Our Stories: Essays on Life, Death, and Free Will* (New York: Oxford University Press, 2009).

The Stoic philosopher Seneca (as with Epicurus, a post-Aristotelian or "Hellenistic" philosopher) provided various insights about death and practical ideas for coming to terms with it. For a useful compilation of his work on death, see *How to Die: An Ancient Guide to the End of Life*, edited, translated, and introduced by James S. Romm (Princeton, NJ: Princeton University Press, 2018).

CHAPTER 4

It's about Time: Timing and Mirror Images

"What's this?" I say to myself. "Does death make trial of me so frequently? Let it: I've done likewise to death, for a long time." When was that, you ask? Before I was born: for death is non-existence. I know what that's like. It will be the same after me as it was before me. If death holds any torment, then that torment must also have existed before we came forth into the light, but back then, we felt nothing troubling. I ask you, wouldn't you call it a very foolish thing if someone judges that a lamp is worse off after it's snuffed out than before it has been lighted? We too are snuffed out and lighted. In the time in between, we have sense and experience; before and after is true peace. We go wrong in this, Lucilius, if I'm not mistaken: we think that death comes after, whereas in fact it comes both before and after. Whatever existed before us was death. What does it matter whether you cease to be, or never begin? The outcome of either is just this: that you don't exist.

—Seneca,
Epistle 54[1]

··········

Introduction

When is death bad, if it is bad? This is a vexing question. Typically, we think that an individual is harmed by a set of events (or states of affairs) *during or after* the events in question. It is important to distinguish the time of the harmful events from the time of the harm. (A time here can be a stretch of time.) So, to pick a horrifying example, torture is a

---

1. Seneca, a Roman stoic philosopher, lived just after Lucretius.

harmful set of events, and it harms the individual being tortured both during and after the torture takes place. During the torture, the individual is in pain and may be physically or emotionally damaged (or both); after the torture, the individual has to deal with the memories and the ongoing pain and physical and emotional damage. Same with other misfortunes, such as being punched in the stomach, falling and breaking one's leg, having a toothache, and so forth: the harm takes place during and/or after the harmful event.

How can the time of the harm of your death be *during* your death? (Again, we are thinking of death here as the status of being dead, rather than the transition, during which the individual arguably still exists.) How can an individual be harmed when he is in the state of being dead, when he does not exist? A slightly different way to ask the question: how can an individual have a property (or characteristic), such as being harmed, when he does not even exist?

Another challenge to the secular view comes from Lucretius's famous Mirror Image Argument (introduced in Chapter Two). The argument presupposes that our lives are a "blip" between two great absences: the time before we were born and the time after we die. Clarence Darrow notoriously said, "Life is an unpleasant interruption of a peaceful nothingness."[2]

The Lucretian argument does not ask us to take an "objective" and "detached" viewpoint on our lives (as in the zoom-out arguments discussed in Chapter One), noting that we are tiny blips or mere specks in an ocean of nothingness. Rather, it assumes that we are living our lives and temporally located "here." It invokes judgments and attitudes we have in our concrete, temporally located situations. It zooms in on our actual thoughts and attitudes in our lives. The basic idea is that since posthumous and prenatal nonexistence are the same to me now, I should make the same judgments and have the same attitudes toward them. Since I am indifferent to past nonexistence, I should not judge my future death bad or fear it.

The Epicureans (including Lucretius) are particularly concerned about our *attitudes*, such as anxiety and fear. They think of philosophy

---

2. Barbara Ehrenreich writes: "You can think of death bitterly or with resignation, as a tragic interruption of your life, and take every possible measure to postpone it. Or, more realistically, you can think of life as an interruption of an eternity of personal nonexistence, and seize it as a brief opportunity to observe and interact with the living, ever-surprising world around us" (*Natural Causes* [New York: Hachette, 2018]: xv).

as a kind of "therapy," which can reduce our concerns about features of our lives—anxieties they believe are confused and irrational.[3] The Mirror Image Argument complements the therapy offered by the no-experience and timing arguments.

The Timing Problem

The timing problem stems from the facts pointed out by the Epicurean: when the person exists, death does not, and when death exists, the person does not. If we say that a person P is harmed at a particular time T (where T can be an interval), we are saying that P has the property, being harmed, at (or during) T. But if P has a property at (or during) T, it would seem that P must exist at (or during) T. So how can death be a bad thing for the individual who dies? It appears to be a harm without a subject: a harm at (or during) T without a subject existing at (or during) T.

This is the "Problem of Predication." A property instance must involve a bearer of the property, and it is plausible to think that a property instance at T must involve a bearer who exists at T. The problem might be put generally: how can an individual who does not exist at T have a property at T? The Problem of Predication, as it applies specifically to death, is as follows: how can an individual who does not exist during the time at which he is dead have the property "being harmed" at that time?

Answers to the Timing Challenge

Priorism. One way to answer this challenge is to say that the time of the harm of death takes place *before* death has taken place. That is, one's (premature) death harms one while one still exists. The subject of the harm is the "antemortem" person (the person as he was while he was alive), who need not be *aware* of the harm.[4] This solves the problem of the harm without a subject: one's death is a harm at a time or times during which one exists. Because this view contends that the harm of

---

3. Steven Luper-Foy, "Annihilation," *Philosophical Quarterly* 37 (1987): 233–252; reprinted in John Martin Fischer, ed., *The Metaphysics of Death* (Stanford, CA: Stanford University Press, 1993): 269–290; and Martha Nussbaum, *The Therapy of Desire: Theory and Practice in Hellenistic Ethics* (Princeton, NJ: Princeton University Press, 1994). These were referred to in Chapter Two.

4. Pitcher introduces the term "antemortem" in George Pitcher, "The Misfortunes of the Dead," *American Philosophical Quarterly* 21 (1984): 183–188; reprinted in John Martin Fischer, ed., *The Metaphysics of Death* (Stanford, CA: Stanford University Press, 1993): 157–168.

death occurs prior to the person's going out of existence, we will call the view "priorism."[5] Although priorism has the manifest virtue of solving the Predication Problem, it has a vice from the get-go: it is implausible. We should note that initial implausibility is not a fatal flaw in a philosophical theory; otherwise we'd be left with very few! But it is at least a strike against a theory.

It just seems strange to think that something could harm you before it actually occurs, even if you are unaware of it. On priorism, your death (especially if it will be premature) is harming you even now, although you don't know this. Of course, one could be harmed by worrying about something or fearing it. The *prospect* of one's death can be a misfortune for one while one still exists. But how can you be harmed by your own death itself (the status of being dead), prior to its occurrence?

Subsequentism. Subsequentism is the view that the harm of death takes place after the individual goes out of existence. The harm of death takes place at (or during) the time of one's death. This makes the time of the harm of death parallel to the times of other harms—during or after the time the harmful events take place. In contrast, priorism treats the time of the harm of death differently from the time of other harms; on priorism, the harm of death takes place *before* the harmful event: harm time-travel.

Being harmed is a property. So, if death harms someone subsequent to his going out of existence, the individual has the property, "being harmed," at (or during) a time when he does not exist. Subsequentism (unlike priorism) faces the Problem of Predication.

Is this problem impossible to solve? I do not think so. We can start by noting that Aristotle has various properties now, even though he does not exist now. Aristotle has the property of being written about by John Fischer, of being a very influential philosopher, and so forth. Aristotle now has these properties, although he does not exist now. This fact would seem to provide an initial step toward an answer to the Problem of Predication.

---

5. This term, together with "subsequentism" and other terms related to the timing problem, were originally introduced by Steven Luper, "Mortal Harm," *Philosophical Quarterly* 57 (2007): 239–251. He here argues for *priorism*. For a critique, see Jens Johansson, "The Timing Problem," in Ben Bradley, Fred Feldman, and Jens Johansson, *The Oxford Handbook of the Philosophy of Death* (New York: Oxford University Press, 2013): 255–273.

Abraham Lincoln is now well regarded for leading the fight against slavery, and Franklin Delano Roosevelt for tackling the Great Depression. Stalin is one of the most notorious leaders in modern history, and Adolf Hitler is hated for his evil.[6] All of these thoughts involve predicating properties of nonexistent persons. Why should we think it is any different when we say that an individual is harmed after she ceases to exist by her own death?

Thus, it is *not* incoherent to suppose that some previously existing person can now have the property of being harmed by death, at least if we take seriously our ordinary views. I have certainly not here provided a full answer to the Problem of Predication, especially if one is skeptical (at a deeper level) about the coherence of our commonsense beliefs. But I have suggested that we do not in general reject the notion that a previously existing individual can now have a property. This is not property time-travel: the property is had now, although the individual existed before.

Atemporalism. "Atemporalism" names the view that death is a harm for the individual who dies, but at no particular time. Thomas Nagel writes:

> There certainly are goods and evils of a simple kind (including some pleasures and pains) that a person possesses at a given time simply in virtue of his condition at that time. But this is not true of all the things we regard as good or bad for a man. Often we need to know his history to tell whether something is a misfortune or not; this applies to ills like deterioration, deprivation, and damage. Sometimes his experiential *state* is relatively unimportant—as in the case of a man who wastes his life in the cheerful pursuit of a method of communicating with asparagus plants.
>
>   . . . It therefore seems to me worth exploring the position that most good and ill fortune has as its subject a person identified by his history and his possibilities, rather than merely by his categorical state of the moment—and that while this subject can be exactly located in a sequence of places and times, the same is not necessarily true of the goods and ills that befall him.[7]

_____

6. Hitler *was* a monstrous person—he *had* this property during his life. But Hitler also *is* reviled now—he has a range of properties now, although he does not exist now.

7. Thomas Nagel, "Death," in Nagel, *Mortal Questions* (Cambridge: Cambridge University Press, 1979): 1–10; reprinted in John Martin Fischer, ed., *The Metaphysics of Death* (Stanford, CA: Stanford University Press 1993): 61–69. The quotation is on p. 65 in the reprinted paper.

Note that atemporalism treats the harm of death differently from many other harms, in that there is no specific time at which the harm of death is located. So, like priorism, atemporalism is committed to a certain lack of uniformity in its views about the time of harms.

None of the contenders here is entirely without difficulties. A bullet must be bitten, and the only question is which one is least unpalatable. In my view, bullet biting, although not rewarding metaphysical gastronomy, is preferable to concluding that death cannot be a bad thing for an individual. I think that *subsequentism* and *atemporalism* would result in less philosophical indigestion than *priorism*.

Lucretius's Mirror Image Argument: The Symmetry Problem

The issues raised by Lucretius's Mirror Image Argument are deep and fascinating. Although we sketched the argument earlier, it will be helpful to have it here as well. The argument can be put in terms of judgments about values (badness/goodness) or attitudes (fear/indifference). Start with the judgments-about-values version. We do not consider it a bad thing for us that we were born when we were actually born, rather than earlier, and upon reflection, this judgment seems reasonable. The time after we die is the mirror image of the time before we were born. Thus, we should not deem it a bad thing that we die when we will actually die, rather than later. Early death has the same value status as late birth.

Here's the "attitudes version." The time after we die is the mirror image of the time before we were born. We are indifferent to the time before we were born. Thus, we should not fear the status of being dead. Here symmetry in metaphysics drives symmetry in psychology.[8]

---

8. Metaphysics is, roughly speaking, the study of what "is" or "exists" in a fundamental sense. Often the term (or its adjective form, *metaphysical*) is used to denote a "descriptive" fact about the way the world is. Metaphysics thus differs from ethics, which points us to reasons for action. Metaphysics is in itself motivationally inert, whereas ethics seeks to guide our actions. "Normativity" is this property of giving us reasons for action. Simplifying greatly, metaphysics is about the realm of descriptive facts, and ethics is about values (the normative realm). We will here take facts about our minds, attitudes such as fear or dread or indifference, as parts of "psychology," rather than metaphysics. So metaphysics would include the fact that prenatal and posthumous nonexistence are similar deprivations, whereas their status as bads (or not) is a normative question; and the issues about fear, dread, and indifference are psychological.

This is a powerful argument, which has engaged many philosophers and writers over the centuries. What are we to make of the Mirror Image Argument? Given the symmetry between prenatal and posthumous nonexistence, one option would be to turn the argument on its head and argue that, since we do in fact deem posthumous nonexistence a bad thing, we should also deem prenatal nonexistence a bad thing. Since we fear posthumous nonexistence, we should regret prenatal nonexistence.

This just seems unduly gloomy. It is intuitively jarring and implausible to suppose that we should think of our late births as a bad thing, or regret our late births. We already have enough problems—why manufacture a new one? The right attitude toward prenatal nonexistence seems to be indifference, not regret. What about someone who regrets missing the Sixties or never having known his grandfather? We will come back to such folks later.

Alternatively, we could give the symmetry a different valence, as Lucretius encourages us to do. On this approach, we should have the same tranquil equipoise toward posthumous nonexistence as we have toward prenatal nonexistence. Any comfort in the face of existential threats is to be welcomed. But wanting something does not make it true, and to many people this argument will seem to be an example of wishful thinking.

Most of us think that, whereas it is inappropriate and irrational to think of prenatal nonexistence as bad or something to be regretted, it is appropriate or rational to deem posthumous nonexistence (at least *premature* death) a bad thing and to fear it (to some reasonable degree). The two periods are indeed mirror images of one another "metaphysically"; prenatal nonexistence is a deprivation in the same way in which posthumous nonexistence is. Early death is a deprivation in the same way as late birth is: holding fixed the time of birth and allowing for a later death might bring life that is, on balance, desirable, and holding fixed the time of death and allowing for an earlier birth might bring life that is, on balance, desirable.

It does *not*, however, follow from *this* symmetry that we should make similar value judgments about the two periods or have similar attitudes toward these periods. I contend that the *metaphysical* (or *descriptive*) symmetry does not entail a *normative* symmetry, and it does not imply a symmetry of attitudes. We think of our early deaths very differently from our late births. This appears to be a basic fact about human beings.

How could we *explain and defend* the widespread asymmetry in human beliefs about, and attitudes toward, prenatal and posthumous nonexistence? How could a proponent of the commonsense asymmetry respond to the Lucretian Mirror Image Argument?

Responses to the Mirror Image Argument

The Asymmetry of Possibility. The Asymmetry of Possibility view answers the Mirror Image Argument by contending that, whereas it is possible for an individual to live longer than he actually lives by dying later, it is impossible for an individual to have been born significantly earlier that he actually was born.[9] That is, it is possible to die later, but impossible to have been born earlier. The idea is that I—the very same "I"—can live longer than I actually live, because we can imagine an additional segment of my life "added on" to my life. In contrast, I could not have been born significantly earlier, because anyone born significantly earlier would not have been me (the particular person I am).

This is an answer to the Mirror Image Argument in all its forms because it denies the premise that states that prenatal nonexistence is the mirror image of posthumous nonexistence. It denies metaphysical symmetry: it is incoherent to suppose that I was born (significantly) earlier than I actually was born, whereas it is coherent to imagine that I will die later than I actually will die. Seeking to imagine an earlier birth is to attempt to imagine the impossible, whereas considering a later death focuses on a possible state of affairs. It is not a bad thing that I wasn't born earlier, since this would have been impossible; it is not to be regretted that I wasn't born earlier, since this would have been impossible. But it is possible that I die later than I actually will die.

Why exactly is it impossible for me to have been born significantly earlier than I actually was born? This is not as straightforward as it might seem. Some think that essential to me—to being the particular person I am—is the fact that I developed from a particular sperm and egg.[10] Then the idea is that anyone born much earlier would not have been the product of that same combination of sperm and egg.

---

9. Thomas Nagel suggested this way of responding to Lucretius's argument: Nagel, "Death."

10. Saul Kripke, *Naming and Necessity* (Hoboken, NJ: Wiley/Blackwell, 1991).

Or perhaps it is essential to me that I have the DNA I actually have. Then the point would be that anyone born significantly earlier would not have the same DNA as I actually have. Or maybe it is essential to me that I have a specific history—that my life corresponds to a specific ongoing narrative. The contention would be that anyone born significantly earlier than I actually was born would have had a different (relatively specific) narrative.

The Asymmetry of Possibility view holds that, on any plausible approach to personal identity (the identity of the *particular* person), I could not have been born significantly earlier than I actually was born. This explains and, more importantly, *justifies* my indifference to the fact that I was not born significantly earlier, but it does *not* warrant an inference to the conclusion that I should be indifferent to my death (or that my death cannot be bad for me). This is because posthumous nonexistence is not the mirror image of prenatal nonexistence; whereas it is impossible, in a very strong sense, for me to have been born earlier than I actually was born, it is *not* impossible that I live longer than I actually will live.

This is a plausible and appealing response to the Lucretian Mirror Image Argument. But is it really true that I could not have been born significantly earlier than I actually was born? It *seems* to me that I could have been born in Athens a long time ago and talked with Plato and Aristotle. (Actually, I would appreciate getting their feedback on my views about free will!) I can imagine it, so it is not *obvious* that I couldn't have been born earlier.

Even if it were true that I could not have been born significantly earlier, does this fact really justify our asymmetric attitudes toward prenatal and posthumous nonexistence? In an intriguing passage in his classic article, "Death," Thomas Nagel explores these questions:

> [Consider the following] suggestion of Robert Nozick. We could imagine discovering that people developed from individual spores that had existed indefinitely far in advance of their birth. In this fantasy, birth never occurs naturally more than a hundred years before the permanent end of the spore's existence. But then we discover a way to trigger the premature hatching of these spores, and people are born who have thousands of years of active life before them. Given such a situation, it would be possible to imagine *oneself* having come into existence thousands of years previously. . . . the consequence appears

> to be that a person's birth at a given time *could* deprive him of many earlier years of possible life. Now while it would be cause for regret that one had been deprived of all those years of life by being born too late, the feeling would be different from that which many people have about death.[11]

Nagel's point is that we can (apparently, at least) imagine a situation or situations in which we come from spores that can be triggered to hatch significantly earlier than they actually hatch. Now imagine that you live in such a world. Although you might have *some* regret about not having been hatched or "born" significantly earlier, your attitude toward this period would be very different from the feeling you would have about death. Thus, Nagel claims that even if we *could* have been born significantly earlier, the asymmetry in our attitudes would *still* be present. This at least suggests that the asymmetry of possibility (the fact that I can die later but could not have been born earlier) is not what explains the asymmetry in our attitudes toward prenatal and posthumous nonexistence: this asymmetry would still exist, in a world in which we could have been born earlier. If this is correct, then we still don't have an adequate answer to the Lucretian Mirror Image Argument.

The example of the spore world raises interesting questions about who exactly we care about, when we consider "our" later deaths and earlier births. Do we care about ourselves, thought of as "thin persons," without particular narratives or personalities? The spores seem to be thin persons, conceptualized as the "essence" of you, but without a particular narrative or rich set of personal characteristics. Nagel's story suggests that you—the very same "essence"—could have been hatched significantly earlier, and thus you could have had a very different narrative and personality. Given that we care about this thin self or essence, abstracted away from a narrative and specific personality traits, the asymmetry of possibility disappears, and thus it cannot provide an adequate response to the Lucretian argument. My thin self could have existed significantly earlier, just as it is possible that my thin self may have a longer life than it actually will.

In contrast, some philosophers insist that we do not care about this sort of thin self or bare essence; rather, on their view we care about our

---

11. Nagel, "Death," endnote 3, pp. 370–371 in the reprinted article (Fischer, ed., *The Metaphysics of Death*).

"thick" selves—with a certain history and personality.[12] They point out that when we consider the possibility of living longer, we are imagining that we as *thick selves* shall live longer. They conclude that to be consistent in our evaluation of the Mirror Image Argument, we need to seek to imagine ourselves as *thick selves* having been born earlier. These philosophers contend that, whereas it might be possible to imagine your thin self having been born considerably earlier, it is *impossible* coherently to imagine your thick self having been born significantly earlier. After all, anyone born considerably earlier would have had a very different history. Invocation of the thick self view of who we care about appears to provide a defense of the asymmetry of possibility answer to Lucretius.

But is it really true that we do not care about the thin self in these matters? Let's suppose you are adopted shortly after your birth by a couple who takes care of you. We can imagine that at some point later in your life you wonder what it would have been like to have been raised by your biological parents. We can even imagine that you very strongly wish that you had indeed been raised by your birth parents.

This is similar to a "baby-switching" case. Imagine that the hospital made a horrific mistake and sent you home with the wrong parents. You are thus raised by a different couple than your biological parents. Later in your life, when you discover that the hospital made this mistake, it is quite possible that you will attempt to find your birth parents and even regret that you were not raised by them. In these sorts of cases, it appears that you care about your thin self. You prefer that your thin self had developed or had been "attached to" a different thick self.[13]

For the sake of our exploration of the issues here, put these points about the thin self aside for now. Is it really so obvious that you, thought of

---

12. For the terminology "thin" and "thick" persons, and its employment as part of the asymmetry of possibility view, I am indebted to Frederick Kaufman, "Pre-Vital and Post-Mortem Non-Existence," *American Philosophical Quarterly* 36 (1999): 1–19. Kaufman has defended the Asymmetry of Possibility approach in various papers. Christopher Belshaw also defends this strategy of response to Lucretius: Christopher Belshaw, "Asymmetry and Nonexistence," *Philosophical Studies* 70 (1993): 103–116. Kaufman and Belshaw are leading proponents of the asymmetry of possibility response to the Mirror Image Argument. In the text I rely especially on Kaufman's development of this view.

13. The comedian Lily Tomlin says in her one-woman theatrical performance *The Search for Signs of Intelligent Life in the Universe:* "When I was young, I thought, 'I really want to be someone.' Now I realize I should have been more careful."

as a thick self, could not have been born considerably earlier than you were actually born? This is a difficult question to answer. If we make the historical or narrative components of the thick self so specific as to include particular dates, then it would indeed be impossible for the thick self to have come into existence earlier. So, if your thick self includes, for example, "Your being in kindergarten on September 1, 1997," then it is impossible for you to have been born significantly earlier than you were actually born.

But why suppose that we care about ourselves as thick selves specified so precisely? Why not think of ourselves as having a certain sort of narrative arc, but where the events are not specified in terms of dates? (So, how about: "Your being in kindergarten when you were five years old"?) We could think of ourselves as having the same narrative arc, even if not all of the particular events, specified very precisely, are the same. This narrative arc might specify a humble beginning leading eventually to great success; or it might go the other way around. Many different narrative arcs can be imagined, and given any particular one, it can be "filled in" by various different specific events. It may well be that, in order to have the same narrative arc (in the relevant sense), many of the events, or certainly most of the important events, must be the same (perhaps we could say, "of the *same type*") as in your actual history. But, as earlier, this does not imply that the events must have taken place at the very same times as they actually occurred. It does not require *precisely* the same events. This is a more plausible way of understanding ourselves as thick selves. It is much more reasonable to think that we care about ourselves, so conceived.

It is not so clear that it is *impossible* that our thick selves, so construed, have come into being significantly earlier than they actually did. It is indeed far-fetched to suppose that our thick selves could have come into being significantly earlier than they actually did. But far-fetchedness is not impossibility. So it seems that the Asymmetry of Possibility answer to the Lucretian Mirror Image Argument is inadequate (or at least not totally convincing) on either the thin or thick interpretation of the self about whom we care. We can imagine both the thin and thick selves having come into being earlier.[14]

---

14. For a nuanced defense of this view, see Travis Timmerman, "Avoiding the Asymmetry Problem," *Ratio* (new series) XXXI (March 2018): 88–102.

Maybe we are not interpreting the asymmetry of possibility view charitably. We might then recast this answer to the Lucretian Mirror Image Argument as invoking a slightly different asymmetry of possibility: the asymmetry of plausible (or perhaps "easily conceivable as occurring") possibility. It is much easier to imagine that I die later than I actually will die than that I came into existence significantly earlier than I actually did. It is rather easy to imagine that an individual dies later than he actually dies; one just extends the life of the thick self, as it actually has been (or will have been). But it is much harder to imagine that an individual's thick self came into existence significantly earlier than it actually did; more features of the world would have to be "adjusted" to produce the same thick self existing earlier. We could put it this way: it would be a greater departure from reality to get to a situation in which an individual's thick self came into existence considerably earlier than to get to a situation in which an individual's thick self dies considerably later.

Is this asymmetry significant? Does it justify the asymmetry in our judgments about and attitudes toward prenatal and posthumous non-existence? Philosophers inclined toward the Asymmetry of Possibility view often dismiss the relevance of the possibility of having been born earlier (as the same thick self), because it is so far-fetched, implausible, or unlikely. But I am not sure that it matters how "far-fetched," implausible, or unlikely a scenario is, for the purpose of underwriting an answer to the Lucretian Mirror Image Argument. After all, our hopes and fears are often attached to possibilities that are highly unlikely. So, for example, I might be afraid that my house will catch on fire, despite the fact that I've taken special precautions and fires in the area in which my house is located are very rare. I might hope to win the Powerball lottery, although I recognize just how unlikely this is. Despite my knowledge that my chance to win the lottery is (say) one in one hundred million, I still go to the donut shop and buy my lottery ticket. (This mainly provides an excuse for getting an old-fashioned donut with icing, but, still, I do hope to win, if only a little bit.)

When the stakes are high, even unlikely scenarios can capture our attention in ways that engage our emotions. Winning the lottery would be an extremely good outcome, and my house's burning down an extremely bad one. Despite the unlikeliness of their occurrence, I can still hope for the lottery win and fear the burning down of my house.

Of course, I shouldn't pay a lot of attention to these possibilities. I shouldn't place a lot of hope on my lottery ticket or become preoccupied with the possibility of my house burning down. But it just doesn't seem out of the ballpark of rationality to hope, at least a little, that my ticket wins the lottery and to fear, at least a little, the catastrophic results of a fire in my neighborhood. Surely it can be rational to buy fire insurance, even if a fire is extremely unlikely. So the asymmetry of plausible possibility doesn't seem to drive an asymmetry in attitudes. It is thus helpful to consider an alternative answer to the Mirror Image Argument.

The Parfit-Style Response. Here we shall be concerned with the version of the Mirror Image Argument that pertains to our *attitudes* toward late birth and early death, rather than the value status of late birth and early death. After all, the primary thrust of the Epicurean arguments, including Lucretius's Mirror Image Argument, is an attempt to assuage our worries and anxieties about death. Consider this example from Derek Parfit:

> I am in some hospital to have some kind of surgery. Since this is completely safe, and always successful, I have no fears about the effects. The surgery may be brief, or it may instead take a long time. Because I have to co-operate with the surgeon, I cannot have anesthetics. I have had this surgery once before, and I can remember how painful it is. Under a new policy, because the operation is so painful, patients are now afterwards made to forget it. Some drug removes their memories of the last few hours.
>
> I have just woken up. I cannot remember going to sleep. I ask my nurse if it has been decided when my operation is to be, and how long it must take. She says that she knows the facts about both me and another patient, but that she cannot remember which facts apply to whom. She can tell me only that the following is true. I may be the patient who had his operation yesterday. In that case, my operation was the longest ever performed, lasting ten hours. I may instead be the patient who is to have a short operation later today. It is either true that I did suffer for ten hours, or true that I shall suffer for one hour.
>
> I ask the nurse to find out which is true. While she is away, it is clear to me which I prefer to be true. If I learn that the first is true, I shall be greatly relieved.[15]

---

15. Derek Parfit, *Reasons and Persons* (Oxford: Clarendon Press, 1984): 165–166.

I agree with Parfit. I would hope that the nurse would come back with the news that the longer, and thus more painful, operation had already taken place, and I would be greatly relieved by this news. We human beings want our pains in the past, other things equal. This seems to be a deep-seated feature of us: we regard our own past and future sufferings asymmetrically. Perhaps this justifies our asymmetric attitudes toward prenatal and posthumous nonexistence, which would then count as a specific instance of a more general asymmetry in our attitudes toward past and future bads.

We will return to this possibility later, but here it will be helpful to pause for a clarification. The asymmetry in our attitudes toward past and future sufferings—we are indifferent to past suffering (followed by amnesia), but we care deeply about future suffering (followed by amnesia)—is present only when we imagine ourselves located at a specific point in time. So, for instance, Parfit's example assumes that he is located at a particular point in time, which is either *after* the ten-hour operation or *before* the one-hour operation. By locating himself in time, Parfit can describe the two possibilities (the ten-hour operation and the one-hour operation) as *past* and *future*. The use of this "tensed" language (past and future) presupposes location at a particular point in time. (By "point," I do not necessarily mean to rule out intervals or periods of temporal duration. I just mean location in the temporal sequence, rather than outside of it.)

In contrast, if you could be extracted from the human temporal sequence and God could present to you two possible lives, each exactly the same except in one you have the ten-hour operation (followed by amnesia) on Monday and in the other you have the one-hour operation on Tuesday (followed by amnesia), you would presumably choose to live the operation-on-Tuesday life, and it would seem *rational* to choose the operation-on-Tuesday world. The point is that the Parfitian asymmetry in our attitudes toward past and future bads—sufferings, in particular—only emerges from a certain *temporally located* perspective.

Does the Parfitian asymmetry help to explain our asymmetric attitudes toward prenatal and posthumous nonexistence? Not on the secular assumption that both periods are experiential blanks. After all, the Parfitian asymmetry pertains to suffering in the future versus suffering in the past. But we are assuming that death does not involve suffering, so it cannot explain our special concern about death (as opposed to prenatal nonexistence).

Consider now this variant on the Parfit-style thought experiment just discussed:

> Imagine that you are in some hospital to test a drug. The drug induces intense pleasure for an hour followed by amnesia. You awaken and ask the nurse about your situation. She says that either you tried the drug yesterday (and had an hour of pleasure) or you will try the drug tomorrow (and will have an hour of pleasure). While she checks on your status, it is clear that you prefer to have the pleasure tomorrow. There is a temporal asymmetry in our attitudes to experienced goods that is parallel to the asymmetry in our attitudes to experienced bads: we are indifferent to past pleasures and look forward to future pleasures.[16]

I think you would even prefer to have one hour of pleasure tomorrow (followed by amnesia) to ten hours of pleasure yesterday (followed by amnesia), given that you are temporally located "at today." Our asymmetric attitude toward pleasures—we want our pleasures in the future, all other things equal—seems to be equally as deep-seated and "basic" as our asymmetric attitudes toward pains.

The asymmetry in our attitudes toward pleasures can help to explain our asymmetric attitudes toward prenatal and posthumous nonexistence. Both periods are deprivations of goods, some of which include pleasures. But prenatal nonexistence deprives us of past pleasures, to which we are relatively indifferent. We care much more about future pleasures, and posthumous nonexistence deprives us of these. So our asymmetric attitudes toward prenatal and posthumous nonexistence can be seen as a special case of a more general asymmetry in our attitudes toward pleasures. Although death itself is an experiential blank, it deprives us of pleasurable experiences, and this is arguably the key (or at least as important) to understanding death's badness (as we have seen in prior chapters). It also helps in understanding our asymmetric attitudes toward early death and late birth.

The deprivation-of-pleasure version of the Parfit-style response to the Mirror Image Argument is promising. One might, however, have

16. Anthony L. Brueckner and John Martin Fischer, "Why Is Death Bad?" *Philosophical Studies* 50 (1986): 213–223; reprinted in Fischer, ed., pp. 221–229.

various worries about it. First, it seems to presuppose a kind of hedonism, according to which the good is identified with pleasure, and all value is reducible to pleasurable experiences. But the Parfit-style strategy of response to the Mirror Image Argument is just that—a response to a particular argument. It does *not* presuppose or seek to articulate any general theory of value. It does not claim or assume that all valuable things are—or can be reduced to—pleasurable experiences. It simply employs the idea that a valuable stretch of life will contain at least *some* pleasurable experiences, and this is plausible to me; it is hard for me to imagine an on-balance worthwhile or desirable stretch of life that does not contain *any* pleasurable experiences.

Another worry is that the Parfit-style response implies that no one *ever* prefers to have been born considerably earlier and that it can *never* be rational to have such a preference. It seems that a serious opera buff of the future could reasonably prefer to have been born (and lived) earlier, so that he could have attended performances by Luciano Pavarotti. A serious baseball fan might prefer to have lived during the time of Babe Ruth. A fan of classic rock music might prefer the 1960s and 70s. (Beatles tribute bands just aren't the Beatles!) Such people could reasonably regret that they weren't born significantly earlier.

Of course, these thoughts raise the question of whether it really is possible for an individual—the very same individual—to have been born significantly earlier than he actually was born. Would it be the same person, if we were to seek to imagine that a person living in the twenty-first century was born in the eighteenth? But let's put these worries aside for now, as we considered them in the last section. Let's assume here that it is possible that an individual (in the sense in which we care about ourselves) has existed significantly prior to the time of his actual existence.

The Parfit-style response is *not* committed to denying the possibility of these sorts of preferences about when to live (or their rationality). This response to Lucretius is a way of defending the idea that death can be a bad thing for the individual who dies. It therefore must address the situation of individuals who are indifferent to the time of their births, given the (apparent) fact that posthumous nonexistence is the mirror image of prenatal nonexistence.

The Parfit-style strategy does not even get engaged in situations of preference for an earlier birth, since in these situations there is no threat to the idea that death can be a bad thing for an individual. If late birth could be a bad thing for a given individual, then granting the mirror image point, death could be a bad thing for the individual. So the existence of a person who prefers to have lived in the 1960s is no counterexample to the Parfit-style response to the Mirror Image Argument.

Finally, a critic of the Parfit-style response might concede that it is in general (although perhaps not universally) true that human beings have asymmetric attitudes toward past and future pleasures. But he might go on to point out that the mere existence of this sort of psychological tendency does not establish its *rationality*. So invocation of the more general asymmetry in our attitudes toward past and future pleasures would, at best, *explain* our asymmetric attitudes toward prenatal and posthumous nonexistence; it would not *justify* them. Without some sort of defense of the rationality of our generally asymmetric attitudes toward prior and future pleasures, we haven't established the *rationality* of our asymmetric attitudes toward prenatal and posthumous nonexistence. After all, many widespread beliefs do not pass the rationality test. Racist attitudes, although prevalent, are not warranted or defensible.

Showing that something is conducive to flourishing, and, at a more basic level, to survival, is one way of establishing its rationality. Having a bias toward future pleasures is indeed conducive to flourishing and survival. Someone who has this sort of future bias will be more attentive to possibilities for opportunities and pleasure in the future, and also to obstacles and dangers. Having this sort of future bias "lights up" these possibilities (along with the obstacles) for the individual, thus making it more likely that she will have more pleasurable experiences, and avoid unpleasant experiences, in the future.

Now I am not saying that possessing a survival advantage is the only kind of rationality, nor am I asserting that having a survival advantage renders a course of action (or propensity), on balance, rational. It might be that a particular feature conducive to survival brings with it *other* features that are (in other ways) irrational, thus rendering the feature in question, on balance, irrational. But possessing a survival advantage at least counts (perhaps significantly) toward rationality. So we have gone some distance toward establishing that a future bias is rational, and thus that the asymmetry in our attitudes toward prenatal and posthumous nonexistence is *justifiable*.[17] Of course, this does not imply that *excessive* fear of or *preoccupation* with death is warranted.

Williams's Solution. Bernard Williams has offered an alternative to the deprivation view of death's badness.[18] On Williams's view, death is a bad thing for an individual when it "frustrates" a certain special sort of preference of the individual—a preference for pursuing projects that propel the individual into the future. (Williams calls these "categorical preferences," and he distinguishes them from mere "conditional preferences," which are preferences about how one's life goes, *assuming* that one will continue to live, but not addressing the question as to whether continued life would be desirable.) Here Williams understands "frustration" of a preference as simply "thwarting" the preference or blocking the satisfaction of the preference, where this would not necessarily involve any suffering or negative experiences.

Williams's approach to the badness of death fits nicely with the ideas about meaningfulness in life discussed in Chapter One. Death's badness, on this view, consists in the frustration of categorical preferences about the future; some of these may be identified with projects at the intersection of subjective attraction and objective attractiveness. It should not be surprising that the badness of death would be connected to meaningfulness in life. Death is bad in part because it thwarts the projects that help to give meaning to our lives.

It is interesting to note that Williams's account of the badness of death has the virtue of providing a relatively straightforward answer to the Mirror Image Argument. Early death thwarts actual preferences, whereas late birth does not. As we live our lives, and even as we get older, we have preferences for pursuing projects that give our lives meaning. These are *actual* preferences. Death now, rather than later, may thwart these preferences. In contrast, if we had been born earlier, perhaps we *would have had* different preferences, and our late births make it the case that we don't have these alternative preferences. But actual preferences

17. For an insightful critical discussion of this approach to justifying the attitudinal asymmetry, see Frederick Kaufman, "Late Birth, Early Death, and the Problem of Lucretian Symmetry," *Social Theory and Practice* 37 (2011): 113–127.

18. Bernard Williams, "The Makropulos Case: Reflections on the Tedium of Immortality," in Bernard Williams, *Problems of the Self* (Cambridge: Cambridge University Press, 1973): 82–100; reprinted in Fischer, ed., *The Metaphysics of Death*, 73–92.

and alternative (or counterfactual) preferences are importantly differ-ent. For example, you are *not* under any obligation to bring a child into existence, despite the fact that she *would have* a good life (and would be able to pursue meaningful projects). In contrast, you have various obligations to your own (actual) children. Blocking the satisfaction on an individual's actual preferences is fundamentally different from failing to bring into existence an individual who would have had preferences.

The preference-thwarting model provides another way in which a commonsense theorist (who believes that our attitudes toward death and prenatal nonexistence should be different) can respond to Lucre-tius. The discussions of the Mirror Image Argument (earlier and in the general literature) have centered on the deprivation theory, but the preference-thwarting theory has a straightforward response. This is not to say that *on balance* the preference-thwarting account is preferable to the deprivation theory of death's badness. It is simply interesting that it gives an elegant response to Lucretius.

Conclusion

In Chapter Three we considered the "no-experience" challenge to the view that death can be bad for the individual who dies. Here we have considered both the timing objection and the Mirror Image Argument. We have explored various promising ways of addressing these chal-lenges. A suite of options for answering the timing problem is available: priorism, subsequentism, and atemporalism. I find subsequentism and atemporalism the most appealing, although none of them is without problems.

I believe that the Parfit-style approach is the most promising can-didate for answering Lucretius's Mirror Image Argument, although the Asymmetry of Possibility strategy has merits. It is also interesting to note that if we accept Williams's preference-thwarting account of death's badness, we have a simple and plausible answer to Lucretius.

Perhaps it is not necessary to find *just one* reason why death is bad, when it is bad. After all, actions and events can be bad for more than one reason: an action can be a betrayal and also a murder, and so forth. A plausible view might be that death is bad for two reasons: it is a depri-vation of what would be, on balance, a good continuation of life, and it thwarts categorical preferences about the future. When only one condi-tion is met, death is bad to some extent; when both are met, it is simply bad (or bad, all things considered). Typically both conditions would be met in a premature death, so death would be bad in an unqualified way, and there would be two complementary ways of responding to the Mirror Image Argument: the fact that death would deprive us of good experiences, and the fact that death thwarts the preferences that would have propelled us into the future.

We now have a way of justifying my claim in Chapter One that it can be a particularly bad thing for a human being, as opposed to a non-human animal, to die. Death can rob a human being of future good experiences (and other goods), and it can also thwart preferences to pursue projects in the future. The death of an animal may rob it of future pleasant experiences, but it cannot thwart the animal's preferences to pursue projects in the future. Non-human animals do not have projects for the future. When a human being dies, both criteria for death's badness may be met, whereas when a non-human animal dies, only one can be met.

Annotated Suggestions for Further Reading

For versions of priorism, see George Pitcher, "The Misfortunes of the Dead," *American Philosophical Quarterly* 21 (1984): 183–188; reprinted in Fischer, ed., pp. 159–168; Joel Feinberg, "Harm to Others," excerpt from Feinberg, *Harm to Others* (New York: Oxford University Press, 1984): 79–95; reprinted in Fischer, ed., pp. 171–190; and Neil Feit, "The Time of Death's Misfortune," *Nous* 36, (2002): 359–383.

For a defense of subsequentism, see Benjamin Bradley, Well-Being and Death (Oxford: Oxford University Press [Clarendon], 2009).

Although the Problem of Predication is widely known and discussed, a nice development of it is Martha C. Nussbaum, "The Damage of Death: Incomplete Arguments and False Consolations," in James Stacey Taylor, ed., *The Metaphysics and Ethics of Death: New Essays* (New York: Oxford University Press, 2013): 25–43.

There is a helpful overview and discussion of the issues about timing in Jens Johansson, "The Timing Problem," in Ben Bradley, Fred Feldman, and Jens Johansson, eds., *The Oxford Handbook of the Philosophy of Death* (New York: Oxford University Press, 2013): 255–273.

The Mirror Image Argument has been discussed widely in philosophy and literature. For some recent discussions, see Shelly Kagan, *Death* (New Haven, CT: Yale University Press, 2012): 224–233; and Fred Feldman, *Confrontations with the Reaper* (New York: Oxford University Press, 1992): 154–156. For a detailed discussion, with close attention to Lucretius's text and arguments presented by others, see James Warren, *Facing Death: Epicurus and His Critics* (Oxford: Clarendon Press, 2006): 57–108.

For defenses of the Asymmetry of (Plausible) Possibility view, see, in addition to the papers by Kaufman referred to in the text: Frederick Kaufman, "Thick and Thin Selves: Reply to Fischer and Speak," in Peter A. French and Howard K. Wettstein, eds., *Midwest Studies in Philosophy* 24 (2000): 94–97; and Christopher Belshaw, *Annihilation: The Sense and Significance of Death* (Stocksfield Hall, UK: Acumen, 2009): 153–174.

A critique of the Asymmetry of (Plausible) Possibility View is presented in John Martin Fischer, "Earlier Birth and Later Death: Symmetry through Thick and Thin," in Richard Feldman, Chris McDaniel, and Jason R. Raibley, eds., *The Good, the Right, Life, and Death* (Aldershot, UK: Ashgate, 2006): 84–93; reprinted in John Martin Fischer, *Our Stories: Essays on Life, Death, and Free Will* (New York: Oxford University Press, 2009): 63–77.

For a more detailed presentation of the Parfitian strategy of response to the Mirror Image Argument, see Anthony L. Brueckner and John Martin Fischer, "Why Is Death Bad?" *Philosophical Studies* 50 (1986): 213–223; reprinted in John Martin Fischer, ed., *The Metaphysics of Death* (Stanford, CA: Stanford University Press, 1993): 221–229. More advanced students (and scholars) will benefit from the development of the Parfitian strategy in F.M. Kamm, *Morality, Mortality Volume I: Death and Whom to Save from It* (New York: Oxford University Press, 1998); and *Morality, Mortality Volume II: Rights, Duties, and Status* (New York: Oxford University Press, 2001).

....

CHAPTER 5

The Meaning of Immortality

"Do you think your death is premature?" he said.

"Every death is premature. There's no sufficient reason why we can't live a hundred and fifty years. Some people actually do it, according to a headline I saw at the supermarket."

"Do you think it's a sense of incompleteness that causes you the deepest regret? There are things you still hope to accomplish. Work to be done, intellectual challenges to be faced."

"The deepest regret is death. The only thing to face is death. This is all I think about. There's only one issue here."

... "So you're saying, Jack, that death would be just as threatening even if you'd accomplished all you'd ever hoped to accomplish in your life and work?"

"Are you crazy? Of course. That's an elitist idea. Would you ask a man who bags groceries if he fears death not because it is death but because there are still some interesting groceries he would like to bag?"

... "This is death. I don't want it to tarry awhile so I can write a monograph. I want it to go away for seventy or eighty years."

... "Do you believe love is stronger than death?"

"Not in a million years."

... "Do you believe life without death is somehow incomplete?"

"How could it be incomplete? Death is what makes it incomplete."

"Doesn't our knowledge of death make life more precious?"

"What good is a preciousness based on fear and anxiety? It's an anxious quivering thing."

—Don DeLillo,
White Noise

....

Introduction

If death can be a bad thing for an individual, then immortality might seem attractive. Of course, it does not *follow* from the possibility that death is a bad thing for an individual that immortality would be desirable. It is possible that both death and immortality could be bad for an individual; it would depend (at least) on the situation of the individual and the nature of the envisaged immortality.

Some, however, think both that death can be a bad thing for an individual and that immortality—of a certain sort—would be desirable. We are here thinking primarily of immortality as living forever and never dying; this is the secular conception of immortality, and I will assume that this does not involve an afterlife or reincarnation. (Later in our discussion of immortality I will consider the afterlife.) The prospect of living forever has been of great interest to human beings throughout history, and this fascination continues unabated.

The Drive to Live Forever

The first literary depiction of the human desire for immortality is in the Epic of Gilgamesh (1800 BC).[1] In this epic, Gilgamesh loses his friend and fellow soldier, Enkidu, and he goes off in search of a way of achieving immortality. An old man offers to tell him the secret of eternal life, but Gilgamesh is not able to do what the old man requires: keep his eyes open for a week. (He closes his eyes at the very last moment.) The old man then tells Gilgamesh where to dive in the river for a weed that would give him immortality, but when Gilgamesh finds the weed, a snake on the riverbank steals it from him when he gets to the shore.[2]

This story illustrates both the human drive toward overcoming death and also its tantalizing elusiveness. Gilgamesh comes close to finding the secret to immortality, but it slips through his fingers. The history of human discussions of immortality in both the Western and Eastern traditions exhibits a thirst for immortality (to be quenched at

---

1. For very helpful discussions of historical treatments of immortality, as well as contemporary developments, see Stephen Cave, *Immortality: The Quest to Live Forever and How It Drives Civilization* (New York: Crown, 2012) and Jonathan Weiner, *Long for This World: The Strange Science of Immortality* (New York: HarperCollins, 2010).

2. In summarizing the Epic of Gilgamesh, I closely follow Weiner, *Long for This World*, 26–27.

the "fountain of youth"), but also significant worries and reservations. We have a deep *ambivalence* toward immortality.

This ambivalence is chronicled in the standard history of the subject, *A History of Ideas about the Prolongation of Life*, by Gerald Gruman.[3] In this book Gruman divides thinkers about immortality into those who endorse the significant extension of our lifespans, "prolongevists," and those who are skeptical about the desirability of such extension and seek to reconcile us to our mortality, "apologists."

One of the first great prolongevists in the Western tradition was the sixteenth-century lawyer and philosopher Francis Bacon, who wrote *The History of Life and Death, or, The Prolongation of Life*.[4] This is a kind of "how-to-live-forever" book, which includes various recipes and potions, not unlike hundreds of other such books throughout history to the present.[5] In our contemporary world, there is no shortage of views about how to extend life, perhaps indefinitely. Some of the most salient contemporary work in the spirit of Francis Bacon is by Ray Kurzweil.[6] Kurzweil reportedly takes something like ninety medicines and "supplements" per day—a considerably updated Baconian regimen.[7] We shall return to a further discussion of Kurzweil.

Bacon's suggestions now seem outlandish and amusing. Bacon advised the wearing of red "long johns":

> Some report that they have found great benefit in the conservation of their health, by wearing scarlet waistcoats next to their skin, and under their shirts, as well down to the nether parts as on the upper.[8]

Although some of Kurzweil's recommendations are sensible, by our current lights, no doubt many will come to seem just as strange as Bacon's.

---

3. Gerald J. Gruman, *A History of Ideas about the Prolongation of Life* (Philadelphia: American Philosophical Society, 1966; reissued by Springer, 2003).

4. Francis Bacon, *The History of Life and Death, or, The Prolongation of Life* (1638; reissued by Kessinger Publishing, Whitefish, MT, 2005). (I am grateful to the discussion of Francis Bacon in Weiner, *Long for This World*, 31–35.)

5. Weiner, *Long for This World*, 33–34.

6. Ray Kurzweil and Terry Grossman, MD, *Fantastic Voyage: Live Long Enough to Live Forever* (New York: Plume, 2005).

7. Stephen Cave, *Immortality: The Quest to Live Forever and How It Drives Civilization* (New York: Crown, 2012): 70.

8. Quoted in Weiner, *Long for This World*, 34.

Human beings have always wanted to overcome death (at least in some moods), and they have shown considerable ingenuity in trying.

Along with the human drive toward living forever, there has always been a countervailing tendency (as in the Epic of Gilgamesh) to think that a decisive victory over death is unattainable, and perhaps even undesirable. In Gruman's terminology, there have always been, and continue to be, "apologists." One of the well-known apologists was Christopher Marlowe, who wrote the play *Doctor Faustus* in the sixteenth century. In this play, the greatest doctor in the world, Faustus, recognizes that even he, as a mere mortal, cannot secure immortality. He realizes that only by selling his soul to the devil will he have a chance to vanquish death. But in the end the devil takes him down to hell. Marlowe's *Doctor Faustus* is a clear and influential statement of the apologist's case, and it is the basis of Goethe's great work, *Faust*.

We shall turn to contemporary apologist arguments, primarily put forward by philosophers, later. But first we'll take a quick look at the remarkable contemporary interest in slowing down aging and even defeating death.

The Immortality Business

Life expectancy has shot up dramatically in the last century, and we continue to make advances. In 1900, life expectancy in the most developed countries of the world, including England and the United States, was forty-seven years.[9] By the end of the twentieth century, life expectancy in these countries reached seventy-six years.[10] Jonathan Weiner writes:

> Throughout the twentieth century, life expectancy changed so fast that for the first time in history, people became aware of it as a phenomenon that was extending their life spans during their own lifetimes. During the twentieth century we gained almost thirty years, or about as much time as our species had gained before in the whole struggle of existence.
>
> In other words, this is a good time to be a mortal. Life expectancy today is roughly eighty years for anyone in the world's developed countries. And life expectancy is still improving, which is why each

---

9. Weiner, *Long for This World*, 11.
10. Weiner, *Long for This World*, 11.

day we live now we are given the gift of more time down the road. It's as if we are all driving on a highway that is still being built, and the roadbuilders are adding to it at a good rate.[11]

Not only is this a good time to be a mortal, but it has seemed to many to be a good time to think about the possibility of immortality. In part because I want to sharpen the characterization implicit in Gruman's distinction between prolongevists and apologists, I will introduce new terminology to mark the distinction: "immortality optimists" (or "optimists," for short) and "immortality curmudgeons" (or "curmudgeons," for short). Immortality optimists deny that basic facts about human character or the nature of human life in themselves show that immortality is impossible or undesirable. They also think that it is plausible that we can achieve immortality in the not-too-distant future. Optimists differ on how far in the future the "not-too-distant" future extends, and they differ on how best to achieve immortality. In contending that immortality can be achieved in the not-too-distant future, optimists are committed to the claim that the prerequisites for immortality (physical and social circumstances that can sustain immortality) will (or probably will) continue to exist (in some form or other).

In contrast, immortality curmudgeons contend that basic facts about human character or the nature of human life show that immortality is either impossible or, in any case, would be undesirable. This is a conceptual, not an empirical, point. Immortality curmudgeons dominate the contemporary philosophical landscape. I shall turn to the curmudgeons and their arguments later, but I will begin by briefly sketching the ideas of some contemporary immortality optimists.

It is not easy to select a small number of optimists on whom to focus, since there is a burgeoning interest in immortality. One might say that the "immortality business" is booming, where this includes anti-aging medicine; cosmetic interventions for people seeking a more youthful appearance; dietary supplements, medications, and exercise to extend life; and biomedical research into curing diseases and otherwise lengthening our lives.[12] In short, there has never been a better time to be

---

11. Weiner, *Long for This World*, 11.
12. For interesting overviews and discussions, see Cave, *Immortality*; Weiner, *Long for This World*; and Tad Friend, "The God Pill: Silicon Valley's Quest for Eternal Life," *The New Yorker*, April 3, 2017: 54–67.

an immortality optimist or to spend some money trying to feel and look younger. We pursue the fountain of youth relentlessly.

One of the most visible and enthusiastic optimists is the Englishman Aubrey de Grey, who was trained as an engineer and did his early work on artificial intelligence.[13] Now he is the chief science officer at Silicon Valley's SENS Research Foundation. SENS stands for Strategies for Engineered Negligible Senescence. The strategies de Grey thinks are most promising are new technologies employing genetics, stem cells, and nanomedicine. In explaining these approaches, Stephen Cave writes:

> Genetic engineering should enable us to rewrite our bodies' instruction books, ensuring many diseases that are now fatal never arise. Stem cells, which have the ability to develop into any kind of tissue, from skin to neurons, hold out the promise of growing healthy tissue to replace that which is diseased or worn out—even whole organs. And nanotechnology (engineering on the scale of atoms or molecules) gives hope of the ability to repair our bodies from the inside out using billions of tiny targeted machines.[14]

Think of it this way. Our bodies engage in a whole host of biological processes. Perhaps the most fundamental is metabolism. Over time, these processes generate indigestible by-products—"damage" or "garbage"—and this damage accumulates, causing diseases of old age and eventually death. Weiner writes:

> If that's what aging really is, the slow accumulation of damage, then it's reasonable to argue that there are three ways to fix it. You can try to repair our metabolism so that it does not generate so much trash; you can try to clean up the trash itself; or you can try to deal with the harm the trash does to the body.[15]

De Grey believes that the second strategy is the most promising—to improve the body's ability to clean up the trash. The first

---

13. Weiner's *Long for This World* contains an extended and fascinating discussion of de Grey's views. For a comprehensive presentation, see Aubrey De Grey, PhD, with Michael Rae, *Ending Aging: The Rejuvenation Breakthroughs That Could Reverse Human Aging in Our Lifetime* (New York: St. Martin's, 2005).

14. Cave, *Immortality*, 64–65.

15. Weiner, *Long for This World*, 124.

approach—repairing our metabolism so that our bodies don't create as much trash—is too difficult. The third approach—dealing with the harmful consequence of the trash—is expensive, inefficient, and allows too much suffering. De Grey opts for the "middle" option; he thinks we need to engineer ways of improving our housekeeping skills, so that we do not die from a pileup of junk (the "garbage catastrophe"[16]).

He argues that there are seven types of physical damage that we will need to figure out how to "fix" or remove more efficiently. We don't have to do this all at once. As we make progress, we buy ourselves more time, until finally we reach "escape velocity." Longevity escape velocity, according to de Grey, is "the point when improvements to the comprehensiveness and safety of human life-extension treatments are being made faster than people are aging . . ."[17] At this point we will have achieved a kind of immortality; biomedicine will be adding to our life expectancy faster than our natural biological decline (our diminishing natural ability to take out the trash) diminishes it.[18] De Grey is remarkably sanguine about the time it will take us to reach escape velocity; he has estimated it as three to (at most) five decades. He writes, ". . . we will probably achieve something equivalent [to longevity escape velocity] within only a few decades from now . . ."[19] De Grey believes that the fountain of youth is literally within our grasp, and he is ready for the plunge (or the gulp).

Tad Friend writes:

> Immortalists fall into two camps. Those who might be called the Meat Puppets, led by de Grey, believe that we can retool our biology and remain in our bodies. The RoboCops, led by Kurzweil, believe that we'll eventually merge with mechanical bodies and/or with the cloud.[20]

Kurzweil is an engineer who invented the flatbed scanner and a machine that reads books aloud for the blind. He is currently a

---

16. I am indebted to Weiner, *Long for This World*, 129, for this term. My wife often has to remind me of the garbage catastrophe in our kitchen, and my lamentable housekeeping skills.

17. De Grey, as quoted in Weiner, *Long for This World*, 208.

18. Weiner, *Long for This World*, 208.

19. De Grey, *Ending Aging*, 334.

20. Friend, "The God Pill," 65.

director of engineering at Google.[21] As mentioned earlier, Kurzweil takes about ninety pills a day, including vitamins, minerals, other supplements, and prescription medications. He calls these efforts, which employ currently available means to slow aging, "Bridge One" to indefinite longevity. Kurzweil believes that personally tailored immune therapies for cancer and organs grown from our own DNA, and other innovations based on biotechnology, will be available soon. He contends that this—Bridge Two—will bring us to longevity escape velocity in just fifteen years; this is more optimistic than even Aubrey de Grey.[22]

In Bridge Three, which Kurzweil thinks we will cross in the 2030s, we will have "nano-bots"—blood-cell-sized devices that will roam the body and brain, cleaning up all the damage that de Grey wants to fix with medical interventions.[23] Style of housekeeping is one salient point on which the RoboCop Kurzweil departs from the Meat Puppet de Grey.

The RoboCop in Kurzweil emerges dramatically at Bridge Four, where the nano-bots will connect our brains to the cloud (a set of computers) and our intelligence will expand a billionfold. This is what Kurzweil describes as the "Singularity," which he estimates will happen in 2045.[24] He holds that in the Singularity our superintelligence will make us like gods. According to Kurzweil, "For a time, we'll be a hybrid of biological and nonbiological thinking, but, as the cloud keeps doubling, the nonbiological intelligence will predominate."[25] Kurzweil's Singularity is parallel to de Grey's longevity escape velocity; on both approaches, we will accelerate our way to infinity (or, at least, much greater longevity).

Not only is Kurzweil wildly optimistic about the possibilities for advancement in medical and mechanical means of extending life, his view that we can somehow be "uploaded" to computers presupposes highly contentious philosophical views about mental states, consciousness, and the nature of persons. For example, it is very controversial whether

21. I am indebted here, and in the later text concerning Kurzweil, to Friend, "The God Pill," 65–66.

22. Friend, "The God Pill," 65.

23. Friend, "The God Pill," 65–66.

24. Friend, "The God Pill," 66.

25. As quoted in Friend, "The God Pill," 65.

computers can have consciousness.[26] Philosophers also disagree about whether a person could survive—as the very same person—without a body at all.

Many believe that *even if* artificially intelligent artifacts (like computers) can have information-bearing states, they cannot have the kind of *consciousness* and *affective states* required for personhood. It may be that the particular way in which we are embodied is essential to our nature as persons. Some even contend that we are identical to our organisms; this view is called "animalism."[27] It is thus extremely controversial to suppose that we could be "uploaded" to computers in the future.

It is completely unclear what kind of "life" it would be if we were uploaded to the cloud. Could we act, pursue projects, fall in love? As we have pointed out in Chapter One, it is not enough that we have experiences that *represent us* as acting, pursuing projects, or falling in love; we do not just want it to *seem* that we are living an active life. We want really to be living such a life. Similarly, it is not obvious that existence as software of a computer, even one that is the CPU of a robot, would be sufficiently similar to human life. It is a big stretch.

In the longevity literature there is, in my view, not enough attention to the dystopian possibilities in a world in which "uploading" of minds is envisaged as possible. Who controls the computer and the uploaded mind? Could an evil person commandeer the computer or software and subject the "trapped" mind to endless repetition of torture?[28]

---

26. There is an excellent overview of the relationship between consciousness and the body, and also discussions about artificial intelligence (A.I.), in a book in the same series (*Fundamentals of Philosophy*) in which the current book appears: John Searle, *Mind* (New York: Oxford University Press: 2004).

27. Eric Olsen is a prominent contemporary animalist: Eric T. Olsen, *What Are We? A Study in Personal Ontology* (New York: Oxford University Press, 2007).

28. This possibility and other similar nightmarish scenarios are explored in the television series *Black Mirror* (a kind of updated version of *The Twilight Zone*). In his article, "Superior Intelligence: Do the Perils of A.I. Exceed Its Promises?" *The New Yorker* (May 14, 2018): 48–51, Tad Friend discusses many of these scenarios and contemporary ways of representing and thinking about them.

For an overview and discussion of science fiction treatments of immortality, together with a bibliography, see John Martin Fischer and Ruth Curl, "Philosophical Models of Immortality in Science Fiction," in George Slusser, Gary Westfahl, and Eric S. Rabkin, eds., *Immortal Engines: Life Extension and Immortality in Science Fiction* (Athens: University of Georgia Press, 1996): 3–12; reprinted in Fischer, *Our Stories*, 93–101.

Although they differ in various ways, de Grey and Kurzweil share an extraordinary optimism and belief in the upward trajectory of the human species. But, just in case things don't work out soon enough, they have both arranged for cryogenic preservation (freezing) at the time of significant deterioration just prior to death, with an eye to being thawed out when their problems are treatable in the future. The belief in our prospects for overcoming aging—whether through biological or mechanical means (or some combination)—is held by a growing contingent of immortality optimists, including some scientists, Silicon Valley billionaires, Russian plutocrats, and many others.[29] The dream of immortality, which goes all the way back (in Western culture) to Gilgamesh and was given significant impetus by Francis Bacon at the dawn of science, is still with us.[30] New technology offers new hope in our enduring quest.

What Is Immortality?

We saw in Chapter Two that it is difficult to define death in a way that is fully adequate. Same with immortality.[31] You might think it is simple: immortality is living forever. But I don't think this quite captures the relevant kind of immortality. What if you live forever, but you are vulnerable to dying? (You are just lucky and you never in fact die.) What if you are invulnerable to dying, but you don't know this? What kind of circumstances will you live in? I think the notion of immortality that is relevant to the question of whether immortality could be desirable is richer than simply the idea of living forever.

---

29. Friend's *New Yorker* article ("The God Pill") contains an interesting discussion, especially of the interest in immorality in the Silicon Valley.

30. The early emperors of China were equally smitten by the immortality bug, and gave their alchemists the project of finding ways to achieve it. These herbal treatments were the ancient versions of the suggestions of Bacon, and the supplements and medications of Kurzweil.

31. Stephen Cave presents an analytic framework that distinguishes different kinds of immortality, and he presents a skeptical view about medical (or true) immortality. Cave distinguishes "staying alive" (secular immortality), resurrection, survival of the soul, and "legacy." Legacy includes fame, which is often considered a type of immortality, and having children.

The relevant kind of immortality includes knowledge of one's invulnerability to death. It will be simpler to begin with the Meat Puppet approach, according to which we live forever as embodied creatures (or perhaps organisms). What kind of invulnerability to death is available? One answer to this question is invulnerability to dying by "natural causes," such as biological aging and deterioration, disease, or catastrophic internally caused biological events, like heart attacks and strokes. It is at least coherent to suppose that we will someday achieve this sort of immortality, which we might call "medical immortality."[32] This is the sort of immortality Aubrey de Grey has in mind. Of course, even a medically immortal person could know that he is vulnerable to death in various ways (other than by natural causes), as we discussed earlier. For instance, he could die as a result of falling off a cliff or a car crash or being shot at point-blank range by a shotgun or being hit directly by a powerful bomb, and so forth; and he could know all of this.

A second kind of immortality is "true immortality," in which one knows that one is not vulnerable to death in *any* way. Whereas it is relatively easy to imagine medical immortality, it is not so easy to conceive of true immortality. True immortality would imply that if someone were to be directly hit by a nuclear bomb, and her body were pulverized, she would somehow not die—perhaps the body could be reassembled from the materials from which it had been made or similar materials, or perhaps her mind could be transferred somehow to a computer or the cloud.[33] But this is far-fetched in the extreme. Even if we could cure all diseases and render people invulnerable to the ravages of increasing age and biological deterioration, why suppose that we could also render human beings able to survive multiple stabbings, being run over by a semi-truck, or being hit directly by a nuclear bomb? (I'll spare you a more comprehensive list of grisly possibilities.)

---

32. I am indebted to Stephen Cave, *Immortality*, for this term. See also John Martin Fischer and Benjamin Mitchell-Yellin, "Immortality and Boredom," *Journal of Ethics* 18 (2014): 353–372.

33. Fischer and Mitchell-Yellin, "Immortality and Boredom," 364.

Sticking with the idea that we are medically immortal (assume about six thousand years), what will our circumstances—internal and external—be? It would obviously be undesirable to be medically immortal but continuously deteriorating biologically. This was the condition of the miserable Struldbrugs in Jonathan Swift's *Gulliver's Travels*:

> At ninety, they lose their teeth and hair; they have at that age no distinction of taste, but eat and drink whatever they can get, without relish or appetite. The diseases they were subject to still continue, without increasing or diminishing. In talking, they forget the common appellation of things, and the names of persons, even of those who are their nearest friends and relations. For the same reason, they never can amuse themselves with reading, because their memory will not serve to carry them from the beginning of a sentence to the end; and by this defect, they are deprived of the only entertainment whereof they might otherwise be capable.
>
> . . . They are despised and hated by all sorts of people. . . . They were the most mortifying sight I ever beheld . . . Besides the usual deformities in extreme old age, they acquired an additional ghastliness, in proportion to their number of years . . . [34]

No one would want to be a Struldbrug. Mere chronological longevity is not enough, if our bodies deteriorate. A myth has it that Eos, a Greek goddess, fell in love with Tithonus, a human being. When Eos asked Zeus to grant Tithonus immortality, she forgot to ask for eternal youth, and thus Tithonus continued to deteriorate and to shrink. Eventually, he took the form of an insect, which Eos put in a little container. A similar lapse doomed Achilles, whose mother immersed him in a "sea of invulnerability," but left out the heel!

When we are averse to immortality, it might be because we are envisaging the infirmities of old age and supposing that we will be so ravaged *forever* in a disastrous downward trajectory. This would be undesirable, but we don't have to conceive of immortality in this way. Even if we can't now achieve endless biological youth, there is no bar to imagining it as a possibility. So, for instance, Bernard Williams famously discussed

---

34. Jonathan Swift, *Gulliver's Travels*, Chapter 26, Chapter X. The Struldbrugs live in Luggnag, located in Lilliput (to which Gulliver travels in this fantasy voyage).

an opera by Leoš Janáček, which was based on a play by Karel Čapek.[35] The play tells of a woman called "Elina Makropulos," who goes by various aliases, all of which have the initials "EM." Her father has given her an elixir of "eternal" life, which causes her to live three hundred years (before she must take it again to ensure another three hundred years). The elixir also prevents her from biological aging or deterioration; biologically she is thirty-seven years old, although she is chronologically three hundred and thirty-seven years old.[36] In the play and opera, she is faced with the question of whether to take the elixir to achieve another three hundred years. We will return to her dilemma later.

I pause to note that the assumption of "endless biological youth" is vague. You take an elixir that prevents biological aging. But does this imply that you would never develop non-life-threatening conditions and maladies? If you eat gluttonously, you won't die, but will you become obese? Maybe you will develop diabetes. You wouldn't die, but you would be impaired in various ways. Or does the elixir make it possible for you to eat whatever you'd like, exercise not at all (if that's your preference), drink to excess, smoke, and so forth, without suffering any harmful biological consequences? A serious evaluation of medical immortality would have to sort out such issues. To sharpen our question about the appeal of immortality, we would want to imagine the most favorable circumstances. Perhaps medical science would have advanced to the point where our "sins," like sloth and gluttony, would not have biological consequences.

Of course, one would not want immortality under various external circumstances, even if one were healthy and not deteriorating biologically. For instance, we would not find it desirable to live in conditions of significant poverty, environmental degradation, lack of adequate food, shelter, medical care, and so forth. It is easy to answer the question of

---

35. Bernard Williams, "The Makropulos Case: Reflections on the Tedium of Immortality," in Williams, *Problems of the Self* (Cambridge: Cambridge University Press, 1973): 82–100; reprinted in John Martin Fischer, ed., *The Metaphysics of Death* (Stanford, CA: Stanford University Press, 1993): 73–92.

36. Williams gave a lecture at the University of California, Berkeley, on which his article is based, when he was forty-two years old. He also attributed to EM the biological age of forty-two, but in the play and opera she is actually said to be thirty-seven years old biologically.

whether we would choose to live in such circumstances: no! So, for the purposes of trying to figure out whether we could find immortality appealing, we will assume that we are considering "favorable" circumstances, that is, no biological deterioration, good economic and environmental conditions, and reasonably high-quality food, shelter, medical care, and so forth.

This is the situation of EM. It is interesting to ask whether immortality, so conceived, could be desirable for human beings. This is basically a "thought experiment" or "philosophical question," because we cannot now achieve even medical immortality. But we can certainly conceive of this as a possibility, and we can ask whether we would choose it, if it were available. This question, EM's dilemma, is compelling, in part because it may well be possible to achieve medical immortality in the future.

Conclusion

As with death, immortality has different meanings. In both the case of death and immortality, however, we can have a tolerably clear grasp of the concepts. It is especially important to distinguish between medical and true immortality; the different notions of immortality will play different roles in the arguments. Also, it is important to keep in mind that in thinking about the potential desirability of immortality, we might be considering various ways of filling in the circumstances of the individual and environment. The most interesting version of the question of whether immortality would be worthy of choice assumes relatively favorable circumstances— biological, social, and environmental. I have suggested a slightly more detailed way of distinguishing the two camps than the pro-longevists and apologists of Gruman: immortality optimists and immortality curmudgeons.

Optimists abound. They are not just Russian plutocrats and Silicon Valley billionaires, but respected scientists and many thoughtful people who hope that human beings can continue to extend our average lifespans and eventually achieve "longevity escape velocity." The immortality business is booming.

Many, however, worry about this drive to longer and longer life. Skeptics are also everywhere—philosophers, scientists, science fiction writers, physicians, and many people who are concerned about the implications of immortality for individuals, societies, and the world. Philosophers are concerned about these issues in a very fundamental way. Would an immortal life be recognizably human? Would the life be *mine*? Would it be engaging, or full of repetition and tedium? In the next two chapters we will explore these issues, as well as the social and environmental implications of immortality.

Annotated Suggestions for Further Reading

Stephen Cave brings together much of the science, and the most important philosophical issues, pertaining to life extension and immortality in his extremely helpful book: Stephen Cave, *Immortality: The Quest to Live Forever and How It Drives Civilization* (New York: Crown, 2012). He also gives some historical background to the contemporary discussions.

Paul Edwards, ed., *Immortality* (Amherst, NY: Prometheus Books, 1997) is a useful collection of classic historical and contemporary philosophical discussions of immortality.

Guy Brown gives a helpful overview of the science of life extension in Guy Brown, *The Living End: The Future of Death, Aging, and Immortality* (London: Macmillan, 2008). Aubrey de Grey has presented his scientific ideas in favor of life extension (and seeking medical immortality) in Aubrey de Grey, with Michael Rae, *Ending Aging: The Rejuvenation Breakthroughs That Could Reverse Human Aging in Our Lifetime* (New York: St. Martin's Griffin, 2008). Jonathan Weiner offers a detailed discussion of de Grey and his ideas in his very helpful book: Jonathan Weiner, *Long for This World: The Strange Science of Immortality* (New York: HarperCollins, 2010). Weiner also sketches the history of ideas about immortality. For another pro-immortality approach, see Ray Kurzweil and Terry Grossman, MD, *Fantastic Voyage: Live Long Enough to Live Forever* (New York: Plume, 2005).

For a less sanguine view of the biological possibility of significant life extension, see S. Jay Olshansky and Bruce A Carnes, *The Quest for Immortality: Science at the Frontiers of Aging* (New York: W.W. Norton, 2001). Similarly skeptical views are presented in Steven N. Austad, *Why We Age: What Science Is Discovering about the Body's Journey through Life* (Hoboken, NJ: John Wiley and Sons, 1997); and Francis Fukuyama, *Our Posthumous Future: Consequences of the Biotechnology Revolution* (New York: Farrar, Strauss, and Giroux, 2002).

There is a philosophical defense of radical life extension, as well as enhancing human capabilities, in John Harris, *Enhancing Evolution: The Ethical Case for Making People Better* (Princeton, NJ: Princeton University Press, 2007). For a helpful, more recent philosophical discussion, see John K. Davis, *The New Methuselahs: The Ethics of Life Extension* (Cambridge, MA: MIT Press, 2018).

CHAPTER 6

Would Immortal Life Be Recognizably Human?

I was 4 years old, and my grandfather had just passed away after a drawn-out battle with cancer. My family tried to console me by explaining that he went to a beautiful, calm, and happy place, where he would be united with all his loved ones, forever and ever.

That night, I lay in bed in pitch darkness and tried to grasp what they had told me. But every time I thought I had a grip on eternity, it slipped further away. The largest number of years I could imagine failed to make a dent in infinity. My primitive brain filled with an existential angst. The idea of living forever was even more unsettling than the idea of no longer existing after death.

—BOBBY AZARIAN,
Apeirophobia: The Fear of Eternity

....

Introduction

You might think it would *obviously* be desirable to be immortal in favorable circumstances. Who could object? What party poopers! But there will always be thoughtful people who disagree about any interesting philosophical question. Recall the characterization I gave earlier: immortality curmudgeons contend that basic facts about human character or the nature of human life show that immortality would be either impossible or undesirable. Arguably, Plato was an immortality curmudgeon, arguing that death liberates us from the realm of the transitory and unreal phenomena and allows us to make contact with what is unchanging and ultimately real: the "forms."[1] On Plato's view, immortal life would necessarily rob one of the greatest good. Many think that Heidegger was an immortality curmudgeon, holding that death gives meaning to our lives.[2]

Contemporary philosophy is filled with immortality curmudgeons. As we saw earlier, Bernard Williams discussed Elina Makropulos's (EM's) daunting choice. He is the paradigmatic curmudgeon, as he defended EM's choice not to take the elixir again, and to destroy it instead. He argued that it would be irrational for *any* human being to choose immortality, even in the most desirable circumstances, simply in virtue of basic facts about the nature of human beings.[3]

We can distill a conceptual framework for evaluating immortality from Williams's seminal discussion. We can identify three conditions for my rationally deeming a proposed or imagined immortal life worthwhile—worthy of choice. First, the proposed immortal life must be *recognizably a human life*. Second, the imagined future person must be *me*, that is, identical to the individual I am now. Finally, the imagined immortal life must be *attractive*. We can call these the recognizability, identity, and attractiveness conditions. Of course, meeting the identity condition implies meeting the recognizability condition, since my life is recognizably human (on most days!). But in analyzing the issues, it will help to distinguish these two conditions. In the rest of this chapter,

---

1. Plato, *Socrates' Defense (Apology)* in Edith Hamilton and Huntington Cairns, eds., *Collected Dialogues of Plato* (Princeton, NJ: Princeton University Press, 1961): 3–26; and *Republic* in Hamilton and Cairns, eds., 575–844.

2. Mark Wrathall has pointed out to me in conversation that Heidegger's use of the term "death" is different from ours, and thus it is not so obvious that he was an immortality curmudgeon in a straightforward sense.

3. In addition to Williams, contemporary immortality curmudgeons include Samuel Scheffler, *Death and the Afterlife,* Niko Kolodny, ed. (New York: Oxford University Press, 2013); Seanna Shiffrin, in Kolodny, ed.: 143–158; Shelly Kagan, *Death* (New Haven, CT: Yale University Press, 2012); and Todd May, *Death* (Stocksfield Hall, UK: Acumen, 2009), and *A Fragile Life: Accepting Our Vulnerability* (Chicago: University of Chicago Press, 2017). In her early work on this subject, Martha Nussbaum developed a curmudgeonly position on immortality: *The Therapy of Desire* (Princeton, NJ: Princeton University Press, 1994), but she has subsequently adopted a different view: Martha Nussbaum, "The Damage of Death: Incomplete Arguments and False Consolations," in James Stacey Taylor, ed., *The Metaphysics and Ethics of Death: New Essays* (New York: Oxford University Press, 2013): 25–43. (We shall return to this work later.)

I will focus on the recognizability condition, and in the next chapter I will turn to the identity and attractiveness conditions.[4]

Note, before we plunge into a more detailed discussion, that Williams demands that the life under consideration be recognizably "human." But it is not obvious that we should restrict our attention to *human* lives. Consider, for example, the possibility of uploading, as discussed earlier. Presumably being uploaded to the cloud would end one's existence *as a human being*. Similarly, in the film *Avatar*, the protagonist becomes a member of another (alien!) species, and yet this seems like a coherent story. Can't an individual remove his flesh suit and still be the same person? Of course, it remains unresolved whether this would be worthy of choice—that's a different question. Williams inserts "human" into his recognizability condition because he is a bodily identity theorist of personal identity over time, but we need not buy into this view. Given all of this, it probably would be better to adjust the condition so that it requires a life that is recognizably that of a *person*. But for simplicity and adherence to the framework put forward by Williams, I will stick to "human life" here.[5]

The Recognizability Condition

Borders. If I consider whether a certain proposed immortal life would be worthy of choice, I must recognize it as a human life. Now a thing is what it is in part because of its borders. A particular table is what it is in part because of its borders, a particular building is what it is in part

---

4. I discuss Williams's article and I offer a related framework for evaluating proposed models of immortality in John Martin Fischer, "Why Immortality Is Not So Bad," *International Journal of Philosophical Studies* 2 (1994): 257–270; reprinted in John Martin Fischer, *Our Stories: Essays on Life, Death, and Free Will* (New York: Oxford University Press, 2009). My discussion of the arguments of the immortality curmudgeons in the rest of this chapter and the following chapter owes much to John Martin Fischer, "Immortality," in Bradley, Feldman, and Johansson, eds., *The Oxford Handbook of the Philosophy of Death* (New York: Oxford University Press, 2013): 336–354.

5. The "transhumanists" would reject Williams's restrictions to human life. They envisage and welcome enhancements to humanity that would eventually transcend our species. For a very helpful overview, see Nick Bostrom, "Transhumanist Values," *Journal for Philosophical Research* 30 (Suppl. 2005): 3–14. Such "enhancements" are frequent themes of science fiction: Fischer and Curl, "Philosophical Models of Immortality in Science Fiction." Bostrom is director of the Future of Humanities Institute at Oxford University.

because of its borders, and so forth. Of course, a table can maintain its identity through *some* changes in its borders (for example, a small chip falls off the corner of the table), but not significant changes; similarly, a particular building can still be the same building, given some, but not significant, changes in its borders. A particular sculpture is *that* particular sculpture in part because of its borders, and a particular carpet is *that* particular carpet in part because of its borders. If we significantly expand the borders of the table in our imaginations, we get a different table, and if we continue the imaginative expansion, eventually we have no table at all. Same with the carpet, the sculpture, and so forth.

Some people apply this logic to immortal life. They claim that an indefinitely long life would not have any determinate content, and thus it would not be a life of a particular human being. Todd May, a leading immortality curmudgeon, writes:

> For humans, an immortal life would be shapeless. It would be without borders or contours. Its color would fade . . . An immortal life would be impossible to make my life, or your life. Because it would drag on end-lessly, it would, sooner or later, just be a string of events lacking all form.[6]

Note, to begin, that it is only reasonable (although, admittedly, somewhat quixotic) to aim for medical immortality, not true immortality. So there would be (and would be understood to be) a limit to the length of our immortal lives. Still, the limit would be so large (say, six thousand years) that one might still worry that the life would not be recognizably human.

But note, also, that when we did the thought experiments involving expansion of the borders of the table, carpet, building, and sculpture in our imaginations, we pictured the expansion of *all* of the borders. In imagining an immortal human life, we are simply imagining an expansion of *one* of the borders—the length of the life, or, metaphorically, the horizontal border. Admittedly, with the table, carpet, and so forth, even (significant) expansion of *one* border will change the nature of the object, making it a different particular table or carpet, or no table or carpet at all. But other sorts of things are different; they can maintain their identity, given a significant expansion of their horizontal dimension.

Consider, for instance, an electrocardiogram—an appropriate example, in that it is a central marker of continued life. Even if we imagine

---

6. May, *Death*, 68–69.

a significant extension of the electrocardiogram, it does *not* follow that it lacks determinate content, especially at any given time. It is still an electrocardiogram. Similarly, the set of natural numbers has a determinate content—a determinate composition and definite properties—even though it is infinite. One might think of it as having an infinite horizontal dimension. Certain objects and processes have a determinate shape, even though one dimension goes to infinity. Human life could be one of these.

Human Lives Are Fraught: The Wave beneath. This worry can be put in different ways. Some have argued that it is an essential feature of human life that we are aware—either explicitly or implicitly—of its finitude. On this view, an awareness (of some sort) of death "haunts" us, and makes life precious and our various projects urgent; the intense beauty of life, and its capacity for poignancy, stem from our sense of its finitude.[7]

Think about human relationships. They would seem to lose much of their significance in an immortal life. We would always have time to correct mistakes we make in our friendships and love relationships, and there would always be time to meet new friends and lovers. When limitations of time are removed, the nature of all of our significant relationships would apparently change.

Similarly, there would always be time to pursue projects, such as writing a great novel or poem, getting in good physical shape, mastering Bach's Two-Part Inventions on the piano, or writing a book that solves (or, perhaps, simply makes a bit of progress on) the Free Will Problem(s). No matter what project we imagine—artistic, athletic, scientific—there would always be more time and indefinitely many opportunities to succeed. Our successes would then seem to be robbed of their significance.

Consider also the moral virtues, which give a kind of structure to human lives. These might be absent in an immortal life. Courage, for instance, seems to be defined at least in part by the way an individual confronts the possibility of death. Martha Nussbaum brings together the worries stemming from the "fraught" feature of human lives:

> The intensity and dedication with which very many human activities are pursued cannot be explained without reference to the awareness that our opportunities are finite, that we cannot choose these

---

7. Some attribute this sort of view to Martin Heidegger, although Heidegger employs the term "death" in a special way (as noted in footnote 2 above), and thus it is difficult to interpret him. See also May, *Death*, 60–63.

activities indefinitely many times. In raising a child, in cherishing a lover, in performing a demanding task of work or thought or artistic creation, we are aware, at some level, of the thought that each of these efforts is structured and constrained by time.[8]

When you are at the beach, or near the shore, you can hear the breaking of the waves in the background. Sometimes they roar, but usually the waves are a barely audible background noise. You are aware of this background noise, and it never goes away. Death is like the relentless background noise of the waves—a sound that is always there and helps to frame your experience. You are aware that the waves will someday engulf you. Death is the wave beneath it all.[9]

But I do not agree that an immortal life would lack intensity, beauty, and poignancy. Recall, first, that we can only aspire to medical, and not true, immortality. In medical immortality we would be vulnerable to early death, even if not by natural causes. Stephen Cave puts the point dramatically:

> The tricky thing about staying alive forever is that it just takes one little fatal accident and it is all over. Surviving is not something you do once then take it easy; you have to do it every day, every hour, every minute. . . . anything from a faulty brake cable to a herd of angry elephants could end it all in a second. When it comes to ways to die,

---

8. Nussbaum, *The Therapy of Desire*, 229.

9. Helen Whitney, the filmmaker (*Into the Night*), used this phrase in personal discussion. Her documentary film *Into the Night* (PBS) is an exploration of the issues we are considering in this book.

The following is an excerpt from Cory Taylor's *Dying: A Memoir* (Edinburgh, UK: Cannongate Books, 2017):

> "Just look where we are!" she shouted, spinning around to take in the sweep of the beach behind us. I realized how far we had walked, how tiny we must look from the land, two dots against the horizon. And I felt a surge of love for my mother, as if at any moment I might lose her to a rogue wave. . . .
>
> That night I went over the scene in my head many times before I went to sleep . . . I pictured my mother's tiny figure surrounded by all that water. I panicked again and my blood pounded. Even my sleep was filled with anxious dreams, where my tiny mother and I were falling off the reef's edge into the fathoms of churning water . . . And then I would wake up and hear the surf in the distance . . . (130–131)

It happened to the wife of an acquaintance of mine. She was walking along a beautiful beach in the small Northern California town, Gualala, and she was swept by a huge wave into the Pacific Ocean—to her death.

your imagination is the limit—as the infamous tramway authority sign reminds us: "Touching wires causes instant death—$200 fine."[10]

It is clear that a medically immortal life can be fraught. Now put aside medical immortality and consider true immortality. The activities that often are central to (some or even many) human lives, such as those discussed earlier (writing a great novel or poem, getting in excellent physical shape, mastering Bach's Two-Part Inventions on the piano, or writing a book that solves the Free Will Problem, and so forth), are very difficult. So are the great scientific challenges, such as figuring out the origin of the universe, the fundamental constituents of the universe, the laws of nature, and so on. They would not lose their difficulty in an immortal life! Merely adding more time does not make them easy. To accomplish any of these tasks, even in a truly immortal life, would still be rewarding and meaningful.

Similarly, merely adding more time does not in itself make it possible to have the sorts of friendships and love relationships that one desires. One can still be rejected, frustrated, and lonely. Adding more time does not in itself guarantee that you will succeed in having a close friendship or love relationship with a certain person. You can certainly try, but additional time might just result in more rejection and disappointment. A meaningful relationship is not a one-way street. It would be challenging to achieve close friendship and love in an immortal life, just as in a mortal life. And it would certainly be difficult to *maintain* this sort of relationship in an immortal life.

Indeed, special challenges would arise in the context of immortality. For instance, it can be difficult to maintain the intensity of feelings over time in a marriage. (We will return to these issues in the following chapter.) Couples often have to do things to "spice up" their marriages. Imagine the challenges for marriage in an immortal life!

Yes, more time provides more opportunities to succeed at various tasks, but it also provides unique difficulties and more opportunities to fail. Immortal life would still have deep challenges, and failure could bring with it frustration, loneliness, and despair that could last a very long time (if not forever). Surely one would be afraid of the consequences of failure in an immortal life, and the bare knowledge that one could keep trying is not much of a consolation.

---

10. Cave, *Immortality*, 74.

The virtues would still be present in an immortal life. With medical immortality, we are free of worries about dying from natural causes, but this still leaves lots of possibilities for premature death (recall that herd of wild elephants), and thus many opportunities for displaying courage in the face of death. Perhaps even more important, courage need not be defined only in terms of confronting the fear of *death*. One can display courage in facing dangers of various kinds and their attendant consequences: injury, loneliness, despair, depression, humiliation, and so forth. Just as one example, it is often thought that it takes courage for someone to testify about her own rape or sexual abuse. This *does* take courage, but not necessarily because of a confrontation, specifically, with death. Similarly, it can take courage to "come out" to your parents about your sexual orientation.

No question about it: life would be *different*, if we were immortal. But it doesn't follow that it would be *so* different as to make it unrecognizable as a human life. We would not fear death from natural causes, but this leaves plenty of room for death anxiety. One could be run over by a truck, and there would be many other terrible things to fear. So life would still be fraught. Fear of death is not the only thing that makes our lives fraught. Think of the phrase "a fate worse than death." If being fraught is necessary for life's being meaningful, an immortal life could still be meaningful.

Our Lives Correspond to Stories. Many people contend that our lives are stories.[11] But stories are abstract, and we are concrete. Also, it seems too fatalistic to think that we *are* our stories, since presumably we could have a different story. It is better to say that we *have* a story, one that we "write" with our free actions. Here we'll reflect on the claim that our lives *correspond to* stories (where this captures the idea that we *have* stories). We saw in Chapter One that a crucial part of living a meaningful life is acting freely and thereby writing the story of our lives. The content of the story can be considered the meaning of the individual's life. What follows are thoughts on how this content is determined.

---

11. Arthur Schopenhauer wrote that "the first forty years of life furnish the text, while the remaining thirty supply the commentary." See Arthur Schopenhauer, "The Ages of Life," in Will Durant, ed., *The Works of Schopenhauer* (New York: Frederick Unger, 1928): 407–431; the quotation is on p. 424.

One can write the "description" or "chronicle" of just about anything. In a broad and loose sense, we can call these "stories," but when people say that our lives correspond to stories, they mean "stories" in a stricter sense. Often they use the term "narratives." What are the relevant characteristics of stories (in this strict sense) and narratives? How are stories in this sense different from mere chronicles? (By the way, I am using "chronicle" in a special sense, so it would turn out that *The Chronicles of Narnia*, by C.S. Lewis, would be classified as a narrative, not a "chronicle.")

First, stories engage our emotions in ways in which mere descriptions or chronicles do not.[12] Stories elicit emotions, and they thus give us a special kind of explanation that reaches the heart.[13] Second, stories (in the strict sense) or narratives contain "meaning holism," whereas mere chronicles do not. In a narrative the meaning or value of an event can be determined, at least in part, by events that occur later.

Examples include hard work being "vindicated" or rendered time well spent by subsequent success (say, admission to medical school); mistakes in a personal or professional relationship that are given a different meaning, when one learns from them and subsequently flourishes as a result of the lessons learned; and risky decisions that are rendered well taken by subsequent success or mistakes by subsequent failure. Meaning holism involves a two-way time travel of meaning: for example, success gets an additional boost of value by resulting from hard work in the past, and the hard work gets a boost in value by issuing ultimately in success.[14]

The possibility of backward time travel of meaning shows that death can be bad not only because it deprives an individual of her future, but also because it deprives her of her past. That is, it deprives her of the capacity to "rewrite" her past—to endow it with a different meaning

---

12. David Velleman, "Narrative Explanation," *Philosophical Review* 112 (2003): 1–26. See also John Martin Fischer, "Free Will, Death, and Immortality: The Role of Narrative," *Philosophical Papers* 34 (2005): 379–405; reprinted in Fischer, *Our Stories*, 145–164.

13. Understanding a person's story is crucial to empathy. It can play an important role in a physician's relationship with a patient: Rita Charon, *Narrative Medicine: Honoring the Stories of Illness* (New York: Oxford University Press, 2006). A defendant in a criminal trial wants the jury to hear her story, a politician tells her story, and so forth; they seek to engage our emotions.

14. For these examples, see J. David Velleman, "Well-Being and Time," *Pacific Philosophical Quarterly* 72 (1991): 48–77, reprinted in John Martin Fischer, ed., *The Metaphysics of Death* (Stanford, CA: Stanford University Press, 1993): 329–357.

through its narrative relationship with the unfolding present. Death is a double deprivation.

Another feature that is characteristically present in stories (construed strictly) and narratives is a structure that involves *endings*. The ending offers a way of tying together the beginning, middle, and last stages of the story; it offers a kind of "totalizing" understanding—an understanding of the whole set of events through the lens of the ending. This sort of understanding gives rise to a distinctive kind of *explanation* of a series of events: narrative explanation.

In genres as different as opera and "western" (cowboy) film, the importance of endings is stressed.[15] The idea is that our lives get meaning from our confrontation with our own mortality. In some cases, especially in the western films, our mortality gives us the opportunity to define our lives in terms of courage. In Wagner's *Ring* cycle of operas, human mortality leads to the recognition of the importance of love. As the title of Shakespeare's play has it, "All's well that ends well."

Note that a medically immortal life *would* have an ending, even if it would be (say) six thousand years down the road. But think of true immortality. We could *concede* that our immortal lives would not have endings and thus that *one* of the typical features of narratives would be absent in immortal life. The other features would still be present: engagement with the emotions and meaning holism. Perhaps having an ending is not an *essential* feature of a narrative, although it is a typical feature. Given that there would still be engagement with the emotions and meaning holism, we could still think of our lives as corresponding to narratives; *enough* of the typical features of narratives would be present.

We could perhaps think of an immortal human life as corresponding to a *series* of novels—a series that never ends. After all, it does not seem to be *essential* to a series of novels that it end, even if all such series do in fact end because of the constraints of human life as it actually is. The series can contain the same protagonist (such as a detective in a series of mystery

---

15. Philip Kitcher and Richard Schacht, *Finding an Ending: Reflections on Wagner's Ring* (New York: Oxford University Press, 2004); and Peter French, *Cowboy Metaphysics: Ethics and Death in Westerns* (Lanham, MD: Rowman and Littlefield, 1997). For a critical discussion of *Cowboy Metaphysics*, see John Martin Fischer and Benjamin Mitchell-Yellin, "(Not) Riding into the Sunset: The Significance of Endings," in Zachary J. Goldberg, ed., *Reflections on Ethics and Responsibility: Essays in Honor of Peter A. French* (Cham, Switzerland: Springer International, 2017): 201–218.

novels) and many of the same characters. Think, for example, of the Harry Potter novels or your favorite series of mysteries. The books may engage our emotions, and there can be meaning holism within the individual novels and in the series more broadly. A series of interlocking stories— short stories, novels, television shows—can exhibit two crucial features of narrativity: engagement with the emotions and meaning holism.

Note also that the stories of the parts of our lives can have endings, which can give narrative explanations to the parts. Søren Kierkegaard pointed out that although we live our lives forward, we understand them backwards. But this point does not imply an ending to a life as a whole, but endings to the various parts.

Endings are important for us for our psychological health. But the point is that endings of particular *stretches* or *parts* of our lives are psychologically important because they affect us in our ongoing lives. This insight obviously cannot be extrapolated to the ending of one's life as a whole, since there would be no issue of psychological effects as one goes forward in life (since one doesn't!). So it is not so clear that the importance of endings *within* life, as emphasized in the positive psychology literature (the study of happiness), applies to death. This point then does not count against immortality.[16]

Some theorists reject the notion that our lives have fixed, "objective" meanings. They emphasize the ambiguities of life—the multiple meanings, the loose ends, its fragmentary nature. They think that narrativity is a Procrustean bed, into which human lives cannot fit comfortably. This is a major theme of "postmodernist" thought. If this is correct, then we don't need to worry about immortality not corresponding to a narrative; our ordinary finite lives don't either.

Even if we assume that our lives correspond to stories, it is still possible that we could be immortal. Although it is "a long story(!)," we have not seen *decisive* reason to agree with the immortality curmudgeons.

---

16. Jennan Ismael argues that we would prefer to live lives that correspond to narratives, and thus have endings: Jennan Ismael, "The Ethical Importance of Death," in Charles Tandy, ed., *Death and Anti-Death*, Vol. 4 (Ann Arbor: University of Michigan Press, 2006); reprinted in John Perry, Michael Bratman, and John Martin Fischer, eds., *Introduction to Philosophy: Classical and Contemporary Readings* (8th ed.) (New York: Oxford University Press, 2018): 820–828. But why is it not enough that our lives have meaning holism, and that there are endings to parts of our lives? Would we really prefer an overall ending to more life?

Infinity Is Fundamentally Different

Some curmudgeons point out that infinite magnitudes are different in kind, and not just degree, from finite magnitudes. This makes it hard to see how we could conceive of an immortal life, and conceiving of something is necessary for desiring or choosing it. Mikel Burley writes:

> . . . [T]here is nothing that could count as an infinite series that has reached its completion, for an infinite series, is, precisely, a series that never reaches a point of completion: it just goes on and on forever. So if one agrees that a necessary condition of being able to assess the desirability of a life is that the life be conceivable as a whole, then it looks as though such an assessment cannot be made in the case of a putative immortal life.[17]

Even if infinite magnitudes are fundamentally different and thus an infinitely long life cannot be conceived as a whole, medical immortality does not imply an infinitely long life. Let's once again focus on true immortality for the sake of our discussion. Even under the assumption of true immortality, I do not think that we need to be able to picture immortal lives "as a whole," in order to evaluate them.

Consider the set of natural numbers, which is an infinite set. Can we conceive of the natural numbers? Yes, but not by somehow picturing or holding before our minds the "complete" set of natural numbers (which does not, in any case, exist). Rather, we grasp the natural numbers by knowing how they are generated: 1 is a natural number, and for any natural number N, N+1 is a natural number. By knowing this algorithm, we can conceive of the natural numbers—an infinite set. Why can't we grasp truly immortal life by knowing that for any day D in the life, there will be a next day—day D+1? This is a rather less elegant way of expressing Scarlett O'Hara's line in *Gone with the Wind*: "Tomorrow is another day."

Human Lives Have Stages. Samuel Scheffler has contended that having stages is essential to a recognizably human life:

> Consider . . . the fact that we understand a human life as having stages, beginning with birth and ending with death, and that we understand each of these stages as having its characteristic tasks, challenge, and

---

17. Mikel Burley, "Immortality and Meaning: Reflections on the Makropulos Debate," *Philosophy* 84 (2009): 529–547, esp. p. 539.

potential rewards. . . . [T]he fact that life is understood as having stages is, I take it, a universal response to the realities of our organic existence and our physical birth, maturation, deterioration, and death. Our collective understanding of the range of goals, activities, and pursuits that are available to a person, the challenges he faces, and the satisfactions that he may reasonably hope for are all indexed to these stages.[18]

An immortal life would lack the stages that characterize ordinary human life. Thus, an immortal life would not be recognizably human.

We do tend to divide our lives, even if somewhat arbitrarily, into stages. In a famous passage from *As You Like It*, Shakespeare puts these words into the mouth of Jaques, addressing the Duke:

All the world's a stage
And all the men and women merely players.
They have their exits and their entrances,
And one man in his time plays many parts,
His acts being seven ages. At first, the infant,
Mewling and puking in the nurse's arms.
Then the whining schoolboy . . .
. . . Last scene of all,
That ends this strange eventful history,
Is second childishness and mere oblivion,
Sans teeth, sans eyes, sans taste, sans everything.[19]

The last stage (prior to death) seems to be missing in an immortal life, and thus the associated challenges and opportunities for reward would be absent. Even in medical immortality, we would not know when we would die. Although the expectation for medical immortality now is something like six thousand years, death could come at any time, and it might not

---

18. Scheffler, *Death and the Afterlife*, 96.
19. William Shakespeare, *As You Like It*, act 2, scene 7. Note that there is an ambiguity in "stage." When Shakespeare writes, "All the world's a stage," he means that we can understand our lives as plays. He uses the term "scene" to mean what I have called "stage." So his point is that corresponding to our lives is a play with various scenes, depicting the stages of human life. Also, Lucretius likened human life to a banquet, with its characteristic stages: appetizers, salad, entrée, and dessert. For a discussion of the Lucretian "Banquet Argument," see Fischer, "Epicureanism about Death and Immortality," reprinted in Fischer, ed., *Our Stories*, 121–124. (I suppose that an immortal life would have to be interpreted as an "all-you-can-eat" buffet: not incoherent, *albeit* unhealthy.)

come until considerably after one's six thousandth birthday party. So there would not be a stage of physical and mental deterioration, with a "second childhood," and a preparation for death. In an ordinary human life, this stage can be challenging, but it can also offer opportunities for deep insights, and for modeling courage and wisdom in the face of death. People who do well during this stage can endow their lives with great value.

Other stages would still be present in an immortal life: to put it in Shakespeare's somewhat uncharitable way, the mewling/puking infant stage, the whining schoolboy stage, and so forth. We would presumably still have adolescence, young adulthood, middle age, older age, and so forth, with their characteristic challenges and opportunities. So we wouldn't be without stages entirely. We would indeed lack the opportunities to model courage and wisdom in the face of death, but many other challenges and opportunities would present themselves: avoiding boredom, loneliness, and lassitude; keeping relationships vital; completing worthwhile projects; and so forth. We could model success in meeting these challenges.

As in our earlier discussion of narrativity, we might think that, although immortal lives would not contain exactly the same stages as our mortal lives, they would still have *enough* similarity to our mortal lives to be recognizably human. Immortal lives would still have stages, even if not exactly the same stages as mortal lives. These stages would have challenges and opportunities, even if not exactly the same as mortal lives.

Think of the seasons of the year: fall, winter, spring, and summer. The change of seasons in the Midwest and the Eastern United States is dramatic (as it is in Europe and most places in the world): the fall foliage, winter snow, the re-emergence of green leaves and bright flowers in spring, and the glorious sunshine (and not-so-glorious humidity) of summer. In contrast, although we have our own versions of fall, winter, and spring in Southern California, it can seem to a visitor or "transplant" that we just have one long season: summer. Some transplants find it jarring and disorienting to live in an area that does not have the seasons. A hot Thanksgiving Day and a warm, sunny New Year's Day just seem bizarre (despite the allure of the Rose Bowl floats).

Life is thus in some ways unrecognizable, but you can get used to the weather in Southern California! After awhile, it becomes the "new normal." Having lived in other places and then moving to Southern California, I do miss the dramatic autumn changes, but I do not miss the extended periods of frigid weather, icy sidewalks and roads in the winter, and the ever-present humidity in the summer. I can deal with the fact that many of our leaves and flowers are lovely all year around, and one doesn't have to bundle up the kids when they want to play outside. Overall, I have adjusted to having one long period of sunny weather, and I am very comfortable with it. One notices differences, even if subtle, between the sunshine in July and in January. It is a human life, and a nice one. I can't see why I couldn't adjust to a long stage of immortal life in which I am in my "prime"!

Note, also, that the stages (or, at least, their relative lengths) have changed significantly as we have increased human longevity. When our average lifespan was forty years at the beginning of the twentieth century, middle and older age were less long than they are now, when average lifespan (in developed countries) is about eighty years. It would not have been true to think that the stages, and their proportionate lengths, at the beginning of the twentieth century were *essential* to human nature. This would have been too conservative.

Conclusion

It goes without saying that immortal life would not be *exactly* the same as mortal life. In considering different proposals for immortal life, the question should not be whether they are *exactly* like mortal human life. The question should be whether they are *sufficiently similar* to count as recognizably human lives.

If you think that our lives as a whole correspond to narratives and that an ending is crucial to a narrative, then you will not find a truly immortal life recognizably human. But if you think that engagement with the emotions and meaning holism render the stories of immortal life sufficiently like narratives, then you will find even a truly immortal life recognizably human (at least as regards narrativity).

Similarly, if you think that having all of the stages of mortal human lives is essential to a human life, you will not find an immortal life recognizably human. But if you think that having many, or almost all, of the stages of mortal human lives is enough to render a life recognizably human, you will find an immortal life recognizably human (at least in respect of having stages).

It is the same with all of the features we have considered in this chapter. Immortal life would be *different* from our mortal human life, but this does not in itself make immortal human life incomprehensible. The question here is whether an immortal life would be *so* different as to render it incomprehensible as a human life. I have suggested that the answer might well be "no." It can seem that the immortality curmudgeons are mired in a stale conservatism.

Would immortality be worthy of choice for creatures like us? In order for the answer to be "yes," it would have to be the life of someone who is recognizably like us—recognizably human (or perhaps, relaxing Williams's constraint, recognizably a person). We have considered the recognizability condition here, and we will turn to the identity and desirability conditions in the next chapter.

Annotated Suggestions for Further Reading

The locus classicus of contemporary philosophical skepticism about the desirability of immortality is Bernard Williams, "The Makropulos Case: Reflections on the Tedium of Immortality," in Williams, *Problems of the Self* (Cambridge: Cambridge University Press, 1973): 82–100; reprinted in John Martin Fischer, ed., *The Metaphysics of Death* (Stanford, CA: Stanford University Press, 1993): 73–92. Williams is the paradigmatic immortality curmudgeon, and many contemporary curmudgeons take their cue from him. We will discuss more elements of his views in the following chapter.

For further reflection on the relationship between narratives, immortality, and meaningfulness of human life, see John Martin Fischer, "Stories and the Meaning of Life," *Philosophic Exchange* 39 (2009): 2–16; reprinted in Fischer, *Our Stories*, 165–177. There is a helpful overview of some of the ways in which people use stories to make sense of their lives in Julie Beck, "Life's Stories," *The Atlantic Monthly* (August 10, 2015): https://www.theatlantic.com/health/archive/2015/08/life-stories-narrative-psychology-redemption-mental-health/400796/. For skepticism about the invocation of narrativity in theorizing about the self, see Galen Strawson, "Against Narrativity," *Ratio* 17 (2004): 428–452.

CHAPTER 7

Identity, Boredom, and Immortality Realism

Millions long for immortality who don't know what to do with themselves on a rainy Sunday afternoon.

—Susan Ertz,
Anger in the Sky

....

Introduction

Would you choose to be immortal? Would you take an elixir of eternal life, or a bunch of pills every day, or even choose to upload your mind to a computer? A positive answer requires that the envisaged life be recognizable as a human being's (or person's) life, that it really be *yours*, and that it be *attractive*. We considered the recognizability requirement in the previous chapter. In this chapter we will consider the identity and attractiveness conditions. How can an individual existing in a million years, perhaps with none of your values or memories, really be *you*? How could you continue to be excited by life, fully engaged in it, in a million years? Or even six thousand?

The Identity Condition

We need to interpret the identity condition in a certain way. That is, we will understand it as requiring that the proposed immortal life describe not just the very same individual, but the very same individual *in the sense in which we care especially about ourselves*. In the previous chapter, we distinguished the thick and thin self, and we considered the issue of which self we care about, in the context of the issues raised by the Mirror Image Argument. We also noted that some argue that we only care about the thick self, whereas others contend that we fundamentally care about the thin self (and how it is attached to a thick self over time). I suggested that we do in fact care about the thin self in this way, as indicated by "baby switching," early adoption, and similar cases. We can wonder what it would have been like to have grown up in very different circumstances. And when we think of ourselves in the future, we allow for considerable changes in our personality, even radical conversions and transformations.

Suppose that I tell you that in the future someone will win the state lottery and receive ten million dollars (before taxes!). You think: that's nice, good for him. But now I tell you that the winner will be *you*; this fundamentally changes your attitude. You have a new lease on life (and maybe a new lease on a fancy car, too!). Similarly, suppose I tell you that someone will be tortured by evil people tomorrow. You think: this is very unfortunate—we haven't really made much progress toward greater civility. But now I tell you that the person will be *you*. Yikes! This fact fundamentally changes your attitude. The point is that we care especially about ourselves. This does not imply that we do not care about other humans (and animals) or that we would never sacrifice our interests on behalf of others; it simply means that we care in *a special and distinctive way* about ourselves.

The identity condition requires that a proposed picture of my immortal life involve *me in the sense in which I care especially about myself*. If this proposal presents another individual, it would be a description of the future for someone else, and it would not be about *my* immortality. Further, the proposal would flunk the test if it posited a "me" that is so alien and different that I just don't care. From now on in our discussion, I will interpret the question "Will it be me?" as "Will it be me in the sense in which I care especially about myself?"

In his important discussion of these issues (which we began to consider in the previous chapter), Bernard Williams claims that I would not care in the special way about an individual with substantially different desires and values.[1] Further, he thinks it inevitable that a future individual (purportedly identical with me) in an immortal life will at some point have significantly different desires and values from mine now.

---

1. Bernard Williams, "The Makropulos Case: Reflections on the Tedium of Immortality," in Williams, *Problems of the Self* (Cambridge: Cambridge University Press, 1973): 82–100; reprinted in John Martin Fischer, ed., *The Metaphysics of Death* (Stanford, CA: Stanford University Press, 1993): 73–92.

But I am not convinced about the not-caring part. In our ordinary, mortal lives, we know that our desires and values will change, sometimes suddenly and radically, over time. I might now value challenge, change, and adventure travel, although I know that later in my life I will place higher value on security, comfort, and proximity to medical care. Whereas I am now progressive, I know that later I may well be more conservative politically.

It is fair to say that we can anticipate some changes of political views, perhaps softening of positions, over time. This doesn't imply that we don't care (in the special sense) about our future, somewhat politically different selves. In our finite lives, we care about our future selves, despite anticipating changes in personality characteristics, political views, and even basic values.

Why then shouldn't the same point apply in a medically or even truly immortal life? (Recall that a medically immortal life is one in which you know you will not die of "natural causes." In a truly immortal life, you know you cannot die in *any* way.) Why should there be a *double standard* as we evaluate our situations in mortal and immortal lives? If I care about my future self in my mortal life, even anticipating significant changes in desires and values, why wouldn't I similarly care about my future self in an immortal life?

Suppose a future individual with a body that is physically continuous with mine now, and a set of memories that are psychologically continuous with mine now, is tortured. By "continuous" I mean that there is an uninterrupted chain of mental states, the adjacent links of which contain a sufficient *overlap* of values and memories. So, for example, the Wednesday-me remembers a lot of what happened on Tuesday, and the Tuesday-me remembers a lot of what happened on Monday. It may turn out that the Monday-2018-me remembers very little, if anything, about what happened to the five-year-old me; but this doesn't matter, as long as the links are related suitably (by overlap). The same goes for values.

Return to the future individual. Suppose that I discover that this individual in the future will have very different desires and values from mine now. After this discovery, will I feel relieved? I do not think so. And imagine that such an individual wins the lottery. Will I not care especially, because he has such different desires and values? Again, I do not think so. I care about this self because, well, it is me. In the terminology of Chapter Four, my thin self has become attached to a new thick self. In an immortal life I could have the right *connection* with my previous self (via a chain of suitably interlocking arrays of values), even if the future individual does not have my 2018 values.

Shifting to memories, I also reject the view that I would not care about my future self, if I were to anticipate that I will share *no memories* with myself now. I worry again about a double standard. I now have no memories of my life when I was four years old. Zero. But presumably this doesn't mean that I am not identical to that four-year-old me, or that the four-year-old shouldn't care about the sixty-five-year-old me. Memory is obviously not perfect. Sometimes we remember *nothing* about ourselves at a previous time, even though there is the right kind of chain with interlocking links of memories. This is in our mortal lives as we actually lead them. And yet our former selves can and do care about our future selves. I now care (especially) about my future self—the self that will (someday) retire and spend time with his family (and [maybe!] grandchildren), travel less, live within range of emergency medical care, and so forth.

Why should it be any different in an immortal life? There is no bar stemming from the identity condition to imagining an immortal life.

The Attractiveness Condition and Secular Immortality

The Problem of Boredom. In order for immortality to be worthy of choice, it must not be unpleasant or miserable. We have assumed relatively favorable external circumstances in our discussion thus far, and we can maintain that assumption for now. Turning to "internal" conditions, many have thought that we would be tormented and miserable. Jonathan Swift writes:

> When they [the Struldbrugs] came to fourscore years, which is reckoned the extremity of living in this country [Luggnagg], they had not only all the follies and infirmities of other old men [Lugnaggians], but many more which arose from the dreadful prospect of never dying. They were not only opinionative, peevish, covetous, morose, vain, talkative, but incapable of friendship, and dead to all natural affection, which never descended below their grandchildren. Envy and impotent desires are their prevailing passions.[2]

---

2. Jonathan Swift, *Gulliver's Travels*, Chapter 26, Chapter X.

Yuck! But supposing these problems can be solved (no mean feat), many have thought that immortal life would inevitably become *boring*. This has been the fundamental concern of the immortality curmudgeons: the alleged tedium of immortality.

In his classic paper that we have been discussing, Bernard Williams developed the boredom worry. As we noted previously, Williams discussed an opera by Janáček, based on a play by Čapek. Recall that the protagonist is a woman who goes under different names or "aliases," for instance, "Elina Makropulos," all of which have the initials "EM." Her father has developed an "elixir of life," which extends life (without biological deterioration) for three hundred years, at which point it must be taken again to ensure another three hundred years, and so forth. Her father has been ordered to test the elixir on Elina, which he has done. The experiment is just that—he treats EM as a guinea pig, without any love for her or any attempt to ensure that she has human connections. She leads a life that leaves her lonely, alienated, and bored, and in the play EM decides not to take the elixir again, but to destroy it instead (much to the dismay of some elderly men!).

Bernard Williams attributes her condition to her longevity:

> Her unending life has come to a state of boredom, indifference, and coldness. Everything is joyless: "In the end it is the same," she says, "singing and silence." . . . Her trouble was, it seems, boredom: a boredom connected with the fact that everything that could happen and make sense to one particular human being of 42 [37] had already happened to her. Or, rather, all the sorts of things that could make sense to one woman of a certain character . . .[3]

Williams thus defends the "Necessary Boredom Thesis," the contention that immortality would inevitably be boring, simply in virtue of facts about human character and human lives. This makes him an immortality curmudgeon. We pointed out in previous chapters that Williams adopts a preference-thwarting model of death's badness (when death is in fact bad). He also presents such a theory of immortality's "badness"—a preference-destroying model. According to Williams, EM lost any preferences that could propel her into the future; endless life became alienating and boring. Everything was the same, and she

---

3. Williams, "The Makropulos Case," 82. In Fischer, ed., *The Metaphysics of Death.*

retreated into herself. This is no way for a human being to live, despite favorable biological and economic circumstances. No wonder she destroyed the elixir.

Samuel Scheffler fills in Williams's argument with a more explicit account of the inevitable boredom of living forever.[4] He writes:

> [When categorical desires eventually die, which they must] . . . one will be left with nothing *but* oneself, and one will be doomed to a kind of boredom from which there is no chance of escape in this world.[5]

He elaborates: ". . . we will be left *with* ourselves, and we ourselves are, terminally boring."[6]

I interpret Scheffler as attributing to Williams the view that, when all the projects that give rise to our categorical desires are subtracted, all we are left with is white noise and a blank screen. The screen is still there, but it is blank; there is still audible noise, but it is white noise. All you would be left with is yourself.

Pleasures and Projects. Is it inevitable that a human being would lose her important projects and associated preferences in an immortal life? Recall our consideration of memory in the previous section of this chapter on identity. Here we observed that memory would fade in immortality. If we were to forget significant chunks of our past, this would seem to vanquish boredom. I argued that an individual can remain the same, despite having few, if any, memories of his distant past. This framework provides one way of replying to Williams: the same person persists, and she can endlessly return to previous projects (or new iterations of them), because she will have forgotten her past pursuit of them. This is an underappreciated, and often ignored, avenue of response to Williams (and other curmudgeons who worry about tedium).[7]

Let's put issues about memory to the side, and consider EM. It seems *incorrect* to suppose that after 337 years she would run out of projects that could propel her into the future. It seems wrong that she has lived so long that no experience can have a positive impact on her

4. Samuel Scheffler, *Death and the Afterlife*, Niko Kolodny, ed. (New York: Oxford University Press, 2015): 88–95.

5. Scheffler, *Death and the Afterlife*, 94.

6. Scheffler, *Death and the Afterlife*, 95.

7. Christopher Belshaw has developed this sort of reply to the curmudgeons: "Immortality, Memory, and Imagination," *Journal of Ethics* 19, no. 3–4 (2015): 323–348.

or even make sense to her. At your age you might find this hard to believe, but 337 years is just not that long. (Trust me!) Do you really think you would run out of projects in that amount of time—that you would simply not care anymore? Williams is unduly pessimistic. Perhaps it is not her longevity *per se* that is the problem for EM, but something more *specific* about her life. After all, her father treated her as a guinea pig, not a human being entitled to respect, and certainly not a daughter to be loved and cherished. *This* mistreatment and loneliness, and not her longevity *per se*, may have led to her narcissism and despair.[8] If so, then we could not extrapolate from her case to *everyone*, as specified in the Necessary Boredom Thesis. Williams might be right about *some* people, but he claims that *all* persons would inevitably run out of projects that could propel them into the future. This is too bleak.

We are assuming that you would not be deteriorating biologically and would be living in favorable economic and social circumstances. (We will go into issues raised by these assumptions later in this chapter.) Under these circumstances, would you choose medical immortality? Would you at least choose to take the elixir again? Presumably, the answers would be "no" if you believed that you would run out of projects and associated categorical desires. But I do not see why we should agree with Williams (and the morose parade of immortality curmudgeons) in thinking that we would indeed run out of such projects and preferences. Spoilsports!

Think, just to begin, of certain salient pleasures, such as the pleasure of eating delicious food, listening to your favorite music, having healthy sex, appreciating a work of art (a painting, sculpture, novel, or poem, or perhaps a compelling film or TV program), and so forth. I am

---

8. Connie Rosati makes this point in her insightful discussion of Williams's paper: Connie S. Rosati, "The Makropulos Case: Reflections on Immortality and Agency," in Ben Bradley, Fred Feldman, and Jens Johansson, eds., *The Oxford Handbook of Philosophy of Death* (New York: Oxford University Press, 2013): 355–390.

In the episode "Death Wish" of the television program *Star Trek*, Quinn is banished to a comet where he is immortal. He gives an impassioned speech in which he describes the boredom of his immortality, saying that it "cheapens and denigrates" his life. He (unsuccessfully) attempts suicide. It is important to note that he is not only immortal, but alone; he is the only person on the entire comet. As with EM, his despair is more plausibly attributed to loneliness than immortality. Even in a finite life, extreme loneliness is profoundly disturbing; this is why solitary confinement is such a terrible punishment.

a "foodie"; the pleasures of delicious food are deeply appealing to me. Similarly, certain pieces of music, or songs, have a profound resonance for me. Perhaps they remind me of a period of my life, a place, or particular people who have meant a lot to me. Or maybe the music just touches me in some way that is hard to describe, but deep.

I cannot imagine ever becoming bored with Bach's Second Unaccompanied Violin Partita. And I cannot imagine ever becoming bored with a steaming hot platter of chile rellenos with refried beans and rice.[9] Of course, if I were to listen to Bach's piece all the time—morning, noon, and night—this would quickly become tedious and hideously oppressive. If I were to eat chile rellenos at every meal, this would quickly become sickening.

So our activities and associated pleasures must be spread out in the right way. Sex, compelling as it is, needs to be spread out appropriately; sex morning, noon, and night, even if possible, would quickly become cold, oppressive, and, frankly, boring—a chore. (The undergraduate reader might find this implausible, but, again: trust me . . .) We are not considering immortal life in which pleasurable activities are repeated obsessively in a compulsive and repetitive fashion. We are envisaging a life with an *appropriate distribution* of activities and associated pleasures. Given this, my enthusiasm for the pleasures of life would not be extinguished.[10]

I ask you to pause and think carefully. Would the pleasures of eating your favorite foods, listening to your favorite music, or having healthy sex really run out—given that they are part of a sensible *distribution* of activities? They seem to be "repeatable" pleasures. Granted, some

---

9. I could have picked various dishes or meals—I don't have one "favorite." You can substitute your own cherished dish. (I use "chile rellenos," rather than the grammatically correct "chiles rellenos.") By the way, many of you might have had an unfortunate "chile rellenos experience" in a restaurant; they can seem to be wilted, soggy, and doused with an undistinguished tomato sauce. It doesn't have to be this way! If made properly, chile rellenos can be delicious—crispy on the outside and creamy on the inside. Various sauces, including a complex mole sauce, can enhance the dish. They are not haute cuisine, but they *are* delicious.

10. Kierkegaard pointed out that the aesthete will "rotate" his pleasures like a farmer will rotate his crops, to get the most out of the respective activities: Søren Kierkegaard, "The Rotation Method," in *Either/Or*, in Robert Bretall, ed., *A Kierkegaard Anthology* (New York: The Modern Library, 1946): 21 and 23–24. Relentlessly planting the same crops year after year will deplete the soil. Similarly, relentlessly pursuing the same activities will deplete our capacity for pleasure.

pleasures, or pleasurable experiences, are not repeatable: for instance, the pleasure of climbing Mt. Whitney for the first time. These pleasures tend to be associated with activities that are defined in terms of particular occasions, or times, or relationships. But not all pleasures are "self-exhausting." Some are repeatable, and these would give some reason for wanting to continue to live in an immortal life.[11]

The philosopher Corliss Lamont highlights this point:

> I deny that repetition as such leads necessarily to "monotony and boredom." Consider, for instance, the basic biological drives of thirst, hunger, and sex. Pure, cool water is the best drink in the world, and I have been drinking it for sixty-two years. If we follow through with [the Necessary Boredom Thesis], I ought to be so tired of water by this time that I seek to quench my thirst solely by wine, beer, and Coca-Cola! Yet I still love water. By the same token, the average person does *not* fall into a state of ennui through the satisfaction of hunger or sexual desire.[12]

As I noted in Chapter Four, I do not hold that the *only* thing that is good in itself is pleasure, or that the *only* reason to continue to live is the accumulation of pleasure. My point is only that this would give us *some* reason, perhaps *sufficient* reason, to continue to live an immortal life. In my view, pleasure does not exhaust goodness or meaningfulness, nor does it count as the only reason for action. Further, I do not claim that goodness or meaningfulness must be defined only in terms of *positive experiences* (other than pleasures); it may be that activities in themselves, apart from the associated experiences, render lives good or meaningful, and give us reasons for wanting to continue to live (and reasons for action). Repeatable pleasures represent only *some* (important) reasons for wanting to continue to live—reasons that I think would also be present in an immortal life.

Many people are less hedonistic and more spiritual, or perhaps they are not exclusively hedonistic and are at least to some extent spiritual.

---

11. For the distinction between "repeatable" and "self-exhausting" pleasures, see John Martin Fischer, "Why Immortality Is Not So Bad," *International Journal of Philosophical Studies* 2 (1994): 257–270; reprinted in John Martin Fischer, *Our Stories: Essays on Life, Death, and Free Will* (New York: Oxford University Press, 2009).

12. Corliss Lamont, "Mistaken Attitudes toward Death," *Journal of Philosophy* 52: 29–36; the quotation is from p. 33.

For them meditation or prayer can be deeply moving and profound. I do not see why prayer, meditation, yoga, or other spiritual practices (such as seeking deeper mindfulness) would inevitably lose their resonance over time. If one were to pray all the time, this would sap life of its rich texture—at least for most of us. The vast majority of us are not ascetic monks who wish to spend every waking moment in prayer. We need not, however, envisage an immortal life totally and exclusively devoted to spirituality in order to see that these experiences could be rewarding and help to propel one forward (when *blended* appropriately with a range of human activities and experiences). In our mortal lives we think it is important to distribute our activities appropriately; why suppose it would be any different in an immortal life? To do so would be to apply a double standard.

Consider now "intellectual" projects, such as seeking to answer questions in the natural and social sciences, mathematics, and philosophy (among countless other areas). Many people are deeply and passionately interested in the origins of the universe. How did everything begin: the Big Bang? But what preceded the Big Bang and precipitated it? Pursuing these questions could keep one engaged in life for many years. Is it really plausible that these questions, and all related cosmological and astronomical questions, will be solved in the future? Is there life elsewhere in the universe? What are the fundamental building blocks or constituents of our physical world? What are the fundamental laws of physics? And so forth. In any case, it would seem that these questions could keep us fascinated for at least six thousand years, and that, if they are solved, other interesting problems in physics will emerge and become salient. It just doesn't seem like we'll run out of important questions in these areas, or that they will lose their power to engage our attention.

The situation is similar in other fields. Why think that the interesting questions in sociology, archeology, anthropology, and political science will have been answered in six thousand years (or longer), or will have lost their ability to fascinate and engage us? Further, our immortality would in no way obviate the need to coordinate our behavior and to live together productively; if anything, it would render these challenges more pressing. So politics—local, national, and global— would still be essential and engaging.

Some (unlucky!) individuals will continue to be interested in philosophy. Some of us are absolutely driven (our spouses think we are crazy) by philosophical problems. How can we understand Aristotle's *Metaphysics Zeta*? Kant's *Critique of Pure Reason*? What is justice, truth, beauty? How can free will and moral responsibility fit into a causally deterministic universe—if at all? I don't see that these questions are in danger of being answered decisively soon. Nor do I think they would stop eliciting interest, even in an immortal life.

You might find these perky ruminations excessively optimistic. Shelly Kagan writes:

> Essentially, the problem with immortality seems to be one of inevitable boredom. The problem is tedium. You get tired of doing math after a while. After a hundred years, a thousand years, a million years, whatever it is, eventually you are going to say, "Yes here's a math problem I haven't solved before, but so what? I've just done *so much* math, it holds no appeal for me anymore." Or, you go through all the great art museums in the world (or the galaxy) and you say, "Yes, I've seen dozens of Picassos. I've seen Rembrandts and Van Goghs, and more. I've seen thousands, millions, billions of incredible works of art. I've gotten what there is to get out of them. Isn't there anything new?" And the problem is that there isn't. There are, of course, things that you haven't seen before—but they are not new in a way that can still engage you afresh.[13]

It is obvious that Kagan is discussing true immortality, rather than medical immortality. But I do not see why (say) math would lose its appeal in immortality of either kind. Of course, math all the time would be a very boring existence, even for the biggest math nerd. But we are not envisaging math all the time—only math sometimes, mixed in with other activities and experiences. Kagan is aware of this point. He concedes that we are not to envisage doing the same thing all the time, day after day. Shelly likes Thai food, but:

> Instead of Thai [food] every day for all eternity, perhaps it could be Thai for lunch on Mondays, Wednesdays, and Fridays, with Italian for lunch on Tuesdays and Thursdays, and Ethiopian for dinner on Saturday night, and so forth and so on. Perhaps we could spend three hours in the morning doing philosophy, and then two hours in the afternoon doing math, and then spend the evening watching a movie or going to the theater. I must say, that sounds like a pretty pleasant life.

---

13. Kagan, *Death*, 243.

But it doesn't really help. Because, again, when I think of doing this, not just for years, or decades, or even centuries, but for all *eternity*, never getting away from it, never being free from it, it all turns sour. The seemingly positive dream of immortality becomes a nightmare, a nightmare from which we can never escape.[14]

We wouldn't, however, have to envisage such a rigidly structured existence. There are so many more kinds of food than Thai, Italian, and Ethiopian, and we could distribute our exploration and enjoyment of them as we'd like—with as much variety and spontaneity as we would prefer. Kagan knows all of this, but he still thinks immortality would inevitably become a nightmare. I am not so confident of this.

Back to Thai food. In a fascinating paper, Phillip Bricker discusses the issue of whether he would want to live longer than an "ordinary immortal," since there are infinitely many orders of infinity greater than "aleph null"—the smallest, and the one corresponding to an unending sequence of years, one for each natural number.[15] He writes:

> There are countless greater infinities that dwarf aleph-null as surely as aleph-null dwarfs our customarily allotted three score and ten. Why settle for a piddling aleph-null years . . . ?[16]

Either Bricker likes Thai food more than Kagan, or, what is more likely, he has a more expansive view of what could propel you onward in an immortal life, even one that dwarfs a piddling true immortality of aleph-null years. I am inclined to agree with him, although perhaps Kagan has a clearer view than either of us of the nature of extremely long life.

Recall that Kagan writes, "I've seen thousands, millions, billions of incredible works of art. I've gotten what there is to get out of them. Isn't there anything new? And the problem is that there isn't." Perhaps he is thinking of "what we get" from appreciating a work of art as a *by-product* of the experience, perhaps something purely cognitive, such as a piece (or pieces) of information or an insight (or insights). But this is surely *not* all we get from appreciating a novel or a work of art. The experience *itself* can be valuable and compelling. I do not see why this sort of valuable experience cannot be reliably repeatable in an immortal life.

---

14. Kagan, *Death*, 240.

15. Phillip Bricker, "On Living Forever," in his collection, *Modal Matters: Essays in Metaphysics* (Oxford University Press, forthcoming).

16. Bricker, "On Living Forever," ms. 1.

The same is true for the experience of doing mathematics. When this activity is rewarding, it is not simply because of some theorem one has proved or insight one has gained; the experience of doing math *itself* is rewarding and engaging. Philosophy is like this for many of us.

The same goes for sex. There can be many valuable "by-products" of sexual activity: reproduction, the expression of love, the strengthening of a relationship, and so forth. But sex is a good example of an activity that gives rise to experiences that are compelling *in themselves*. (To say that they are valuable in themselves does not imply that they would be so, in any context; it just means, in suitable and healthy circumstances, sex gives rise to experiences that are valuable, but not because they result in something else.) It would be bizarre to say, "I've tried all of the positions in the *Kama Sutra*, and even more (it would take some imagination to think of these!), and I've gotten what there is to get out of them. Isn't there anything new?" Sex is not just about different positions and partners or some insight gained from the activity. The experience *itself* can be rich and deeply engaging. We do not think that once all of the positions and partners have been tried out, there is "nothing left to get out of sex," nothing that can "engage us afresh." Sex is just not like that. It seems to me that it is not that way with many activities that are reliably and repeatedly compelling: prayer and meditation, engaging with art and music, doing philosophy, and, yes, maybe even immersing oneself in mathematics. (Not sure about organic chemistry, though!)

Similar considerations apply to friendship and love. Could you imagine saying, "I've loved many, many people. At this point I've gotten what there is to get out of love. Isn't there anything new?" This would be wildly reductionistic; it leaves out the magic and mystery of love and the compelling beauty of friendship and their irreducible experiential features. Love and friendship would not lose their transformational and inspiring qualities in an immortal life.

It is interesting to ask whether *marriage* could be sustained in an immortal life. (I don't mean a brutally unhappy marriage—a shell of a marriage. I mean a reasonably happy and rewarding marriage.) In the case of the Strudlbrugs in Swift's *Gulliver's Travels*, marriages were automatically annulled when one member of the couple becomes eighty years of age:

> If a Struldbrug happens to marry one of his own kind, the marriage is dissolved of course, by the courtesy of the kingdom, as soon as the younger of the two comes to be fourscore; for the law thinks it a

reasonable indulgence, that those who are condemned, without any fault of their own, to a perpetual continuance in the world, should not have their misery doubled by the load of a [spouse].[17]

Although this is no doubt a grumpy passage, it highlights some vexing questions. Could marriage be sustained in an immortal life?[18] In our weddings we pledge loyalty "til death do us part," but how do we understand the commitment in an immortal life? Some think that immortal marriage (to the same person) is impossible or highly unlikely, because of the challenges of maintaining interest and passion over time. Also many distractions and temptations would present themselves. These are challenges even in our mortal lives, and couples often divorce because of them.

This sad reality is to some extent counterbalanced by the indisputable fact that the more time people spend with each other in a relationship, the more precious the relationship becomes (all other things equal), and the more difficult it is to break up. More is at stake. Does one really want to throw away (say) two thousand years of a relationship, with all its ups and downs? Could a human being even do this—walk away from a relationship of two thousand years? We will have to leave the question of the sustainability of healthy marriage in immortality unresolved here.[19]

Let's take stock. We wouldn't have to run out of projects in an immortal life. Bernard Williams is way too pessimistic about our prospects in immortality. Maybe he was confused by the particular facts about Elina Makropulos that made her lonely and depressed—facts about her troubled relationship with her father. In any case, it is hard to believe that all human beings would have exhausted their projects in a mere 337 years. Shelly Kagan is also too pessimistic. Maybe he was implicitly thinking of our activities as valuable only *instrumentally*—as leading to some separate and valuable by-product. But many of our activities are treasured because of the nature of the experiences involved in them— experiences that, arguably at least, provide reliably repeatable rewards (when distributed appropriately).

---

17. Jonathan Swift, *Gulliver's Travels*, Chapter 26, Chapter X.

18. The *institution* of marriage could still exist, even if one particular marriage does not last forever. As in our mortal lives, we could have various marriages or none at all.

19. The Netflix series *Forever* is a fascinating exploration of marriage "forever," but in an afterlife of a certain sort. The question of boredom is in the foreground.

Imagine that you have lived a long time under relatively favorable circumstances: say, four thousand years. Now you are given a choice. One possibility is that you continue to live for at least awhile (perhaps two thousand more years, give or take a few) under similarly favorable circumstances, with a mixture of experiences, some of which are of eating delicious food, listening to beautiful music, spending time with friends, and participating in loving relationships. These experiences will be distributed according to your wishes, and not necessarily in a rigidly regimented or densely compressed way. The other possibility is that you die painlessly, after a relatively short period during which you can say goodbye and arrange your affairs. The immortality curmudgeons are committed to thinking that it would not be rational or even attractive to choose the first option. They are party poopers! They think that at a certain point you will have lost the zest to pursue or appreciate these experiences. I don't agree. Some pleasures are repeatable, and some activities are repeatedly rewarding.

Attractiveness and the Afterlife

Before we proceed, I want briefly to consider immortality from the religious viewpoint, according to which we have an afterlife (in which our personal identity is preserved and we have conscious experiences). It is not easy to establish that immortality would be desirable for human beings, on the secular view (although I believe we can come close). It is also difficult to establish the desirability of immortality, given a religious framework. Perhaps surprisingly, it will emerge that the secular and religious friends of immortality have similar (although not exactly the same) challenges, and similar resources to address them.

There are too many religious conceptions of immortality for me to give a comprehensive, fair treatment of them here. I will thus oversimplify greatly, but I hope that my form of analysis can be applied to many of the most salient pictures of the afterlife. Let's begin by focusing on the Christian conception of the afterlife (although it is already an oversimplification to refer to "the" Christian conception). In particular, we'll consider the Christian conception of heaven. Although I think that the analysis I develop here can be applied widely, I certainly do *not* think that it is applicable to *all* important religious conceptions of the afterlife and, in particular, heaven.

The basic description of heaven in (many forms of) Christianity is that it involves a special, enhanced relationship or "communion" with God. But how can this be endlessly wonderful? As with EM's life, wouldn't it become alienating and boring?[20] What is the relationship with God supposed to be?

Let's begin by thinking of it as a kind of *dialogue*; here we are thinking of communion by conversation. The idea is that in heaven we are in dialogue with God forever. In this context we are thinking of something like true immortality, rather than medical immortality. The religious view has it that we exist forever, rather than, say six thousand years, and thus the dialogue is envisaged as literally going on *forever*.

How could dialogue with *anyone* be endlessly fascinating and engaging—literally forever? Of course, God is perfect in the mainstream Christian tradition. Still, being in dialogue *forever* with even the Best Possible Conversationalist would not seem attractive. Shelly Kagan writes:

> [A friend] suggested that I should think of God as being like an *infinitely* fascinating and understanding friend. Communing with God would be like having an incredibly satisfying conversation, one that you would literally want to continue forever.
>
> Well, I can say the words, but when I try to imagine that possibility and take it seriously, I find that I just can't see it. No friend that I've ever talked with is one that I would actually *want* to spend eternity talking to.[21]

---

20. Mark Twain captured these worries about heaven: "Singing hymns and waving palm branches throughout eternity is pretty when you hear about it in the pulpit, but it's as poor a way to put in valuable time as a body could contrive" (Mark Twain, "Captain Stormfield's Visit to Heaven," in *Mark Twain's Quarrel with Heaven: "Captain Stormfield's Visit to Heaven" and Other Stories.* Masterworks of Literature Series [Lanham, MD: Rowman and Littlefield, 1970]).

He also noted that both heaven and hell have their advantages: "heaven for climate, hell for society" (Mark Twain, *Notebooks and Journals*, Volume 3: 1883–1891 [The Mark Twain Papers], Berkeley: University of California Press, 1980).

It seems that Mark Twain was an "apeirophobe." Apeirophobia is the fear (roughly speaking) of heaven (or infinitely long existence): Bobby Azarian, "Apeirophobia: The Fear of Eternity," *The Atlantic Magazine* (Online), September 2016). Azarian, himself an apeirophobe, asks, "What is scarier, death or eternal life?"

21. Kagan, *Death*, 240–241.

To be frank, the same point applies to a spouse or close friend, no matter how engaging and wonderful.[22]

So far I have briefly explored one view about the relationship between the individual and God in heaven. Perhaps it is too restrictive to think of one's communion, or communication, with God as a literal conversation or dialogue.[23] Rather, this is supposed to be a kind of communication that involves more than just words. It is "dialogue" in which "heart speaks to heart" (words of St. Francis de Sales, adopted by Cardinal John Henry Newman as his motto), and it is more like sexual union than a conversation.

One would also have relationships with others in heaven, and other beings, such as saints. Heaven is a "communion of saints," as the Apostles' Creed puts it, not just a union of self with God. Whether there are enough diverse and compelling projects to make existence in heaven attractive is unclear. Some of the resources available to the secularist will not be available, as heaven is a more restricted context, with fewer sorts of opportunities. But the opportunities for deep communion with God, and the development of relationships with others in heaven, may compensate sufficiently.

Note that this conception of heaven is beginning to look like the secular immortal life I described earlier. In the quasi-sexual (perhaps "erotic") union with God, and the relationships with others in heaven, perhaps one will find "repeatable pleasures" and reliably meaningful activities. Friendship, solidarity, and love can propel one forward in a secular immortality. Why not also in the afterlife? We can at least note that the Christian religious tradition essentially invokes similar ingredients to those that we identified earlier as possibly making a secular immortality worthwhile for a human being. The challenges are similar, and so are the responses.

---

22. The prospects for endlessly fascinating conversation in heaven might not be as bleak as I have suggested. If it is possible to remain engaged in projects in an immortal secular life, why couldn't one find endless fascination in discussing (say mathematics, philosophy, music, art, etc.) with an all-knowing conversationalist? You could learn about the sorts of topics that could engage one in a secular immortal life through dialogue with God. I thank Travis Timmerman for this suggestion. But it is worth thinking about whether there is a crucial difference between active *engagement* in a project and discussion of the issues involved in it.

23. I am indebted to Aaron Preston for helping me to see this point.

The Koran presents heaven as a place of sensual pleasures, again pointing to the attractiveness of repeatable pleasures in immortality—this time in the Islamic tradition. The imagery of heaven is of two gardens, filled with abundance. The righteous recline ". . . on beds whose linings are of silk brocade and the fruit of the two gardens is hanging low" (Koran 55: 54). As is famous (and also infamous), there is imagery of beautiful and virtuous maidens throughout the Koran's description of heaven. We can interpret this more broadly as a nod to the importance of repeatable pleasures, such as those of sexual union, without accepting any asymmetry between men and women in this respect. In short, both the Christian and Islamic conceptions of heaven contain repeatable pleasures, among other activities that arguably could keep one from getting bored.

Consider, now, a more intimate kind of union with God: one *merges* with God and is forever in an ecstatic state. On this view we are in ecstatic *union* with God in heaven, not just *communion*. Here boredom just isn't a possibility; by its very nature, one's state is (forever) perfectly engaging and compelling.

On this view of the relationship with God, it seems that the identity condition would be difficult to meet. But it is *not obvious* that we can't make sense of an ecstatic union with God in which one's individuality is maintained. This sort of union might be modeled on mystical experience, in which the self *seems* to dissolve. The *experience* suggests a dissolution of the self, and yet the self actually persists. The phenomenology—the experiences—are not *about* a self, but they are *had by* a self. Perhaps we can understand the ecstatic union with God along these lines, as in Christian mysticism.[24] It is thus unclear that, on the communion-as-union picture, the identity condition cannot be met. The condition is not about the content of experience; it is about the subject of experience.

We will discuss this feature of spiritual experiences again in Chapter Nine. Note, here, that this signature characteristic of mystical or spiritual experiences (the lack of self-focus) makes them the "opposite" of the experience of boredom, as discussed earlier. In a spiritual experience,

---

24. For an excellent development of this sort of picture, see Nelson Pike, *Mystic Union: An Essay on the Phenomenology of Mysticism* (Ithaca, NY: Cornell University Press, 1992).

the self is still "there"—the screen is still present, but the focus is on the rich content depicted on it. In contrast, in boredom there is nothing but the self (in Scheffler's way of putting it)—nothing but a blank screen. Boredom leaves us isolated and alone, trapped in ourselves.

The skeptic Mark Twain wrote, "I have never seen what to me seemed an atom of truth that there is a future life . . . and yet . . . I am strongly inclined to expect one."[25] Religion remains important in human life throughout the world, and its role in terror management is a significant benefit for many. There are, however, difficulties in seeing exactly how the afterlife can play this role. We have noted the striking similarities between the challenges for the secular and religious views of immortality. Do we continue to exist as the particular human beings or persons we actually are? Would we avoid the pitfalls of tedium? It is also fascinating to see how parallel answers can be offered for our consideration.[26]

Immortality and the Environment

Return to the secular conception of immortality. In Chapter Six and thus far in this chapter I have explored many of the arguments of the immortality curmudgeons. These arguments are widely adopted in contemporary philosophy, but I have suggested that they are not decisive. Of course, different individuals will evaluate the considerations differently, but in the end I am no immortality curmudgeon. Does it follow that I am an immortality optimist?

Not quite. Recall the way in which I characterized immortality optimism previously (in Chapter Five). First, the optimist denies the curmudgeon's view that basic facts about human character or the nature of human life imply that immortality is necessarily undesirable. So far, so good. But there is more to immortality optimism. Optimists also think that it is plausible that we can achieve immortality in the not-too-distant future. Optimists are thus committed to the claim that the prerequisites for immortality—physical and social circumstances that can sustain immortality—will (or probably will) continue to exist in some form or other.

---

25. Albert Bigelow Paine, *Mark Twain, A Biography, 1835–1910, Complete* (CreateSpace Independent Publishing Platform, 2012).

26. In this section I am deeply indebted to Aaron Preston.

The idea that the environmental conditions required for a desirable immortality will or probably will continue to exist in the future—for at least six thousand years—seems dubious to me. Now I don't mean to be a skunk at the garden party. I'm not saying that it is *impossible* for us to save our planet (its viability) or even that it is highly unlikely that humankind will solve our pressing environmental problems. But, then again, I do not think it is definite or probable that we will. Given the mess the planet is in, I think that it is unreasonable to be confident that we will solve the environmental challenges that threaten to extinguish us.

It will be helpful to be clearer about certain aspects of our imagined immortal lives that we have thus far put aside. Who will be immortal? Will it just be me? Will it include some others? Everyone?[27] The lone immortal picture is unattractive. Although as a lone immortal you could make friends and have love relationships, your friends and lovers would biologically deteriorate and eventually die. You could make new friends and have new love relationships, but you might well be very lonely: you are the only immortal, the only person who is living an immortal life with all its rewards and challenges, whereas everyone else faces the human difficulties of deterioration and death. New friendships will eventually reinscribe the same patterns. This was presumably one of EM's problems: she was a *lone* immortal. She was alienated from others. As she put it, "Everything is the same."

Suppose that some others are immortal, but not everyone. Now you can have relationships of friendship and love with other immortals. But a situation in which only some, but not all, have access to immortality would be unhealthy and politically unstable. It has always been—from the ancient Chinese emperors to the contemporary Russian plutocrats and Silicon Valley billionaires—primarily the wealthy and privileged classes who have pursued greater longevity and immortality (in the secular sense). This is because their lives tend to be considerably better than the lives of those in poverty, and they have the resources to take many of the required steps: supplementation with vitamins, medical care, cosmetic treatments, cryogenic preservation, and so forth.

---

27. Nussbaum raises these issues in Martha C. Nussbaum, "The Damage of Death: Incomplete Arguments and False Consolations," in James Stacey Taylor, ed., *The Metaphysics and Ethics of Death: New Essays* (New York: Oxford University Press, 2013): 25–43.

Access to medical care in many countries is based on income, and the means required to achieve greater longevity are expensive. Poor people, indeed, most of us, are not getting skin rejuvenations or taking ninety supplements per day to achieve a more youthful appearance or greater longevity; we are just trying to make ends meet. As anti-aging medicine develops further, access to this kind of medicine will increasingly be restricted to the very wealthy. This will exacerbate the social and economic inequality and magnify their destabilizing effects.

So perhaps the most promising answer to the question of who will be immortal is: "Everyone." This obviates the problems of loneliness and injustice that afflict the other models, but now the problems associated with overpopulation become pressing. If we are all immortal, and we can have children (who are also immortal), the planet will soon become intolerably overcrowded, and its resources depleted disastrously.[28] Some extremely optimistic folks might (and do) say that we will be able to use our limited resources much more efficiently, and perhaps we'll even be able to colonize other planets. We'll evolve (quickly!) and become superintelligent, as in Kurzweil's Singularity. But these possibilities just seem outlandish.

So if everyone is to be immortal, no one can be allowed to have children. After all, if only some, but not all, are allowed to have children, this would again cause intolerable tensions and instability. More important, it would be deeply unjust. Not all people want children, but many do, and for them it is an important good. It seems that prohibiting *everyone* from having children (and raising families) would be the only *fair* way to address the problems of overpopulation and depletion of resources. Aubrey de Grey and others have endorsed this model of immortality.

Would this sort of life, without the possibility of raising children, be desirable? We have already considered the worry that a human life without the sorts of stages we have in our mortal lives would be unrecognizable. If we add to the picture that no one will have any children, we increase both the concerns about recognizability and attractiveness. Would you trade your opportunity to raise a family for immortal life?

---

28. This problem would presumably not afflict heaven. No overpopulation or traffic jams in heaven. For *some* religious folks this diminishes their concerns about the environment.

That's a difficult question, and I doubt that everyone would answer in the same way. Even if you answer positively, you must concede that the immortal life in question would be significantly different from our mortal human lives—different in ways that raise big questions about its recognizability and desirability.

Let's suppose, as seems reasonable, that some—perhaps many—will opt for immortal life, even though it would lack the normal stages of human life and the possibility of having children. Although this model of immortal life avoids some of the problems of overpopulation and resource depletion of the alternative models, it still faces daunting environmental challenges. We will still have to address the pressing problems of global climate change; actually, we will have had to make considerable progress on these (and related) problems well before the time of universal medical immortality (if that comes at all).

The environmental problems we face threaten to make our planet uninhabitable. They have to be addressed soon; as I write this book, the glaciers and ice fields in Greenland and Antarctica are melting, and the seas are rising. Fires, storms, and floods are getting more frequent and worse. The world's nations have difficulty coordinating their behavior in the ways required to make genuine progress. I thus reject immortality optimism. I do not think that it is likely that the environmental (and social) conditions required for continued desirable life will be achieved. (Remember that, in order to be an immortality optimist, one must believe that these conditions will or will likely be satisfied.) As far as I'm concerned, the immortality optimists might as well be called "immortality Pollyannas."

But I have not (yet) fallen into despair and pessimism. With the consequences of continued dereliction becoming clearer and more frightening, and with redoubled and concerted effort, we might well come together to solve these problems. We should indeed become more efficient in using resources, and human ingenuity cannot be dismissed. Note that if everyone were medically immortal, this would provide a strong incentive to solve the environmental problems. We would have something big to lose—even bigger than the lives we currently lead. Currently it is possible for many to be irresponsible, knowing that they will not be around to suffer the consequences. That would change in an immortal life.

I am not an immortality curmudgeon. Further, I do not think it likely—more probable than not—that we will solve the problems of society and the environment in time. I am thus neither a curmudgeon nor an optimist. It has become clear that we need a *third* category, which I will call "immortality realism." I am an immortality realist. The problems are huge, and human beings tend to wait until the last moment to face problems that require sacrifice. Many are still in denial about the dire situation of our planet's environment, and by the time we face up to the environmental challenges, it might be too late.

Conclusion

In this chapter we have considered the immortality curmudgeons' identity and attractiveness challenges. I have suggested that these challenges, like the recognizability worry discussed in the previous chapter, are not decisive. An important theme in my discussion of all of these worries is that it is unfair and inappropriate to apply a double standard to immortal and mortal life. For example, we change our personality characteristics and values over time in our *mortal* lives. We lose memories in our *mortal* lives, sometimes resulting in *no* memories of previous times in our lives. And from time to time we are bored and depressed in our *mortal* lives. Nevertheless, we think our mortal lives can be meaningful and worth living. Why think otherwise about *immortal* lives? Further, many of the same resources of the secularist friend of immortality are available to the religious person.

I do not, however, think that the curmudgeons' arguments can be *decisively* refuted. A recurring theme here is that it is not straightforward to extrapolate evaluations about a mortal life to an immortal life. What is appealing in a mortal life may not continue to be appealing in a much longer life. Those pesky immortality curmudgeons will remind us that it is hard to get our minds around the fact that an immortal life would go on and on and on. Six thousand years is a very long time, and forever is even longer. And forevers of even higher orders than aleph null are pretty tough![29] The difficulty and profundity of these issues should make

---

29. We do, however, know the mathematical algorithm that generates the higher-order infinities from aleph null, just as we know the algorithm for generating the natural numbers.

us slow down, think carefully, and not jump to conclusions; to fail to do so would be to violate the philosophical speed limit.

So have we reached a stalemate? I do not think so. I do not accept the dreary philosophical landscape of the curmudgeons.[30] This doesn't imply that I am an immortality optimist. I believe that there is nothing incoherent about aspiring to immortality, but I also know that the tasks will be very difficult, and that the jury is still out as to whether human beings will succeed in saving our planet. I am an immortality realist.

The immortality optimist believes that the glass is half-full. The immortality pessimist (curmudgeon) thinks that it is half-empty. The immortality realist thinks that the glass is (say) forty percent full.

Annotated Suggestions for Further Reading

Martin Heidegger discussed boredom in *The Fundamental Concepts of Metaphysics* (Bloomington: Indiana University Press, 1995 [originally 1983]). He distinguished three kinds of boredom: becoming bored by something, being bored by something, and profound boredom. A key element in Heidegger's analysis is that boredom involves a focus on time's slowing down. (The German word for *boredom* is, appropriately enough, *langweillig*—a long time or while.) The following snappy slogan is sometimes attributed to Heidegger: "Boredom is the awareness of the passage of time." A very helpful resource is Mark A. Wrathall, *Cambridge Heidegger Lexicon* (Cambridge: Cambridge University Press, forthcoming).

There is a nice discussion of boredom in Cheshire Calhoun, *Doing Valuable Time: The Present, the Future, and Meaningful Living* (New York: Oxford University Press, 2018): "Living with Boredom": 212–242.

The primary source (in contemporary philosophy) for the identity and boredom worries is the Bernard Williams's paper, "The Makropulos Case: Reflections on the Tedium of Immortality." An interpretation and alternative formulation of Williams's argument is offered by Samuel Scheffler: *Death and the Afterlife*, Niko Kolodny, ed. (New York: Oxford University Press, 2015): 88–95. Shelly Kagan discusses Williams's view and presents a version of immortality curmudgeonliness in Shelly Kagan, *Death* (New Haven, CT: Yale University Press, 2012): 234–246.

---

30. I have sought to *remove* the nails from the coffins of the curmudgeons' arguments, thereby liberating them. They might find immortal life rewarding!

For critical discussion of Williams's paper, see John Martin Fischer, "Why Immortality Is Not So Bad," *International Journal of Philosophical Studies* 2 (1994): 257–270; reprinted in John Martin Fischer, *Our Stories: Essays on Life, Death, and Free Will* (New York: Oxford University Press, 2009): 79–92; and Connie S. Rosati, "The Makropulos Case: Reflections on Immortality and Agency," in Ben Bradley, Fred Feldman, and Jens Johansson, eds., *The Oxford Handbook of Philosophy of Death* (New York: Oxford University Press, 2013): 355–390.

Further reflections—many critical—on Williams-style immortality curmudgeonliness can be found in John Martin Fischer, "Immortality," in Ben Bradley, Fred Feldman, and Jens Johansson, eds., *The Oxford Handbook of Philosophy of Death* (New York: Oxford University Press, 2013): 336–354; John Martin Fischer and Benjamin Mitchell-Yellin, "Immortality and Boredom," *Journal of Ethics* 18 (2014): 353–372 (from which I borrow in this chapter); David Beglin, "Should I Choose to Never Die? Williams, Boredom, and the Significance of Mortality," *Philosophical Studies* 174 (2017): 2009–2028; Amanda Gorman, "Williams and the Desirability of Body-Bound Immortality Revisited," *European Journal of Philosophy* 25 (2017): 1062–1083; and Preston Greene, "Value in Very Long Lives," *Journal of Moral Philosophy* 14 (2016): 1–19. Jeremy Wiznewski connects issues in these discussions of Williams's "necessary boredom thesis" with Heidegger's theory of boredom, and Mikel Burley replies: J. Jeremy Wisnewski, "Is the Immortal Life Worth Living?" *International Journal for Philosophy of Religion* 58 (2005): 27–36; and Mikel Burley, "Immortality and Boredom: A Reply to Wisnewski," *International Journal for Philosophy of Religion* 65 (2009): 77–85.

For some contemporary treatments of heaven by theologically well-informed religious philosophers, see Peter Kreeft, *Heaven: The Heart's Deepest Longing* (San Francisco, CA: Ignatius Press, 1989); and Jerry L. Walls, *Heaven: The Logic of Eternal Joy* (New York: Oxford University Press, 2002) and *Heaven, Hell, and Purgatory: Rethinking the Things That Matter Most* (Grand Rapids, MI: Brazos Press, 2015). A helpful collection that issued from the Paradise Project (supported by the Immortality Project) is T. Ryan Byerly and Eric Silverman, eds., *Paradise Understood: New Philosophical Essays about Heaven* (Oxford: Oxford University Press, 2017).

Martha Nussbaum presents a pithy and potent version of the (widely discussed) environmental concerns about immortality in Martha C. Nussbaum, "The Damage of Death: Incomplete Arguments and False Consolations," in James Stacey Taylor, ed., *The Metaphysics and Ethics of Death: New Essays* (New York: Oxford University Press, 2013): 25–43.

Aubrey de Grey offers more sanguine reflections on the environmental challenges in Aubrey de Grey, "The Foreseeability of Real Anti-Aging Medicine: Focusing the Debate," *Environmental Gerontology* 38 (2003): 927–934; and "Editorial: Aging, Childlessness, or Overpopulation: The Future's Right to Choose," *Rejuvenation Research* 7 (November 4, 2004): 237–238. The authors provide a recipe for saving the planet in Paul Hawken and Tom Steyer, *Drawdown: The Most Comprehensive Plan Ever Proposed to Reverse Global Warming* (New York: Penguin Books, 2017).

CHAPTER 8

Near-Death Experiences and Supernaturalism

What I'd experienced was more real than the house I sat in, more real than the logs burning in the fireplace. Yet there was no room for that reality in the medically trained scientific worldview that I'd spent years acquiring.

—EBEN ALEXANDER,
Proof of Heaven

··········

Introduction

Human beings are afraid of death, and we yearn for immortality (even if we have some ambivalence toward it). We have seen that immortality, even true immortality, might well be desirable. Religion offers the prospect of immortality in an afterlife. Near-death experiences (NDEs) are significant for many reasons, but perhaps the main reason is that they seem to indicate the possibility of an afterlife and, thus, a kind of immortality. Indeed, most NDEs point to a very attractive immortality. Given that NDEs have been reported throughout history and across cultures, and because they appear to be a portal to a beautiful immortality, they are of tremendous interest.

Are the reports of NDEs sincere and reliable? Do they really provide a view of the afterlife? For those who have them, NDEs are extraordinarily meaningful and transformative. How can we understand the significance of NDEs? In this chapter we will consider the first two questions (about the evidence for NDEs), and in the next chapter we will explore the meaning of NDEs—the stories they tell.

Near-Death Experiences

NDEs take place in near-death contexts: situations in which an individual's life is in jeopardy. Not all people in near-death contexts have NDEs; roughly ten percent of those in near-death contexts report having NDEs, although this is hard to confirm. The Dutch cardiologist and NDE researcher Pim van Lommel describes them as involving

> . . . a range of impressions during a special state of consciousness, including a number of special elements such as an out-of-body experience, pleasant feelings, seeing a tunnel, a light, deceased relatives or a life review, or a conscious return to the body.[1]

I will define an NDE as taking place in a near-death context and having a sufficient number of the characteristics identified by van Lommel. Three salient elements are an out-of-body experience (OBE), that is, an experience of floating above one's body and seeing it from above, a life review, and an experience of traveling toward a light in a dark tunnel or perhaps crossing a river or otherwise proceeding toward a different realm. Typically, one is guided in this "voyage" toward a different realm by deceased loved ones or loving religious figures.

About ninety percent of NDEs are described as (very) positive experiences, and those who have had NDEs have significant changes in their behavior. Pim van Lommel has studied people who have had NDEs in the context of cardiac arrest, and he has observed that the NDEs have had significant transformational effects. Those who have experienced NDEs have less death anxiety and are more spiritual. They are more "prosocial," appreciating relationships and spending more time with family, friends, and relatives. They are also more compassionate and attuned to morality and justice. The transformations are often profound.[2]

NDEs are amazing, and not just because of their capacity to transform. People who were in cardiac arrest or in comas report having had rich experiences during these times—times during which their brains

---

1. Pim van Lommel, MD, "Non-local Consciousness: A Concept Based on Scientific Research on Near-Death Experiences during Cardiac Arrest," *Journal of Consciousness Studies* 20 (2013): 8.

2. Pim van Lommel, *Consciousness beyond Life: The Science of the Near-Death Experience* (New York: HarperOne, 2010), esp. pp. 45–69.

were apparently offline. Sometimes they report events that cannot be independently confirmed, but often they report events or facts that can and are indeed corroborated. (We will describe some of these later.) The fact that some NDEs can be checked against the facts, and that NDEs have very similar patterns of content (as sketched earlier), at least suggests that even the NDEs that cannot be independently corroborated must be taken seriously. Many of the latter sorts of NDEs describe communication with deceased relatives and confrontation with a heavenly or other-worldly realm—an environment hospitable to immortality.

Consider, for example, the neurosurgeon Eben Alexander's NDE, in which he found himself in a "beautiful, incredible dream-world, except it wasn't a dream."[3] He describes himself flying along with "a beautiful girl with high cheek-bones and deep blue eyes."[4] (Sometime after his NDE, Alexander recognized this girl as his deceased sister, whom he had never met.) He writes:

> We were riding along together on an intricately patterned surface, alive with indescribable and vivid colors—the wing of a butterfly. In fact, millions of butterflies were all around us—vast fluttering waves of them, dipping down into the greenery and coming back up around us again . . .
> Without using any words, she spoke to me . . . The message had three parts . . . :
> "You are loved and cherished, dearly, forever."
> "You have nothing to fear."
> "There is nothing you can do wrong."[5]

Alexander holds that this rich set of experiences occurred while he was in a coma and his brain was not capable of having experiences. He writes:

> But while I was in a coma my brain hadn't been working improperly. *It hadn't been working at all.* The part of my brain that years of

---

3. Eben Alexander, MD, *Proof of Heaven: A Neurosurgeon's Journey into the Afterlife* (New York: Simon and Schuster, 2012): 40.

4. Alexander, *Proof of Heaven*, 40.

5. Alexander, *Proof of Heaven*, 40–41.

medical school had taught me was responsible for creating the world I lived and moved around in and for taking the raw data that came in through my senses and fashioning it into a meaningful universe: that part of my brain was down, and out. And yet despite all of this, I had been alive, and aware, *truly aware*, in a universe characterized above all by love, consciousness, and reality. . . . There was, for me, simply no arguing this fact. I knew it so completely that I ached.

What I had experienced was more real than the house I sat in, more real than the logs burning in the fireplace.[6]

Eben Alexander's *Proof of Heaven: A Neurosurgeon's Journey into the Afterlife*, in which he discusses his NDE, has sold millions of copies and has influenced many people across the world. Alexander himself reports many transformative effects. Although he had grown up in a religious family, prior to his NDE he was skeptical about religion. After his NDE he became a believer in religion and the afterlife (although, of course, the content of his NDE was not exactly theologically orthodox). He repeatedly describes his NDE as "real," and there is even a chapter of *Proof of Heaven* called "The Ultra-Real." (We will return to this point, when we discuss general features of spiritual experiences, in Chapter Nine.)

Colton Burpo's NDE is described in the book co-written by his father, Todd Burpo.[7] This book has also sold millions of copies, and it was made into a motion picture that was widely distributed and viewed by millions. Colton became ill a few months shy of his fourth birthday. He was diagnosed with a burst appendix and underwent two surgeries. After he recovered (miraculously), Colton began recollecting and reporting experiences he had while undergoing the first surgery (and under anesthesia). He had visited heaven and personally met Jesus, God, and the Holy Spirit. He claimed to have met various deceased relatives, one of whom was a sister who had never been born due to a miscarriage. He saw angels and John the Baptist, and he even saw his

---

6. Alexander, *Proof of Heaven*, 129–130.

7. Todd Burpo (with Lynn Vincent), *Heaven Is for Real: A Little Boy's Astounding Story of His Trip to Heaven and Back* (Nashville, TN: Thomas Nelson, 2010). For another interpretation of NDEs as roundtrips to heaven, see Mary C. Neal, MD, *To Heaven and Back: A Doctor's Extraordinary Account of Her Death, Heaven, Angels, and Life Again* (Colorado Springs, CO: Waterbrook Press, 2012 [originally published in 2011]).

parents in the hospital at the time of his surgery, his father and mother in different rooms praying.[8]

These are extraordinary and awe-inspiring experiences. The contents of these NDEs cannot be independently verified, but, as I wrote earlier, there are many NDEs whose contents can indeed be independently checked. Consider, for example, the famous story of Pam Reynolds.[9] She underwent surgery for a brain aneurysm. She was under anesthesia, blood was drained from her brain, and her body temperature was

---

8. I believe it is important to respect the sincerity of the majority of NDE reports. But I also think we have to call out the dishonest ones. For a particularly sad account of such a report, see https://www.theguardian.com/books/2018/apr/12/boy-who-came-back-from-heaven-author-sues-books-christian/publisher:

> Alex Malarkey, the American boy who disavowed his bestselling account of meeting Jesus after an accident, has launched a lawsuit against the book's Christian specialist publisher. While the publisher has "made millions of dollars," the suit alleges, it has "paid Alex, a paralysed young man, nothing."
>
> The car accident that almost killed Malarkey happened in 2004 in Ohio, when he was six years old. Two months later he woke up from a coma to find himself paralyzed from the neck down. He and his father, Kevin, a Christian therapist, wrote *The Boy Who Came Back from Heaven* together. According to Chicago's Tyndale House, the firm that bought the book in 2010, Malarkey wrote of "the angels that took him through the gates of heaven itself. Of the unearthly music that sounded just 'terrible' to a six-year-old. And, most amazing of all . . . of meeting and talking to Jesus."
>
> But when he was sixteen, Malarkey revealed on his blog that he had made it all up. "I did not die. I did not go to heaven," he said. "When I made the claims, I had never read the Bible. People have profited from lies, and continue to. They should read the Bible, which is enough."
>
> Tyndale House pulled the book, which had already sold a reported one million copies, saying in a statement that it was "saddened to learn [Alex is] now saying that he made up the story of dying and going to heaven."
>
> Malarkey, who is now twenty, filed a lawsuit against the publisher earlier this week, claiming his father "concoct[ed] a story that, during the time Alex was in a coma, he had gone to Heaven, communicated with God the Father, Jesus, angels, and the devil, and then returned," and alleging that while Tyndale House has "made millions of dollars off Alex's identity and an alleged autobiographical story of his life, [it has] paid Alex, a paralysed young man, nothing."

The article goes on to point out that Alex and his mother, who supports him, are on the verge of homelessness. For interesting background, see https://www.theguardian.com/books/2015/jan/21/boy-who-came-back-from-heaven-alex-malarkey.

9. For details see Janice Miner Holden, "Veridical Perception in Near-Death Experience," in Janice Miner Holden, Bruce Greyson, and Debbie James, eds., *The Handbook of Near-Death Experiences* (Santa Barbara, CA: Praeger, 2009): 183–212.

reduced to 60 degrees. The EEG (electroencephalograph) registered no brain activity sufficient for consciousness, and yet Pam reported specific conversations of the medical team, as she was being prepped for surgery. For example, she reported that the medical team discussed the problems posed by her small arteries. This conversation actually did take place. She also reported having an incredible experience. After witnessing the medical personnel prepping her body, she left the operating room for someplace else, bathed in bright light, and encountered deceased relatives who communicated to her without words.

Consider, also, the remarkable story of the man with the missing dentures.[10] This man watched his body from a location above it while undergoing CPR for a cardiac arrest. When the hospital staff couldn't find his dentures the next day, he reminded the nurse that they were placed in a drawer. The man was able to locate the dentures because he recalled seeing the procedures during his cardiac arrest from a position outside his body (an OBE).

Really? There are myriad examples of NDEs reported throughout the centuries and across cultures. As Eben Alexander repeatedly emphasizes, they are "real," even "more real" than his house and fireplace: "ultra-real." It is, however, extremely important to distinguish two senses of "real." First, "real" could mean that the individual (Eben Alexander, in this case) *really had* the experience in question. I have no doubt that this is so; Alexander really had the experience, Colton Burpo really had the experience, and so did the man with the missing dentures (whose name we are not told). In this sense NDEs are real; people really have them and sincerely report their contents, as they recollect them. I am thus no NDE denier. (An NDE denier contends that individuals really do not have the experiences they report, or, at least, that they are substantially incorrect in their reports of these experiences.)

Second, "real" could mean "accurate." That is, it could mean that the contents of the experience accurately depict external reality. This is a very different notion of "real," and I claim that in the popular literature on NDEs there is a tendency to "slide" from real in the first sense (the individual really had the experience) to real in the second sense (the content is accurate). Eben Alexander clearly makes this slide. This

---

10. This case is discussed in various places, including van Lommel, *Consciousness beyond Life* and "Non-local Consciousness."

is a spurious (and analytically pernicious) transition. Dreams are real in the first sense: people really dream. But this does not imply that the contents of the dreams correspond to external reality. They might, but probably do not (in any detailed way).

The distinction between the two senses of "real" is important in evaluating the significance of NDEs. It might also be helpful in addressing some of the concerns of those who have had NDEs. They often feel that their reports are dismissed and that they are written off as "kooks" or even psychotic.

Such individuals should be able to take great comfort in fully grasping that their experiences are, and are thought to be, completely real in the first sense: they *really had these experiences*, with the contents they report. They are *not* kooks or psychotics (simply in virtue of having had NDEs). Although the literal accuracy of the reports—their reflecting external, heavenly reality—is in question, it certainly does not follow that it is in question whether the individuals actually *had* these experiences.

I am not an NDE denier. But I am dubious about whether the contents of NDEs are accurate reflections of external reality, when taken literally as providing nonphysical access to a heavenly realm. I thus reject "supernaturalism" about NDEs. For our discussion here, an important claim of the supernaturalists about NDEs is that through NDEs we have access to a supernatural realm, such as heaven—one separate from our ordinary physical world. Another supernaturalist claim is that our minds are not just our brains. Perhaps our minds are "souls," but in any case they are not just physical parts of us. Thus, our access to the supernatural (as well as the physical) realm is via nonphysical means, and our consciousness is nonphysical.[11] The supernaturalist thus denies "physicalism," the view that our minds and consciousness are entirely physical (our brains and processes in our brains). I shall use "physicalism" and "naturalism" interchangeably.

Because of the important distinction between the two senses of "real," one could avoid being an NDE denier without thereby committing to supernaturalism. You could really have an NDE, one that *depicts* or *represents* floating above oneself and observing or having access to a supernatural realm, without its being *accurate* that you perceived yourself from above or that you actually had contact with a heavenly realm.

---

11. For a critical discussion of supernaturalism, see John Martin Fischer and Benjamin Mitchell-Yellin, *Near-Death Experiences: Understanding Visions of the Afterlife* (New York: Oxford University Press, 2016). I rely here especially on pp. 7–8.

This is just like in a dream; the dream can depict or represent a certain set of events, but these events may not have actually happened.

Accepting that people really have NDEs does *not* imply supernaturalism. In order to defend the viability of naturalism, one needs to evaluate the most salient arguments for supernaturalism. I shall now turn to these arguments.

When and How Do They Know?

When? It seems to people who have had NDEs that their rich and detailed experiences occurred when their brains were "offline," that is, incapable of supporting conscious experiences. The individual may be in a coma due to a stroke, cardiac arrest, or accident, or the individual may be under anesthesia. During these periods the brain is incapable of conscious experience, and yet it seems that the NDEs occur during these times. If the brain is offline during the NDEs, it seems that there must be some nonphysical mechanism that produces them. Assuming a soul or other nonphysical way of generating experiences appears to be the best explanation of how NDEs occur at times when the brain is not functioning in the way required for conscious experience.

I do not, however, think it is obvious that supernaturalism is the best way to explain these phenomena. First, note that we often wake up from a dream, thinking that we have been dreaming for a long time. But the dreams might have occurred in the short time just prior to awakening. In the case of dreams, the time at which it *seems* to the individual that they occur may be different from the time at which they *do in fact* occur. Similarly, the times at which the dreams actually occur may differ from the times of the events *depicted* in the dreams.

The same is true of NDEs. That is, the experiences may occur in the relatively short time that the brain is ramping up after being offline due to a coma or anesthesia. It may *seem* to the individual who has had the NDE that the experiences took place during the time the brain was offline; but, just as with dreams, we have to distinguish between the time the experience *seems* to have occurred and the time at which it *actually* occurred. We must distinguish between the time of the NDE and the time of the events *depicted* in the NDE. In an NDE the experiences might well occur at a time during which the brain is *not* offline, but, rather, is ramping up for awakening. Thus, we don't have to assume some sort of nonphysical mechanism; brain activity can explain the experiences.

How? We are not forced to invoke nonphysical mental mechanisms to explain cases like those of Pam Reynolds and the man with the missing dentures. This is a good thing, because it is mysterious how these mechanisms are supposed to work, and, specifically, how they would interact with the physical world. We can explain how the brain functions to support experience, and how the brain interacts with the rest of the physical world. It is much more difficult to explain how the soul would interact with the body and the rest of the physical world. Where there is causation, there is a mechanism whereby it occurs, but the mechanism that would allow the nonphysical realm to interact with the physical is mysterious.

Causation implies a mechanism, understanding causation implies understanding the mechanism, and the mechanism of interaction across the physical and nonphysical realms is obscure—perhaps essentially so. It is then *not* a better explanation of NDEs to assume a nonphysical basis for them, as this introduces deep mysteries. It is preferable to stick with physical explanations, even if such explanations are currently incomplete. Given a choice between an incomplete naturalistic explanation of a phenomenon and an explanation that invokes causation without a mechanism—indeed, causation in (say) human perception without any way, even in principle, to make sense of this causation—I choose the naturalistic explanation.

Can we explain how Pam Reynolds and the man with the missing dentures were able to report accurate information that apparently could only have been acquired during the times when their brains were offline? These matters are delicate and controversial, and, due to the very nature of the cases, we must engage in some speculation. But this shouldn't stop us.

Let's start with the easier case: the man with the missing dentures. There are lots of ways he could have known the location of the dentures. Perhaps he saw a nurse put someone else's dentures in the drawer after that individual's surgery, as he was in the hospital several days (and the report did not occur immediately after the surgery). Maybe he overheard nurses discussing where they put patients' belongings, such as dentures. There are myriad ways he could have truly reported the location of the dentures, short of having an OBE. Although we must speculate here, it is not speculation to note that invocation of nonphysical mechanisms of perception introduces a whole host of complications and mysteries. Again, it is preferable to stick with what is simpler and better understood: physical forms of perception of our physical world.

How can we explain Pam Reynolds's true reports of specific conversations of her medical team during the time she was being prepped for brain surgery (and already under general anesthesia)? It is possible that the sounds of the conversations *registered* in her brain, even during her anesthesia. The claim here is not that she had a *conscious* experience of hearing the conversations. Rather, the idea is that it is possible for the auditory impressions to have registered in her brain, like visual impressions can register in our brains when we are driving on "autopilot." It is possible that these auditory impressions came to her *later*, just as one can recall visual impressions after having driven on autopilot and not being consciously aware of these impressions.

It is at least possible that she was later able to recall auditory impressions that she received while unconscious. This explanation is speculative, and perhaps some will find it a "stretch." In my view, however, it is less a stretch than embracing the explanatory mysteries about the mechanism whereby the soul interacts with the body and nonphysical and physical phenomena interact.

How did Colton Burpo know the verifiable fact that his parents were praying (separately) during his surgery? Well, Colton would have seen his parents praying on a number of occasions, especially in difficult times, and he might well have seen them pray separately. It is not a big mystery as to how he could come up with this. Further, his father, Todd, is a pastor, and Colton attends church services every Sunday with his family. Todd reads Bible stories to Colton every night at bedtime. Colton could have absorbed various details he reported as part of his NDE from the many hours he had spent learning, directly or indirectly, about what the Bible says. A smart four-year-old can absorb these details and would find it appealing to report them to authority figures who he senses would welcome such reports. It is well known that children of that age are highly suggestible and that they want to please authority figures, especially their parents.[12]

---

12. For an elaboration of this point, see Fischer and Mitchell-Yellin, *Near-Death Experiences*, 131–147.

The supernaturalist needs cases in which individuals report something that is verifiably true and could not possibly have been acquired by physical mechanisms. In general, I believe that it is sensible to consider carefully whether there is some possible physical means of acquiring the relevant information, when presented with a case in which it initially does not appear possible to get the information via physical means. It will then be preferable to take seriously an explanation that invokes this sort of means, rather than precipitously embracing the dark obscurity of interaction between the physical and nonphysical worlds. The physical explanation is located in a framework that is better understood.

I am not convinced that there is *any* case in which it is obvious that an individual has acquired a piece of information in an NDE, and he could not have acquired it via a physical mechanism. Sam Parnia, the MD and neuroscientist, is doing some fascinating research on precisely this topic.[13] Parnia and his team place computer monitors in cardiac care rooms in places where they are not visible to the patients from their beds. After the previously unconscious patients have regained wakeful consciousness, they are asked whether they saw a number. If these experiments were to show that such patients can indeed see the numbers, this would have to be via an OBE, since the monitors are not visible to the patients. (Here we are thinking of an OBE supernaturalistically interpreted, not just the *experience* of floating above one's body.)

This result would be exactly what is required by the supernaturalist. Thus far the jury is out, as the research is still being conducted. Note that even if a patient reported that he had seen the number, we would have to make sure he didn't come up with this information by other means, for example, a nurse. I believe that physicalism should be our presumption, and we should work from there. It is a *defeasible* presumption, but it

---

13. Sam Parnia, MD, is directing the AWARE studies, some supported by the Immortality Project, a grant from the John Templeton Foundation described in the Acknowledgments section of this book. Parnia's project builds in some ways on earlier work by Bruce Greyson, MD. For a description of these studies, see Sam Parnia, MD, *What Happens When We Die: A Ground-Breaking Study into the Nature of Life and Death* (Carlsbad, CA: Hay House, 2008 [originally published in the United Kingdom in 2005]); and Sam Parnia with Josh Young, *Erasing Death: The Science That Is Rewriting the Boundaries between Life and Death* (New York: HarperOne, 2013).

would take a lot to defeat it, given the power of the naturalistic framework and the mysteries associated with dualism.

We *do* know that certain OBEs (again: experiences *as if* floating above one's body) are uncontrovertibly induced by physical phenomena. A good example is that fighter pilots have experienced OBEs, and so have epilepsy patients who have had a specific part of their brain stimulated in order to seek to cure the epilepsy. Why couldn't the OBEs in NDEs also be caused by, and constituted by, physical phenomena? As with NDEs in general, we could then say that the OBErs *really had* OBEs; it seemed to them that they floated above their bodies. But it does not follow that they *really did* float above their bodies—that their souls detached themselves from their bodies (and the physical world) and nevertheless perceived features of our physical world.[14]

Naturalistic Explanations of NDEs?

Neurophysiology and Culture. We don't *yet* have an adequate neurophysiological explanation of NDEs. But this does not imply that no such explanation will be developed in the future. Science marches on, sometimes in fits and starts, sometimes more slowly than we'd like, but it marches on. What cannot be explained now may be explained in the future. In particular, neuroscience is in its infancy, but with better imaging tools, we are making huge strides. It is totally unreasonable to give up on a physical explanation of the brain processes that underlie NDEs, just because we don't have one *now*. It is better to bet on science in this matter. What is more sensible: to believe that eventually science will generate an adequate understanding of the neurophysiology underlying NDEs, or that the mind is nonphysical and grasps facts about the physical and supernatural realms via nonphysical means?

---

14. There is a fascinating discussion of OBEs, and the contemporary research on them, in Joshua Rothman, "As Real as It Gets," *The New Yorker* (April 2, 2018): 30–36. Some of this research involves "embodied virtual reality." Mel Slater and Mavi Sanchez-Vives are leaders in this field, and some of their work has been supported by the Immortality Project.

Kevin Nelson is a neurologist who has developed a neurophysiological explanation of core elements of NDEs.[15] Nelson holds that the "dark tunnel" is associated with the compromise of blood flow to the retinas. Nelson attributes the "bright light" to a flow of neuronal excitement moving from a part of the brain stem to subcortical visual relay stations and then to the occipital cortex.[16]

Nelson also seeks to explain why these neurophysiological changes would be elicited in a near-death episode. In his view, they are produced in part by the "fight-or-flight" impulse, and they are evolutionarily advantageous. Nelson thus employs a multifactorial explanation that invokes an array of different kinds of factors. This is the most promising kind of approach, and it is entirely compatible with rejecting supernaturalism.

Let's suppose that in an NDE you see a bright light in a dark tunnel. The visual impressions may be explained by reference to compromised blood flow to the retinas and unusual neuronal activity. But why are the impressions *interpreted* as a light in a tunnel? Here is where cultural "tropes" or stories interact with neurophysiological changes; certain metaphors and commonly shared ideas in an individual's culture may structure and shape his raw impressions. In all Western cultures, we have a saying to the effect that, no matter how bad things are, there's always light at the end of the tunnel.[17] There's always hope. Somehow our minds are able to invoke this reassuring metaphor at a time of crisis.

It is interesting that in Japan people who have had NDEs do not typically report seeing a light at the end of a tunnel. Rather, some report that they experience themselves as tending a rock garden with friends and loved ones. It turns out that in Japan, rather than the trope of the light at the end of the tunnel, there is a popular idea of buying and

---

15. A succinct and helpful overview of his work can be found in Kevin Nelson, "Near-Death Experience: Arising from the Borderlands of Consciousness in Crisis," *Annals of the New York Academy of Sciences* 1330 (2014): 111–119.

16. For further discussion, see Oliver Sacks, *Hallucinations* (New York: Alfred A. Knopf, 2012): 261.

17. On a somewhat less perky note, there is also the saying, "It is always darkest just before it turns totally black." In the text we'll keep it more optimistic!

tending a rock garden with friends and loved ones in old age.[18] Presumably individuals in Japan who are experiencing an NDE may well see a light or flash or light in darkness, but they do not typically *interpret* these impressions as a light at the end of a tunnel. They do not find the impressions salient. Rather, they interpret other visual impressions as tending a rock garden, given their background acceptance of this comforting thought.

There are certain patterns that are universal (or nearly so) across cultures in the reports of NDEs. There are also cross-cultural differences as described earlier. These are good examples in which various factors, including neurophysiological changes and culturally dependent background beliefs, work together to produce core features of NDEs. In near-death contexts, something causes these physical changes and also activates the mind in a specific way. Somehow the mind (which, if we reject supernaturalism, is the brain) can reach for a comforting metaphor—a light at the end of a tunnel, an elegant and peaceful rock garden—in a time of crisis. The comforting thoughts help to give shape and meaning to the raw visual impressions.

Evolution. Can we give *possible* evolutionary explanations of the various features of NDEs? This would help to establish that they are parts of the natural world. For example, it is clear that an OBE would be advantageous in a near-death context. Someone who is about to be attacked by a ferocious beast (or human being!) may benefit psychologically from "detaching" herself from her body (at least in her mind). This detachment helps to protect her psychologically, and to allow her to avoid panic. The detachment in the face of physical assault is parallel to the psychological detachment (or "dissociation") on the part of individuals who suffer from emotional abuse. These moves to separate "oneself" from "the individual under attack" are a defense mechanism that protects us in crises (although in the psychological context it can lead to "dissociative disorders").

It is clear why it would be an evolutionary advantage to remain calm in a crisis. It would not be surprising if this tendency would manifest itself in a context in which the individual is called on to *act* in a calm

---

18. I thank Bruce Greyson for mentioning these fascinating points in a presentation to the International Board of Advisors of the John Templeton Foundation, June 2010, and in personal correspondence.

and rational way in the face of a lethal threat. Swiss geologist Albert Heim, motivated by his own nearly seventy-foot fall in the Alps, published the first empirical study of the "psychophysiological" changes that take place in contexts of seemingly imminent death: "Remarks on Fatal Falls."[19] He interviewed people (Alpinists) who (like him) had falls while hiking or climbing, and also workers who had fallen from scaffolding. Heim noted that certain features characterized individuals in near-death contexts:

> Mental activity became enormous, rising to a 100-fold velocity of intensity . . . The relationships of events and their probable outcomes were overviewed with objective clarity. No confusion entered at all. Time became greatly expanded. The individual acted with lightning-quickness in accord with accurate judgment of his situation [and exhibited an absence of] paralyzing fright of the sort that can happen in instances of lesser danger. [Instead, the individual felt] calm seriousness, profound acceptance, and a dominant mental quickness and sense of surety.[20]

This state could be described as "calm alertness in the face of extreme danger."[21]

The tendency to be in a state of calm alertness in a situation of extreme danger is obviously a survival advantage. A perhaps *unavoidable concomitant* of this disposition would be a tendency to find peace, serenity, and comforting metaphors even in an NDE

---

19. For an interesting discussion, see John Seabrook, "Six Strikes: The Danger of Black Ice," *The New Yorker* (April 9, 2018): 30–35; the reference to Heim's article is on p. 33. Seabrook had an almost-fatal accident on black ice on a cold New England day. He did not have an NDE, as we have been describing them. He did not lose wakeful consciousness, as in an NDE, and:

> I had no panoramic life review, no tunnel, no roseate clouds, no reunions with relatives (thank goodness), nor meet-ups with beings of the light, and no unwelcome return to the body. (35)

He did, however, experience the enhanced physical and psychological powers characteristic of individuals in near-death contexts. These experiences might be called "near near-death experiences" (NNDEs); they occur in near-death contexts and have some, but not all, of the hallmark characteristics of NDEs.

20. Seabrook, "Six Strikes," 33. Seabrook is here quoting Heim's article, "Remarks on Fatal Falls."

21. Seabrook, "Six Strikes," 35.

(in which one is not able to be active). This would be an evolutionary "spandrel"—an unavoidable consequence of something that is evolutionarily advantageous. A spandrel is not *itself* evolutionarily advantageous, but it is a necessary (given the way nature works) consequence of something that is: a spandrel comes along for the ride, so to speak. Put in other words, a spandrel is a side effect—an unavoidable (and sometimes welcome) side effect.

The term "spandrel" is an architectural term for the triangular space between the tops of two adjacent arches and the ceiling of a building. Saint Mark's Cathedral in Venice, Italy, is famous for its spandrels. Stephen Jay Gould and Richard Lewontin made the analogy between the spandrels in Saint Mark's Cathedral and certain biological features of organisms in the context of evolutionary theory in a classic paper.[22] Another famous example of spandrels in architecture is the Sagrada Familia Cathedral in Barcelona, Spain, designed by the Spanish architect Gaudi and unfinished.

The tendency of the mind to grasp comforting metaphors and thoughts while the individual is in an NDE is a spandrel. It is a misfiring of the tendency to be calm in a crisis—a misfiring because it takes place when the individual is not awake and mobile. Given that we are wired for staying calm in a crisis, it is perhaps inevitable that the underlying mechanism will sometimes activate, even when not needed. This is like a car alarm that sometimes goes off as a result of an earthquake or other perturbation irrelevant to potential burglary. Might the entire configuration of psychological and neurophysiological features of an NDE be a spandrel? My speculation: NDEs are spandrels through and through.

We actually have a combination of psychological tendencies that may be manifested in a near-death context: the fight-or-flight impulse (discussed by Nelson) and what I might dub the "stay-calm-and-carry-on" disposition. Both confer a survival advantage, especially when combined. We are creatures endowed with the ability to fight or flee, and to remain calm and sensible in the process. Maybe we'll even stay put peacefully. In any case, the twin psychological impulses, manifested

---

22. Stephen Jay Gould and Richard Lewontin, "The Spandrels of San Marco and the Panglossian Paradigm: A Critique of the Adaptationist Programme," *Proceedings of the Royal Society of London B* 205 (1979): 581–598.

appropriately, give us a key advantage in natural selection.[23] Given the way we are wired, these advantages come with spandrels—such as NDEs. Not all spandrels are unwelcome, and NDEs should be considered "welcome spandrels." Positive NDEs are deeply transformative, leading to less death anxiety, more spirituality, and a greater concern for others (among other desirable changes). But what about negative NDEs?[24] Why do some people have them, and how are they explained as a necessary concomitant of an advantageous propensity?

Just as positive NDEs are a misfiring of the stay-calm-and-carry-on tendency, so are negative NDEs. Just as with positive NDEs, negative NDEs can be interpreted as spandrels. They occur when the individual is not awake and in need of calm, cool reflection: they occur in the "wrong" context. Note also that they do not *in themselves* enhance calmness. Frankly, they are alarming. But just as with positive NDEs, negative NDEs are welcome spandrels.

Why welcome? Negative NDEs cause us to reflect on our lives, and to change elements that are not consistent with ultimate connection with a perfectly good being. Such reflection should issue in a reorientation toward goodness. For individuals who feel ashamed and guilty, negative NDEs give vivid evidence of the need to change. Even those who are anxious and depressed, but not because of behavior for which they feel guilty, are encouraged to rethink their lives and their attitudes toward their lives. All of this need not be interpreted as issuing from a recognition that God is wrathful, and one needs insurance for the fire and brimstone that might await. Rather, the motivation to transform can come from a simple recognition that one's life is off course—that one is not oriented toward goodness, but is confused, distracted, and off course.

In most cases an individual oriented toward goodness will behave in ways that are conducive to flourishing. Plato and Aristotle argued that this is *necessarily* the case. There is then some evolutionary support for NDEs. Better: we can at least sketch *possible* evolutionary explanations

---

23. In his article, "Artificial Intelligence: Do the Perils of A.I. Exceed Its Promise?" *The New Yorker* (May 14, 2018): 44–51, Tad Friend writes:

> The Texas Horned Lizard, when threatened, shoots blood out of its eyes; we, when threatened, think. (48)

24. Negative NDEs are disturbing—and intriguing. For interesting discussions, see Nancy Evans Bush, *Dancing Past the Dark: Distressing Near-Death Experiences* (Parson's Porch Books, 2012); and *The Buddha in Hell and Other Alarms* (IngramSpark, 2016).

of NDEs. Showing how it is at least *possible* that a given phenomenon has evolved via natural selection is an important component of a defense of naturalism. Some questions remain, however: Why do some have positive NDEs, whereas others have negative NDEs? Why do only *some* in a near-death context have NDEs, positive or negative? We don't have a fully adequate (or even almost fully adequate) scientific explanation of NDEs. Not *yet*.

I pause to reiterate and emphasize the fundamental problem for supernaturalism about the mind (dualism). This is often overlooked or pushed aside in popular discussions of NDEs, so I will try the reader's patience by reiterating—in slightly different words—a point I have already made. I am now looking out my window, and I see a beautiful tree (as well as my neighbor's yappy dog). On the assumption of supernaturalism, how exactly would my nonphysical mind process the physical signals provided by my perceptual system? How does that beautiful tree (and annoying dog) get into my nonphysical mind? Assume that the tree causes some mental states (that represent the tree) in me; the actual physical tree causes my nonphysical mind (or soul) to have certain (nonphysical) impressions or experiences.

How does this happen? Again: where there is causation, there is a mechanism. What is the mechanism whereby the physical world, and, in particular, the tree, causes me to have nonphysical mental states? We don't have to understand the mechanism in detail, but the problem is that we just have no clue about it. So supernaturalism is *not* obviously simpler and more elegant; if anything, it is more complicated, and it leads to a murky quicksand of obscurity. Dualism is a frondy philosophical ecosystem, and in need of pruning. It is better, and ultimately *simpler*, to stick with the framework of science. This is why I am a default physicalist, and why I think the burden of proof is on the supernaturalist. This burden could be met, but given the philosophical "price" of dualism, it would take strong and clear evidence. We do not have this. It is better to stick with naturalism—a gluten-free metaphysics, so to speak.

NDEs Are Vivid Experiences

Dreams can present themselves as less detailed and vivid than real perception. They often have a "blurry" character. NDEs are unlike dreams in this respect. Often they are lucid and vivid, presenting details of images and colors in a particularly sharp and clear way. NDEs can even be sharper and clearer than ordinary perception, as in surrealist art, such as that of Salvador Dali. The NDE researcher Bruce Greyson and his colleagues write:

> Near-death experiencers often describe their mental processes during the NDE as remarkably clear and lucid and their sensory experiences as unusually vivid, surpassing those of their normal waking state.[25]

Some have taken the extra vividness of NDEs as evidence that these experiences are not produced in the normal way. The oncologist and NDE researcher Jeffrey Long writes:

> People who have had near-death experiences often describe enhanced and even supernormal vision. This is powerful evidence that something other than the physical brain is responsible for vision during NDEs.[26]

Long's claim is that the lucidity of NDEs supports one tenet of supernaturalism: the operation of nonphysical mechanisms. Others (including Eben Alexander) have taken the lucidity of NDEs to support the other tenet: that NDEs give us access to a supernatural realm. The lucidity of NDE reports is presumably part of the reason why those who experience NDEs report that they are "real"—they present themselves in a forceful and vivid way.

But dreams can be vivid, and no one has suggested that an especially vivid dream must be generated by a nonphysical mechanism. Dreams, vivid or not, come from our brains (and are based in some way that is hard to specify on our natures and experiences). Nor should anyone suppose that a vivid dream, in virtue of its vividness, must accurately reflect external reality. It would be a wild coincidence if a dream, vivid or not, happened to coincide with external reality in a detailed way.

In his book *Hallucinations*, Oliver Sacks points out that it is a mistake to suppose that all hallucinations have a dreamlike quality.

---

25. Bruce Greyson, Emily Williams Kelly, and Edward F. Kelly, "Explanatory Models for Near-Death Experiences," in Holden, Greyson, and James, eds., *The Handbook of Near-Death Experiences* (Santa Barbara, CA: Praeger, 2009): 229.

26. Jeffrey Long (with Paul Perry), *Evidence of the Afterlife: The Science of Near-Death Experience* (New York: HarperCollins, 2010): 61.

He writes, "To the hallucinatory . . . hallucinations seem very real; they can mimic perception in every respect . . ."[27] In describing research on hallucinations of subjects who had undergone various kinds of sensory deprivation, Sacks writes:

> Several subjects spoke of the brilliance and colors of their hallucinations; one described "resplendent peacock feathers and buildings." Another saw sunsets almost too bright to bear and luminous landscapes of extraordinary beauty, "much prettier, I think, than anything I have ever seen."[28]

So hallucinations can be very lucid and vivid, and yet be caused by physical phenomena, such as "sensory deprivation, Parkinsonism, migraine, epilepsy, drug intoxication, and [the state just prior to falling asleep]."[29] A person's experience of virtual reality can be quite clear and sharp, and yet virtual reality is not (necessarily) an accurate depiction of external reality. It is wrong to think that the lucidity or vividness of an experience implies that it is caused by nonphysical phenomena, or that it is an accurate depiction of external reality. Vividness is a *mode of presentation* of information; but this does not necessarily indicate the *accuracy* of the information.

The Universality of NDEs Is Best Explained by Supernaturalism

People have reported NDEs throughout the history of the human species. There is a famous account of an NDE at the end of Plato's *Republic*: the Myth of Er. Also, the reports come from all across the world; they are a cultural "universal." Whereas the specifics of an NDE differ from individual to individual, and also from culture to culture, there are basic similarities in the structure and content of NDEs worldwide (as we have noted). Some people think that the best explanation of these similarities is that human beings who have had NDEs throughout time and across cultures are in contact (via nonphysical means) with a single heavenly realm. How else can we explain the universality of NDEs?

---

27. Sacks, *Hallucinations*, ix.
28. Sacks, *Hallucinations*, 39.
29. Sacks, *Hallucinations*, 229.

Jeffrey Long writes:

> The core NDE experience is the same all over the world. Whether it's a near-death experience of a Hindu in India, a Muslim in Egypt, or a Christian in the United States, the same core elements are present in all, including out-of-body experience, tunnel experience, feelings of peace, beings of light, a life review, reluctance to return, and transformation after the NDE.
>
> . . . It is amazing to think that no matter what country we call home, perhaps our real home is in the wondrous unearthly realms consistently described by NDErs around the world.[30]

But if everyone throughout the world were in contact with the *same* heavenly realm, then we would expect their reports of their NDEs to be similar. Note that Long refers to "heavenly *realms*," and indeed the details of various NDEs make it implausible that all those who experience NDEs are in contact with the *same* heavenly realm. Think, for example, of the differences between Eben Alexander's and Colton Burpo's NDEs.

In any case, supernaturalism (and, specifically, access to a single nonphysical realm) just is *not* the best explanation of the cross-cultural similarities in NDEs. The argument for supernaturalism in this context invokes purported similarity in the *objects* of experience. But it seems equally, if not *more* plausible, to invoke similarities in the *experiencers*. Human beings throughout the world have similar brains and central nervous systems. Further, they have similar basic psychological tendencies and needs.

It is not surprising that human beings throughout history and across cultures should have structurally similar NDEs (if not exactly the same in all details). Similar conscious beings will have similar experiences in similar contexts. We need not make extravagant assumptions about the objects of these experiences or the nature of the means of relating to the world. A perceptual context has a perceiver and an object of perception. The supernaturalist finds an explanation of the phenomenon of universality in the purported nature of the apparently perceived object. He thereby buys into a problematic and underdeveloped intellectual framework. It is better to look to the nature of the perceiver.

---

30. Long, *Evidence of the Afterlife*, 171.

Conclusion

NDEs are fascinating, and they raise important questions about the nature of the human mind and the prospects of an afterlife. We have explored some of the most influential arguments on behalf of supernaturalism: the combination of dualism about the relationship between the mind and the body and the claim that in an NDE we are in contact with a nonphysical realm. Despite the wide acceptance of supernaturalism on the basis of such arguments, I have highlighted the gaps between the evidence and the supernaturalist conclusions. I have essentially challenged Eben Alexander's claim quoted in the epigram to this chapter: "Yet there was no room for that reality in the medically trained scientific worldview that I'd spent years acquiring."[31]

Still, NDEs are extraordinarily profound, and they have potent transformational effects. Is supernaturalism the only plausible explanation of the *meaning* and *profound significance* of NDEs? We turn to this question in the following chapter. The key will be understanding the stories NDEs tell.

Annotated Suggestions for Further Reading

A helpful overview of conceptions of the afterlife is *The Palgrave Handbook of the Afterlife* (London: Palgrave, 2017). Just for fun, check out Mary Roach's history of attempts to prove the existence of an afterlife: *Spook: Science Tackles the Afterlife* (New York: W.W. Norton, 2005). She has also written about the bizarre case of Thomas Lynn Bradford, who killed himself with the intention of communicating with his research colleague after he had died: Mary Roach, "What Happens after You Die?" *New Scientist* (November 15, 2006). They wanted to prove the existence of an afterlife, so he committed suicide and intended to send a message to his colleague from heaven (assuming the best). Sadly, no message was received. It was a big price to pay.

A classic early treatment of NDEs and related phenomena is Raymond Moody, *Life after Life* (New York: Mockingbird Books, 1975). Moody coined the term "near-death experience." The psychologist Kenneth Ring was influenced by Moody's book, and he was particularly fascinated by the transformational power of NDEs. His first two books on NDEs are Kenneth Ring, *Life at Death: A Scientific Investigation of the Near-Death Experience* (New York: William Morrow and Company, 1980); and *Heading toward*

---

31. Alexander, *Proof of Heaven: A Neurosurgeon's Journey into the Afterlife*, 130.

Omega (New York: William Morrow and Company, 1984). Ring was the founding editor of *The Journal of Near-Death Studies*, a resource for work in this field. An excellent, relatively early presentation of a careful philosophical analysis of NDEs is R.W.K. Paterson, *Philosophy and the Belief in a Life after Death* (London: Palgrave/Macmillan, 1995).

The two most salient, and dramatic, contemporary presentations of NDEs in popular literature are Eben Alexander, MD, *Proof of Heaven: A Neurosurgeon's Journey into the Afterlife* (New York: Simon and Schuster, 2012); and Todd Burpo (with Lynn Vincent), *Heaven Is for Real: A Little Boy's Astounding Story of His Trip to Heaven and Back* (Nashville, TN: Thomas Nelson, 2010). (This book was made into a motion picture.) A discussion sympathetic to a supernaturalist interpretation of NDEs is Jeffrey Long (with Paul Perry), *Evidence of the Afterlife: The Science of Near-Death Experience* (New York: HarperCollins, 2010). Eben Alexander has written a follow-up book to *Proof of Heaven: The Map of Heaven: How Science, Religion, and Ordinary People Are Proving the Afterlife* (New York: Simon and Schuster, 2014).

Two helpful academic analyses of these phenomena, generally sympathetic to a supernaturalist, or at least nonphysicalist, interpretation of NDEs are Janice Miner Holden, Bruce Greyson, and Debbie James, eds., *The Handbook of Near-Death Experiences* (Santa Barbara, CA: Praeger, 2009); and Pim van Lommel, *Consciousness Beyond Life: The Science of the Near-Death Experience* (New York: HarperOne, 2010). Also see John C. Hagen III, MD, *The Science of Near-Death Experiences* (Columbia, MO: University of Missouri Press, 2017).

Two very important and thoughtful treatments of NDEs, and, in particular, their OBE component, are Sam Parnia, MD, *What Happens When We Die: A Ground-Breaking Study into the Nature of Life and Death* (Carlsbad, CA: Hay House, 2008 [originally published in the United Kingdom in 2005]); and Sam Parnia with Josh Young, *Erasing Death: The Science That Is Rewriting the Boundaries between Life and Death* (New York: HarperOne, 2013).

A skeptical view about NDEs, and especially their supernaturalist interpretation, is found in Susan Blackmore, *Dying to Live* (New York: Prometheus Books, 1993). A helpful discussion of NDEs and related phenomena from a physicalist perspective is found in Oliver Sacks, *Hallucinations* (New York: Alfred A. Knopf, 2012). In this (and the following) chapter I have borrowed much from John Martin Fischer and Benjamin Mitchell-Yellin, *Near-Death Experiences: Understanding Visions of the Afterlife* (New York: Oxford University Press, 2016); in this book we give a more detailed discussion of the philosophical issues pertaining to NDEs than is possible in this chapter.

There are excellent discussions of many of the most important books on NDEs in two "literature review" articles: Robert Gottlieb, "To Heaven and Back!" *The New York Review of Books* (October 23, 2014): http://www.nybooks. com/articles/2014/10/23/heaven-and-back/; and "Back from Heaven—the Science," *The New York Review of Books* (November 6, 2014): http://www .nybooks.com/articles/2014/11/06/back-heaven-science/.

CHAPTER 9

Near-Death Experiences: Their Significance

There are things known, and there are things unknown, and in between are the doors of perception.

—ALDOUS HUXLEY,
The Doors of Perception

....

Introduction

Near-death experiences (NDEs) inspire deep awe, and those who have had NDEs (NDErs) are often transformed in profound ways. Recall that NDErs have less death anxiety and are more spiritual. They tend to appreciate relationships more and cherish time with family, friends, and relatives. They are also more compassionate and attuned to morality and justice. Many have thought that supernaturalism is the best explanation for the awe and wonder that NDEs inspire and the profound transformations they cause. How can a mere physical phenomenon be so meaningful and transformative? It seems that the awe derives at least in part from the NDEr's experience of being in contact with a greater being or realm—a perfect being or realm—and the realization that we will eventually be part of this realm or united with this being.

On this view, the transformations are related to the experience of being in contact with a perfect being or heavenly realm. This leads to a recognition of the need to cultivate practices in ordinary life that orient one toward this being (or realm), including adherence to moral rules. This explains why someone who has had an NDE is more spiritual and moral (including being more attentive to others, and not just oneself).

In short, many contend that contact with the realm of a perfect being causes a reorientation of one's life toward that being.

Are Awe and Transformation Best Explained by Supernaturalism?

I do not however think that supernaturalism is the best explanation of these important phenomena. I do not even think that a *belief* in supernaturalism is the best explanation of the changes we often see in people who have had NDEs. I wish to sketch an interpretation of NDEs that provides an alternative framework for explaining the phenomena.

We often feel awe at the wonders of nature and also the incredible accomplishments of human beings.[1] Think, for example, of the awe we feel when we see a beautiful sunset over the ocean, the majesty of the Grand Canyon, a snowy mountain peak in the Alps, and so forth. Consider, also, the awe we feel when we see the Great Wall in China, visit the pyramids in Egypt, share a milestone with our children or parents, or simply witness the strength and bravery of a person who finds the inner resources to overcome adversity. We feel the awe while fully realizing that these phenomena are parts of the physical world.

Consider also this extraordinary report of an experience induced by the hallucinogenic drug LSD, as reported to Oliver Sacks:

> I was in my late twenties when a friend and I took some LSD. I had tripped many times before but this acid was different . . .
>
> . . . I left my body and hovered in the room above the whole scene, then found myself traveling through a tunnel of beautiful light into space and was filled with a feeling of total love and acceptance. The light was the most beautiful, warm and inviting light I ever felt. I heard a voice ask me if I wanted to go back to Earth and finish my life or . . . to go in to the beautiful love and light in the sky. In the love and light was every person that ever lived. Then my whole life flashed in my mind from birth to the present, with every detail that ever happened, every feeling and thought, visual and emotional was there in an instant. The voice told me that humans are "Love and Light." . . .

---

1. For an insightful discussion of awe, see Howard Wettstein, *The Significance of Religious Experience* (New York: Oxford University Press, 2012). For a discussion of awe, wonder, and hope in the context of NDEs, see John Martin Fischer and Benjamin Mitchell-Yellin, *Near-Death Experiences: Understanding Visions of the Afterlife* (New York: Oxford University Press, 2016): 157–179.

That day will live with me forever; I feel I was shown a side of life that most people can't even imagine. I feel a special connection to every day, that even the simple and mundane have such power and meaning.[2]

I find this experience remarkable for various reasons. It has many of the features of an NDE: an out-of-body experience, a life review, traveling through a tunnel of light, pleasant feelings, deceased persons, transformation, and so forth. This in itself is significant, because the experience is caused by the taking of LSD—a physical fact. Presumably the individual knows that it is caused by a physical fact, even during the experience. Certainly he knows this after the "trip," and yet it has transformed him deeply. Such transformations, involving a reduction in death anxiety and acquiring a sense of peace and tranquility, are reported by people who are being treated (experimentally) with hallucinogenic drugs for terminal illnesses.[3]

In an important discussion of these reports, *How to Change Your Mind*, Michael Pollan points to two hallmarks of LSD experiences, as well as spiritual experiences in general. The first is that the self is not the focus of the experience (it seems to "dissolve," at least in conscious awareness). This is very similar to the interpretation we suggested in Chapter Seven of the religious view of heaven in which the individual merges with God in an "ecstatic union." Recall that the view is that the experience is not *of* the self, although it is *had by* a self. The second is that the content is presented as "objectively true"—ultra-real, in Eben Alexander's phrase. These elements are also distinctive features of NDEs. Again, an indisputably physical agent—LSD—can produce precisely these effects. Spiritual experiences in general—even those induced by physical means—share these properties.

Now some might argue that these drugs usher one into a nonphysical realm; in the famous words of Aldous Huxley, they open "the doors of perception," and perhaps these doors open to a nonphysical realm. It is not clear, however, that the doors open to a new realm, rather than a

---

2. Oliver Sacks, *Hallucinations* (New York: Alfred A. Knopf, 2012): 101–102.

3. For an earlier treatment of these issues, with historical background, see Don Lattin, *The Harvard Psychedelic Club* (New York: HarperOne, 2010). For discussions of more recent research, see Michael Pollan, "The Trip Treatment," *The New Yorker* (February 9, 2015): 36–47; and his comprehensive book, *How to Change Your Mind* (New York: Penguin Press, 2018).

new way of experiencing our physical realm. I think that the most plausible interpretation is one that fits with our well-established physical paradigm. The idea that hallucinogenic drugs cause new ways of perceiving and experiencing our physical world is much more promising than the notion that they give us access to a totally different world—a world that is nonphysical but that we somehow can perceive (and thus have causal interaction with). These drugs open the doors of perception in the sense that they change the mechanisms of physical perception. They give rise to new ways of perceiving *our* world.

In her extraordinary book *My Stroke of Insight: A Brain Scientist's Personal Journey*, Jill Bolte Taylor describes her stroke in ways strikingly similar to aspects of Eben Alexander's NDE and the LSD experience reported to Oliver Sacks.[4] She holds that her stroke took the left half of her brain offline and empowered the right half, leading to greater spiritualism, empathy, and a sense of well-being. It is as if her stroke opened the doors of emotional perception by empowering a previously constrained part of her brain.

The Meaning of NDEs

Explanation and Storytelling. Let's think about how we might come to understand NDEs. Consider the difference between explanation and storytelling. These are two deep-seated aspects of human nature, distinct ways in which we seek to come to grips with the world and ourselves in it. Storytelling helps us to sort out this experience we call living, and it does so by placing events into emotionally recognizable patterns. We feel the pull of narratives because they take us—both in body and in mind—through recognizable emotional landscapes. We feel the tension of drama, the crushing pain of tragedy, the comic release. This is the distinctive way in which stories make sense to us—they give us a kind of emotional understanding. As we discussed earlier (in Chapter Six), this is what makes something a story, and not a mere description of a sequence of events or "chronicle."[5]

---

4. Jill Bolte Taylor, *My Stroke of Insight: A Brain Scientist's Personal Journey* (London: Penguin Books, reprinted in 2009).

5. For an important work that links narrativity to emotional understanding, see J. David Velleman, "Narrative Explanation," *The Philosophical Review* 112 (2003): 1–25.

We don't just tell stories. We use the tools of science to discover what is out there—and in here—and how it all fits together. We observe, hypothesize, and test. We refine our vocabulary for describing what we find, and we constantly revise our explanations of why things are the way they are. In doing so, we are searching for the truth. Unlike our drive to find meaning, our drive to explain is not satisfied by fictional representations. A good explanation grasps the world, just as a good story touches the heart.

When it comes to making sense of the world and ourselves, human nature is multifaceted. We want to understand the way things work, and we want to grasp the meaning of it all. These two pursuits are not necessarily in tension. Sometimes they work in tandem. Placing an explanation in the context of a narrative can be a powerful way of getting the message out and making it comprehensible. It can help to communicate the deep significance of the events being explained and to help people feel the importance of the topic. Explanation and storytelling are two aspects of understanding. Explanation yields cognitive understanding, and storytelling yields affective or emotional understanding. To grasp an explanation is to have a representation of the world. To grasp a story is to be apt to experience a certain range of emotions.

Thus, even if NDEs are entirely physical experiences with physical causes, we can achieve an affective grasp of them by attending to the stories they tell. The meaning provided by a narrative grasp of things does not depend on an assumption that the events being placed in a narrative frame are real (in the sense that they really occurred in our concrete world). Fiction can be meaningful in this way, even fiction understood as such. We emotionally connect with made-up characters and their lives, and we do so knowing full well that they are figments of someone's imagination and projections in our own imaginations. The connection between the events depicted in the stories and an independent reality is beside the narrative point. A good narrative maps onto our emotional templates.[6]

Think of the first time you saw *Romeo and Juliet*. Recall your anxious excitement as they see each other for the first time, feverish expectation at their courtship, crushing heartache at their deaths. The story of young lovers facing the daunting obstacles posed by race, class, and family is universally recognizable. Everyone knows a Romeo and a Juliet. Or perhaps

---

6. Again, see Velleman, "Narrative Explanation."

a Romeo and Julio, or a Juliet and Julia. Presumably none of these friends really climbs on balconies, and so forth. The world often gets in the way of their love, all right, but it typically does not end in deadly confusion for them. They mourn and move on, as people do, or at least they try to do. We console them and help them along their way, and yet we grasp the significance of what they are going through because we are familiar with the tale. The pattern is familiar. This story, like others, meshes with our emotional sensibilities; the stories elicit or activate an emotional template in us. By grasping the story, we get an affective understanding.

Stories render events emotionally meaningful, thereby allowing us to comprehend them, and come to grips with them, in a distinctive way. Hollywood love stories take a trajectory that is the "opposite" of Romeo and Juliet. They are stories of improbably overcoming huge obstacles on the path to living happily ever after. The genre of the romantic comedy ("rom-com") has a distinctive structure that we recognize emotionally: "meeting cute" (by bumping into each other—maybe umbrellas get entangled on a rainy day, or a woman meets a man who lives downstairs in the apartment building who is a slovenly, boorish oaf, or . . .); a significant obstacle (different social classes, races, religions, politics, geographical separation, and so forth); conversation and banter, and, somehow, voilà: love! (The oaf turns out to have a heart of gold, and he had just gotten out of the shower . . .) The loving couple lives happily ever after.

We can recognize familiar kinds of stories of high hopes dashed, of hard work rewarded, of the comeuppance that is one's due, of coming home, of being foiled by an absurd accident (such as slipping on a banana peel), of failing precisely because of the way you attempt to succeed, and so on.

Failing precisely because of the way you try to succeed is a universally recognizable story. For example, it is the story of maladies caused by doctors. A person takes an antidepressant for moderate depression and becomes agitated and suicidal. Another goes to a chiropractor for lower back pain and comes home with piercing neck pain. You switch to a low-fat diet because your doctor and the American Heart Association recommend it, but your high carbohydrate intake leads to obesity and diabetes.[7]

---

7. A true story: I recently purchased a rather heavy piece of exercise equipment to help me to strengthen my back; I had to carry it to another room, and in doing so I strained my back.

Here is a famous story of this kind, from Somerset Maugham's play *Sheppey*:

> SHEPPEY: I wish I'd gone down to the Isle of Sheppey when the doctor advised it. You wouldn't 'ave thought of looking for me there.
>
> DEATH: There was a merchant in Baghdad who sent his servant to market to buy provisions and in a little while the servant came back, white and trembling, and said, Master, just now when I was in the market-place I was jostled by a woman in the crowd and when I turned I saw it was Death that jostled me. She looked at me and made a threatening gesture; now, lend me your horse, and I will ride away from this city and avoid my fate. I will go to Samarra and there Death will not find me. The merchant lent him his horse, and the servant mounted it, and he dug his spurs in its flanks and as fast as the horse could gallop he went. Then the merchant went down to the market-place and he saw me standing in the crowd and he came to me and said, Why did you make a threatening gesture to my servant when you saw him this morning? That was not a threatening gesture, I said, it was only a start of surprise. I was astonished to see him in Baghdad, for I had an appointment with him to-night in Samarra.[8]

The story is instantly recognizable as one in which your best efforts are for naught: you are foiled by the way you attempt to succeed. It also evokes a fatalistic feeling of despair and the futility of our best efforts.

Lest we dwell on the half-empty glass, there are more uplifting stories that resonate with us. The discovery of antibiotics is a great story of serendipity. Early antidepressants were used to treat another malady, and they didn't work; but the patients felt better about their plight! We also recognize stories of lucky breaks. At the inaugural performance of Haydn's "Miracle Symphony," the audience members were so thrilled by the piece that they surged onto the stage. Fortunately for them, because the roof collapsed shortly thereafter—the roof above the seats, not the

---

8. W.S. Maugham, *The Collected Plays of W. Somerset Maugham* (London, 1931). The quotation is from *Sheppey*, act 3, as quoted in Peter van Inwagen, *An Essay on Free Will* (Oxford: Clarendon Press, 1983): 24.

stage! We all love the great American story (myth?) of hard work paying off in the end.

What unites the various kinds of stories is that they allow us to fit sequences of events into familiar emotional patterns. The important feature of a story is not how it describes reality—that is certainly not what we want in a good tale—but how it makes us feel. Explanations allow us to wrap our minds around things. Stories allow us to wrap our hearts around them.

The Stories Told by NDErs. We can understand the meaning of an NDE in part by interpreting the story it tells. NDErs are profoundly moved by the NDE's story. This story includes a heavenly realm and perfect being. It seems then that the story of the NDE is *essentially* supernatural. Can we interpret the story of NDEs in a different way? That is, can we understand this story without requiring it to involve intended reference to certain metaphysically real elements—elements that are supernatural?

I want to show how NDEs can be meaningful and transformative in part due to the stories they tell, where this is all compatible with a rejection of supernaturalism. The distinctive meaning and potency of NDEs need not come from a supernaturalist story. Put in other words: even if the story involves supernatural entities at the superficial level, we do not have to take this as an *indispensable* part of the story. Perhaps the apparent or "surface" story in an NDE is just a vehicle for expressing a deeper meaning—a story that is meaningful to us, quite apart from supernatural content.

I contend that the story at the core of NDEs is a voyage from a known (or familiar) place to a relatively unknown (or unfamiliar) situation or status, guided by a benevolent parental (or authority) figure (or figures). Our voyage is guided by what I have called a benevolent "parental figure," but this need not literally be a parent. It can be an "authority" figure (or even figures) in the sense that it is someone more experienced (in the relevant sphere) and who promotes your best interests. It is someone you rely on and trust. Perhaps parents paradigmatically play this role (when things are going well), but others can fulfill the "normative role" of parents as well. As an abbreviation, I shall continue to speak of guidance by a parent or "parental" figure.

This is a narrative that is capable of resonating deeply with human beings. Stories depicting voyages go back at least as far as *The Epic of Gilgamesh*, discussed previously, and Homer's *Iliad* and *Odyssey*. Healthy human development involves making a transition (taking a "voyage") in adolescence from the familiar territory of the family to the broader and less familiar world of other people and relationships. A psychologically healthy individual learns how to "differentiate" himself from his parents and to live independently of his family. Ideally, this transition is supervised and guided by a knowledgeable and benevolent authority figure (typically, a parent or parents). The story told by an NDE taps into an ancient genre of the voyage, but it also recapitulates or echoes our development from dependence on the family to integration into the wider world, as guided by our parents (or parental figures). An NDE is, you might say, the trip of an after-lifetime.

We can understand an NDE by reference to the way in which we relate to the parental guide. Our guides both teach and model greater prosocial and moral behavior. In an NDE we are reminded of the sacrifices and love of our parents (or those who have raised us benevolently), and we are filled with awe. Their example of love and sacrifice is salient and admirable, and thus we want to follow the lessons they sought to teach as we made the journey from the family to the wider world. Awe and wonder come from recognition of the love and sacrifice of our parents, and increased prosociality and moral concern comes from a desire to learn from their teachings and to follow their example.

The story of NDEs, on my interpretation, does not presuppose supernaturalism or a belief in supernaturalism at a deeper level. In the NDEs reported by Eben Alexander and Colton Burpo, purported details of the heavenly realm(s) and beings are revealed. But in many—perhaps most—NDEs the subject experiences traveling toward a barrier that guards some sort of destination, and before the individual actually negotiates the barrier, she awakens, typically with regret that she has awakened prematurely (and a desire to return and experience the completion of the voyage). This is like waking up from a wonderful dream—you wish it could go on longer. If heaven is for real, it is a gated community, at least in many NDEs. The point is that the importance of NDEs is *not* that they depict a supernatural destination; rather, their deeper meaning is that they tell the story of a recognizable and resonant kind of human journey.

In a sense our lives are really a *set* of journeys from the known and comfortable to the unknown and challenging. Of course, these voyages are not the same for all people, but there are some important similarities. We "travel" from the family to the wider world of relationships and active engagement with the challenges of the broader world guided by (say) our parents. Perhaps we go from the safety and comfort of our family to college or university life. Here we seek friends and perhaps clubs and associations (including fraternities and sororities) to take the place of our families. They then help to usher us from the by now familiar and relatively comfortable world of college to the new and more challenging environment of graduate school or the wider world of employment. Of course, our parents are still there (perhaps in the background), helping us along our way. A graduating senior at an American university captures the essence of this transition: "Leaving a known place. Off to the world we go. To discover more."[9] She probably felt the same way when she left home for college.

If things go well in our lives, we are guided by parents, authority figures, family, and friends. Perhaps the most challenging and frightening transition for us to get our minds around is the voyage from life to death—our last voyage (unless there is reincarnation or an afterlife that allows for change and development). The stories of NDEs help to assuage our anxieties about this daunting journey. Just as our parents ushered us into this world, they usher us out. And just as our parents take us on our first journey into independence (from our family to the wider world), they guide us on our last one—from life to whatever lies ahead (even if it is nothingness). The mind is able to bring our parents back from the dead, as it were, to guide us along this last journey. Not

9. Kimberly Chang-Haines, quoted in the *Stanford Magazine* (July/August 2017): 26.

only are we not alone in this journey, but we are accompanied by people who love us.

In Chapter Eight we briefly considered how negative NDEs might be explained in a naturalistic way. Although negative NDEs are superficially different from positive NDEs, they do in fact share important characteristics. Just as in positive NDEs, negative NDEs often involve life reviews and a journey from the known to the unknown, guided by a benevolent parental (or authority) figure. In a positive NDE, the voyage is typically from darkness into or toward light; also, it is often an ascent toward a barrier that appears to guard a heavenly domain. In negative NDEs these elements are present but reversed: the voyage is a descent into darkness toward a void.

How is one's guide in this descent benevolent? As we pointed out in Chapter Eight, the descent toward a void offers important lessons. Often the individual observes terrible suffering as he makes the descent, but it is important that it is others, and not the NDEr himself, who is being tortured. The negative NDEr learns about the suffering he or she has caused and is given strong motivation to change: to achieve a reorientation toward goodness. The guide then is benevolent insofar as he shows the individual that he is not properly aligned with goodness, and what the consequences will be, unless there is a positive transformation. Tough love!

The stories of positive and negative NDEs are the same at a deeper level: a voyage from the known to the unknown, guided by a benevolent parent figure. Both sorts of NDEs produce significant transformations, helping to reorient the individual toward morality, justice, and spirituality. Arguably, this sort of orientation is a survival advantage.

Return to the LSD experiences (and, in particular, the one reported to Oliver Sacks) discussed earlier. It is worth noting that we call them "trips." An LSD experience is indeed the story of travel from the known to the unknown in a way that is elevating and even ecstatic. The experiences induced by psychedelic drugs, including psilocybin and LSD, thus share this important feature, in addition to the two mentioned earlier in the chapter (the "no-self" content of the experience and the presentation of the contents of the experience as "ultra-real"—objectively true).

Many kinds of spiritual experiences are conceptualized as voyages—journeys to enlightenment.[10]

NDEs then are not unique. They are an instance of a spiritual or mystical experience, and they have the signature characteristics of these experiences. An NDE is similar to meditation, prayer, or the ingestion of psychedelic substances: they are all means of inducing a spiritual experience with similar content. They are different ways of "shaking the snow globe," changing modes and contents of consciousness, and resulting in profound transformations.[11]

The reported contents of NDEs, including supernatural realms and beings, can be understood as *metaphors* or, at least, as nonliteral. These stories can have profound meaning for us, even if we do not take them to refer to really existing heavenly realms and beings. Of course, we interpret many stories, including biblical stories, metaphorically (and not strictly literally). For instance, we can find the story of Adam and Eve in the Garden of Eden meaningful, even if we do not believe that Adam and Eve were literally the first persons or that the Garden of Eden really existed. Same with the story of Abraham and Isaac, and so forth. The distinctive potency of stories does not depend on their literal truth. Similarly, we can find NDEs deeply meaningful, even if we do not take references to other-worldly realms or beings literally.

We often don't know where we are going in life's journey, but it is even *more* mysterious where we are going in dying. NDEs don't tell us where we are going, but they offer comfort on the journey: it is guided by a benevolent parental figure. We are not traveling alone. NDEs are metaphorical narratives that capture this idea of travel into the unknown guided by a benevolent parental figure. The voyage is in a context—death—that magnifies and intensifies the normal anxiety

---

10. See, for example: Ram Dass and Daniel Goleman, *Journey of Awakening: A Meditator's Guidebook* (New York: Bantam Books, 1990 [revised and updated edition]). Ram Dass is the individual formerly called "Richard Alpert," who was one of the Harvard psychologists discussed in Lattin, *The Harvard Psychedelic Club*. He is also the author of *Be Here Now*, referred to in Chapter One.

11. The phrase "shaking the snow globe" is used by the neuroscientist Robin Carhart-Harris to refer to spiritual experiences induced by psychedelics. I am indebted to Pollan, *How To Change Your Mind,* for highlighting it.

associated with uncertainty about the next step in our lives. So NDEs tap into and address some of our deepest concerns.

Conclusion: Stories of Hope

NDEs may well be wholly physical events. We need not assume that they are a portal into another realm or are caused by contact with a heavenly realm. The picture here is that there is just one realm, but elements of this realm have various kinds of properties, and there are different perspectives on this realm. The sequence of physical events that count as the NDE has a special property: it exemplifies, or "tells," a story. This story elicits a certain sort of reaction—an experience of awe and wonder—in the individual having an NDE. There is a match between the story and the individual's emotional templates, in virtue of which the story elicits these kinds of reactions. Being aware that another individual has had an NDE with its characteristic story can also elicit an emotional reaction in the observer.

We can understand the remarkable and profound significance of NDEs in a way parallel to our understanding of the sublime beauty of the Grand Canyon or a sunset over the Pacific Ocean. The Grand Canyon and sunset are physical, but this in no way diminishes their meaning to human beings. LSD experiences are physical, but they can be spiritually deep and transformative in remarkable ways. NDEs can be placed in our physical world, but this would not render them without meaning or diminish their transformative power. Sometimes naturalism is equated with a certain deflating "reductionism," which seems to drain NDEs of their beauty and meaning. But this is no truer of NDEs than of the Grand Canyon or a sunset over the Pacific. A naturalist seeks to *situate* awe, not *eliminate* it.

How exactly does the story of a voyage to the unknown, guided by benevolent authorities (or parental figures), help to explain the diminished death anxiety and, indeed, serenity in the contemplation of death? Perhaps we feel that a benevolent authority would not lead us into a dark or unpleasant status, but we can't be sure of this, since our parents sometimes need to take us to the dentist or, worse yet, to the hospital for difficult treatments.

Rather than providing assurance about the ultimate destination, they tell the story of solidarity and loving guidance along the path forward, wherever that will lead us. We do not face the next part of our journey alone. Kate Bowler writes, summarizing findings of the Near Death Experience Research Foundation:

> Thousands of people were interviewed about their brushes with death in every kind of situation—being in a car accident, giving birth, attempting suicide, et cetera—and many descriptions described the same [odd] thing: love.[12]

A supernaturalistic interpretation of NDEs helps to assuage our worries. I have offered a different way of interpreting the stories NDEs tell. They are stories of loving companionship and guidance. This naturalistic interpretation *also* offers comfort in the face an uncertain future, and it can thus help in terror management.[13]

NDEs tell stories of love in the face of perhaps the most terrifying challenge: death. These stories resonate with us, comfort us, and transform us. Narratives reach our emotions; their power does not depend on the literal truth of the events depicted. The supernaturalist interpretation of NDEs is like a Hollywood love story: after all the joys and obstacles of life, we live happily forever after. We want happy endings, and we are deeply attracted to these stories. But the naturalistic story also points to a happy ending. It is a different kind of love story, but no less profound. It is the story of love in the face of the unknown.

It is important that my claim is *not* simply that NDEs help us to see the point about solidarity and love. They do not just issue in a new piece of information. Rather, the stories they tell give us an *emotional* understanding of this point. They get us to see it via a story, and thus we do not just have cognitive understanding, but an affective grasp of the insight. It is a deeper kind of understanding, one that combines the intellectual with the emotional—explanation and storytelling.

---

12. Kate Bowler, *Everything Happens for a Reason and Other Lies I've Loved* (New York: Random House, 2018).

13. As I pointed out in Chapter Two, Ernest Becker introduced the term "terror management theory."

I am not an NDE denier. Does this force me to be a supernatural-ist? No. I hold that NDEs are real in the sense that people really have them, but not in the sense that they (literally construed) are accurate depictions of the external world. The stories and transformative power of NDEs can be explained without invoking supernaturalism. To unlock their magic, we have to understand the stories NDEs tell. Thus, I am an NDE realist, just as I am an immortality realist. The middle ground allows us to be respectful of the reality of NDEs without accepting the literal accuracy of their contents. An NDE is a spandrel—a welcome spandrel that shakes the snow globe.

Annotated Suggestions for Further Reading

A good description of the transformational effects of NDEs is in Pim van Lommel's research: *Consciousness beyond Life: The Science of the Near-Death Experience* (New York: HarperOne, 2010). Oliver Sacks's book, *Hallucinations* (New York: Alfred A. Knopf, 2012) contains a discussion of an LSD trip as reported to Sacks. Don Lattin discusses the group of psychologists at Harvard, including Timothy Leary, who did research (firsthand!) on LSD: *The Harvard Psychedelic Club* (New York: HarperOne, 2010). The most comprehensive presentation of the history of research on psychedelics, as well as contemporary work on these substances (also including first-person reports!), is Michael Pollan, *How To Change Your Mind* (New York: Penguin Press, 2018). There is a fascinating discussion of the spiritual experience caused by her stroke in Jill Bolte Taylor, *My Stroke of Insight: A Brain Scientist's Personal Journey* (London: Penguin Books, reprinted in 2009).

As discussed in previous chapters, David Velleman has done seminal (but challenging) work on the nature of narrative explanation. See "Well-Being and Time," *Pacific Philosophical Quarterly* 72 (1991): 48–77, reprinted in John Martin Fischer, ed., *The Metaphysics of Death* (Stanford, CA: Stanford University Press, 1993): 329–357; and "Narrative Explanation," *The Philosophical Review* 112 (2003): 1–25. I seek to build on Velleman's insights in John Martin Fischer, *Our Stories: Essays on Life, Death, and Free Will* (New York: Oxford University Press, 2009).

In this chapter I have relied on John Martin Fischer, "University Professor Lecture: Near-Death Experiences: The Stories They Tell," *Journal of Ethics* 22 (2018): 97–112; and John Martin Fischer and Benjamin Mitchell-Yellin, *Near-Death Experiences: Understanding Visions of the Afterlife* (New York: Oxford University Press, 2016).

CHAPTER 10

....

The Final Chapter

I've had hundreds of people tell me the reason for my [stage-four colon] cancer. Because of my sin. Because of my unfaithfulness. Because God is fair. Because God is unfair. Because of my aversion to Brussels sprouts. I mean, no one is short of reasons. So if people tell you this, make sure you are there when they go through the cruelest moments of their lives, and start offering your own. When someone is drowning, the only thing worse than failing to throw them a life preserver is handing them a reason.

—KATE BOWLER,
Everything Happens for a Reason: And Other Lies I've Loved

....

Brief Overview of the Book (So Far)

We typically (although not always) take premature death to be bad for the individual who dies—especially for those beings (like us) capable of living meaningful lives. I have argued that a meaningful life requires that one be in suitable contact with reality and have the capacity for acting freely. These are prerequisites for writing one's own story. One writes the story of one's life by acting freely, and we can think of the meaning of an individual's life as the content of the story. (No agent writes the story of our species by acting freely, and thus there is no meaning of life in general.) The story of an individual's life has the hallmarks of a narrative, including, most important, meaning holism (meaning time-travel in which events at other times can affect the meaning of events at a certain time).

It is plausible that meaningfulness in life comes from the intersection of subjective attraction and objective attractiveness, as suggested by Susan Wolf. This suggestion is schematic and vague in important ways, but it points us in the right direction. The activities that make our lives more meaningful are recognizable from a perspective outside of our own, and they include important relationships and active engagement with projects that are larger than ourselves (in some suitable sense).

The arguments for nihilism are not compelling. The zoom-out argument takes us to a perspective akin to the view from outer space. But outer space has no gravity, and untethered objects and persons float away. Philosophical outer space is like that; when we abstract away from details that matter, we lose the proper perspective. From our more rooted, grounded perspective, life is a rich texture of meaning-conferring activities and projects.

Many of us fear death, and sometimes this fear is a central fact of our lives. But when we think carefully about death, it is puzzling how it can be a bad thing for the deceased. She's not around anymore. If it were not a bad thing, it would seem that we shouldn't fear death at all. The puzzles about death's badness give rise to a strategy pioneered by Epicurus for alleviating our anxieties about death (given a secular framework).

The Epicurean contends that death cannot be a bad thing for the individual who dies, because there is no individual left to be the subject of this purported misfortune. The Epicurean dictum is as follows: when death is, the person is not, and when the person is, death is not.

On the secular view, death (the status of being dead, not the process of dying) involves no unpleasant experiences on the part of the individual who dies, and thus the Epicurean contends that it cannot be bad for her. Also, unlike other harms, it doesn't seem that there is a time at which the badness of death occurs. Further, as Lucretius pointed out, death and the time before we were born appear to be metaphysically symmetric: they are both extended periods of nonexistence, and late birth and early death appear to be parallel deprivations—mirror images. Given this metaphysical symmetry, it seems that we should have psychological symmetry—symmetric attitudes toward these two periods. Since we don't regret the time before we were born, we should not deem death a bad thing for the individual who dies. For these reasons, the Epicurean contends that death cannot be a bad thing for an individual, and if so, then there is nothing to fear.

I suppose it would be nice if these Epicurean points were uncontroversial and decisive, since they would provide comfort. But this may be wishful thinking. We have considered ways of responding to the

Epicureans, many of which are quite cogent. Various things can be bad for an individual, even though he doesn't have negative experiences as a result: experience is not all there is to harm or badness (just as it is not all there is to goodness). It is unclear that it is necessary to specify the time of death's badness, but in any case there are viable options, especially subsequentism and atemporalism. Similarly, we have seen that there are attractive strategies for responding to Lucretius's Mirror Image Argument: the Parfit-style response, which appeals to a reasonable psychological asymmetry (we care about the future in a way in which we don't care about the past), the asymmetry of (plausible) possibility response (it is relatively easy to imagine a later death, but hard to imagine an early birth), and the preference-thwarting response (death thwarts preferences, while late birth does not).

So why is death bad for the individual who dies, when it is indeed bad? Typically, premature death is bad because it *both* deprives the individual of good experiences in the future (as part of an, on balance, good continuation of life), and it thwarts preferences to pursue projects that give meaning to life. When only one condition is met (as with non-human animals), death is bad to some extent; when both are met (as with many human beings), death is bad in an unqualified sense. Epicurean skepticism about the badness of death is not persuasive.

It is not surprising that the badness of death is specified in part in terms of the thwarting of certain kinds of preferences—preferences that are "categorical," and thus propel the individual into the future. These are preferences to pursue projects that, we have seen, give meaning to life. The analysis of meaning in life thus helps to explain why death is bad, when it is bad. This analysis also helps in evaluating immortality: when one's projects run out, immortality is not attractive, as Elina Makropolis discovered.

It is difficult to vanquish our *fear* of death. We fear more than just pain. Surely the thought that I will not exist at all is at least daunting, if not frightening. Even so, it would not follow that it would be rational to fear death so much that it gets in the way of leading our lives—to be preoccupied with this fear. Although the Epicureans sought to eliminate *all* fear of death, it is more reasonable simply to reduce excessive and pathological fear of death. After all, if it is a bad, it is very different from boredom or torture. We can take at least some consolation from this.

Jeffrie Murphy distinguishes between a fear of the fact that we will die *at some point* and the fear of *premature* death.[1] He points out that a fear of premature death can lead us (for example) to take steps to achieve greater health, and thus this fear can be rational. Fear is not by its very nature irrational, and fear of a premature death could be rational. A fear that paralyzed us, and prevented us from protecting our health and thriving, would be irrational. We could accept this insight, and we might reinterpret the Epicurean as chipping away at our dread of death, keeping it manageable. Even if death is bad and worthy of *some* fear, the insight that we will not suffer could damp down the fear, allowing us to live in the face of death.

Murphy holds that *only* a fear of *premature* death can be rational. But I believe that at least *some* fear of death *itself* is not unreasonable. This is because death robs us of a point of view; it robs us of ourselves. We are not there to suffer, because we are not there at all. That itself is frightening. It is not just premature death that is frightening; the fact we will die, sooner or later, is scary too.

If death is indeed bad and to be feared (at least to some extent), would immortality be good? From the beginning of human existence, we have had a profoundly ambiguous attitude toward immortality. Gruman distinguished between prolongevists and apologists. I have proposed a related, but slightly different, distinction between immortality optimists and curmudgeons. (This refinement is rendered necessary by imminent environmental crises.) We considered a panoply of arguments by the curmudgeons, but, although reasonable people can disagree, I find none of them persuasive.

I do not, however, embrace immortality optimism. Rather, I think that the most reasonable view is in the middle: immortality realism. The immortality realist does not believe that basic facts of human character and our nature imply that immortal human life is either incoherent or undesirable. The picture is not that bleak, but neither is it rosy. The immortality realist does not accept the optimist's view that it is more likely than not that we will be able to sustain the environmental conditions required for a good immortal life (even a medically immortal life). The immortality

---

1. Jeffrie G. Murphy, "Rationality and the Fear of Death," *The Monist* 59 (1976): 187–203; reprinted in John Martin Fischer, ed., *The Metaphysics of Death* (Stanford, CA: Stanford University Press, 1993): 43–58.

realist has a healthy fear for the future of the human race—a fear that can help to galvanize us to action to save our planet. It is a rational fear, but not despair. In some ways it is parallel to an individual's rational fear of premature death—the fear of a premature death of the species is based in real worries, and it can energize one in efforts to achieve better health.

There are different routes to immortality: secular and religious. Some think that near-death experiences (NDEs) are a portal into immortality in the religious sense. They adopt supernaturalism, according to which our minds are nonphysical and grasp a heavenly realm in NDEs. We canvassed a suite of arguments for supernaturalism, but found them unconvincing. I do not however embrace NDE denialism (the view that people do not have the NDEs they report). I believe that people *really have* NDEs with the contents they report, but that these contents are not necessarily literal and accurate depictions of external reality. I am an NDE realist. The NDE realist can explain the awe-inspiring and transformative capacities of NDEs by reference to a story that these experiences tell—a story that does not imply or presuppose supernaturalism (but is compatible with it).

The story NDEs tell is a story of loving guidance. In facing the most daunting part of our journey—from life to death—we are not alone. The social nature of humanity has been a theme of this book. We find meaning in life in part through pursuing activities that can be seen to be valuable from a perspective outside ourselves. These activities include love, friendship, and accomplishments that are appreciated by others in a lasting way. We are thus not alone in the space of meaning and the projects that matter to us.

Another theme of the book is the key idea of stories or narratives. We started by suggesting that only free creatures can write a life story. Later we filled in the notion of a story by highlighting three features: having a structure involving an ending, engagement with the emotions, and meaning holism. We saw that an immortal life could at least have the latter two. We have also told the story of an NDE in a way that does not require supernaturalism.

I have sought the middle ground in various debates. I defended a view "in between" the extreme views that death is to be dreaded and that it is not to be feared at all. I have also found immortality realism the most plausible position. The curmudgeons are immortality grouches, whereas optimists are immortality Pollyannas. Nobody wants to spend time with a grouch, or, for that matter, a perky Pollyanna. As usual, the truth is in between. As with immortality realism, NDE realism is a middle ground that is more appealing than the two extremes: NDE denialism and NDE supernaturalism.[2]

These compromises might seem like a bowl of mushy metaphysical oatmeal. But threading the needle can sometimes crystallize the wisdom of the opposing sides without the excess baggage of each. It can allow us to be more nuanced in our views. Gautama Buddha endorsed a Middle Way in his sermon in the Deer Park at Benares. He renounced the extremes of excessive sensual indulgence and self-abnegation. He thus achieved enlightenment.[3] The middle ground is often the path of wisdom.

Dying Well

Advances in sanitation and medicine have led to a doubling of the average life expectancy in developed Western nations in the last century. But as we develop medicines and medical technology that can keep elderly people alive longer and longer, there is the danger that this added life is not good. Often the person is stuck in a hospital or other nursing-care facility, and the quality of life is poor. Sherwin Nuland, MD, writes about a very ill woman under his care, for whom he ordered high-tech means of seeking to prolong life:

> No matter her lack of family, the nurses and I could have seen to it that she did not die alone . . . Instead, she suffered the fate of so many of today's hospitalized dying, which is to be separated from reality by the very biotechnology and professional standards that are meant to return people to a meaningful life.
>
> The beeping and squealing monitors, the hissings of respirators and pistoned mattresses, the flashing multicolored electronic signals—the whole technological panoply is background for the tactics by which we are deprived of the tranquility we have every right to hope for, and separated from those few who would not let us die alone.[4]

---

2. NDE reports are not (necessarily) malarkey (recall the discussion in Chapter Eight, footnote 8, of the hoax involving the Malarkey family), nor are they indisputably accurate descriptions of trips to heaven and back.

3. Speaking of oatmeal, the Buddha's wisdom is echoed in the wisdom of Goldilocks: not too much porridge, not too little, not too hot, not too cold . . . but just right.

4. Sherwin Nuland, *How We Die: Reflections on Life's Final Chapter* (New York: Alfred A. Knopf, 1994): 253–254.

Many, including physicians who are intimately familiar with the process of dying, have emphasized the importance of taking a close look at where our life-prolonging technology has brought us.[5] They point out that heroic efforts to prolong life in the "final chapter" often lead to sterility and loneliness, and they can deprive the individual of the opportunity to die in a humane and dignified way. It is not always better to engage in attempts to prolong life. As Nuland puts it, "I speak . . . of the useless vanity that lies in attempts to fend off the certainties that are necessary ingredients of the human condition."[6] Echoing the arguments of the immortality curmudgeons (especially Scheffler's argument from the stages of human life [discussed in Chapter Six] and the similar Banquet Argument presented by Lucretius and referred to in Chapter Six), Nuland writes:

> When it is accepted that there are clearly defined limits to life, then life will be seen to have a symmetry . . . There is a framework of living into which all pleasures and accomplishments fit—and pain, too. Those who would live beyond their nature-given span lose their framework . . .[7]

It is not just the very final chapter of our lives that needs to be reevaluated. We also need to consider our treatment of people as they approach this chapter. In *Being Mortal* Atul Gawande makes a strong case that life for the elderly is too "medicalized" and sterile; he contends that we need to rethink living arrangements for older people so that they are able to lead more active, robust lives, connected to activities and people they love.[8] (Recall that these activities involve the kinds of projects that give meaning to life.)

I agree that there is a pressing need to re-evaluate our ways of treating older people—our "warehousing" approach to long-term care and our aggressive efforts to prolong life at almost any cost. Haider Warraich quotes another doctor who in 1960 described nursing homes and their

---

5. Nuland, *How We Die*; Atul Gawande, MD, *Being Mortal: Medicine and What Matters in the End* (New York: Metropolitan Books, 2014); Haider Warraich, MD, *Modern Death: How Medicine Changed the End of Life* (New York: St. Martin's Press, 2017); and Stephen Cave, *Immortality: The Quest to Live Forever and How It Drives Civilization* (New York: Crown, 2012).

6. Nuland, *How We Die*, 87.

7. Nuland, *How We Die*, 87.

8. Gawande, *Being Mortal*.

predecessors, geriatric units in hospitals, as "forbidding when viewed from [a] distance." The doctor went on to say, "[T]he long wards with their regular lines of closely placed beds, oddly mimic the silent mounds in the neighboring cemetery."[9] In terms of our discussion of boredom in Chapter Seven, we could say that these institutions, by their very nature, move people inexorably toward a blank slate and white noise. As such, they can lead to profound boredom and alienation from life. No wonder we dread living in these places. As our connections to colleagues and loved ones are severed, and our capacity to be active in the world is squashed, our lives are robbed of meaning, and all we are left with is ourselves (as Scheffler put it).

We need to find more humane ways of allowing older people to thrive, and not simply wait for death. We should enable, not constrain them. And we need to recognize that not all efforts to prolong life are worthwhile; the medical impetus to increase longevity in the face of deteriorating quality of life must be tempered. I agree that we need to pause before we employ aggressive means to prolong life as we approach these limits. We must reflect on whether these efforts are worthwhile. In some situations they will be, in others not. Given the limits to the human lifespan, it is important to age gracefully and accept our condition with serenity and wisdom.[10]

Wisdom and grace require us to accept our condition, insofar as it is fixed and immutable. As we currently live our lives, we know that we cannot expect to live much past ninety years (at the most). Let's call the perspective from which we hold fixed (roughly) our current expectation of lifespan the "constrained perspective." We need to adopt this perspective in living our lives—in facing obstacles and challenges, striving to achieve as much as we can, and accepting our limitations. In adopting this perspective, we accept the "framework" of our lives (roughly as it is currently), and we aspire to live courageously, with wisdom and grace,

---

9. Warraich, *Modern Death*, 45.

10. Betty Freidan, *The Fountain of Aging* (New York: Simon and Schuster, 1993); Lynne Segal, *Out of Time: The Pleasures and Perils of Aging* (London: Verso, 2013); and Barbara Ehrenreich, *Natural Causes* (New York: Hatchette Book Group, 2018) all make the case for a graceful acceptance of aging and mortality. They also point to the wisdom we acquire in maturity. These arguments complement those of Nuland, Gawande, Warraich, and Cave. Some people seek the Fountain of Youth; others embrace the Fountain of Aging. Averaging it out, maybe life is a fountain, after all!

within this framework. We can thus write the final chapter of our lives with dignity, and we can be models for our children, grandchildren, and others. You might say that the constrained perspective is "rooted"—rooted in human life as we lead it.

It is also important to see that we can legitimately take another perspective, not constrained by the current limits on our lifespan. We should not take this relatively unconstrained perspective as we live our actual lives, confront challenges, and strive to achieve as much as we can in our limited time. But this does *not* imply that we cannot take the unconstrained perspective when in more reflective moments and contexts. In appropriate contexts we can step back from our current limitations and reflect on whether it would be desirable to seek to change them.

In playing a game, we need to obey its rules. This does not imply that, at least occasionally, we cannot step back and reflect on whether it might be better if the rules were different. Are we in a position to change the rules? We can engage in such reflection from time to time, and then return to playing the game by the extant rules—at least until such time as the rules change, if they ever do.

We should probably not stop to ruminate about changing the rules of the game as we approach the end of it. Similarly, we should not waste our precious time at the end of our lives reflecting on far-fetched ideas about uploading our minds into computers, or asking whether a regimen of medications and vitamins could extend our lives until we can achieve longevity escape velocity. The time for that sort of rumination is over.

A mature human being approaching death is rooted in the reality of finitude. He adopts the constrained perspective. Nuland is clearly right about this. But this does not imply that in certain moments and at certain times of our lives we cannot step back from the constraints and take a more expansive view. Wisdom requires accepting our limitations in appropriate contexts; but it does not counsel a kind of conservatism that would *never in any context* allow reflection on those limitations. We can, and certainly should, distinguish the context of the death bed from the scientific lab or philosopher's study.

Of course, if it were impossible—in a very strong sense—to change the rules of life (at least our average expectation of lifespan), it would not be particularly interesting or fruitful to reflect on life from the unconstrained perspective. Why bother? Nuland contends that it is indeed impossible for human beings to extend our lifespan much past the current expectation:

> Whether the result of wear, tear, and exhaustion of resources or whether genetically programmed, all life has a finite span and each species has its own particular longevity. For human beings, this would appear to be approximately 100 to 110 years. This means that even were it possible to prevent or cure every disease that carries people off before the ravages of senescence do, virtually no one would live beyond a century or a bit more.[11]

He asserts that medical immortality could only last about 100 to 110 years. This is a very different view from that of Aubrey de Grey and others. Recall that de Grey argues that if we can figure out how to clean up the "garbage" in our bodies created by metabolism, we can live for thousands of years (if we are not run over by a truck or . . .). Some researchers take seriously the possibility of a medical immortality that is considerably longer than 100 to 110 years, but I am not in a position to make a helpful contribution here. It is a matter of science, not philosophy.

If it were at least an open question whether we can achieve a medical immortality of thousands of years, then it would not be inappropriate—in certain contexts—to take the unconstrained perspective and to reflect seriously about the possibility and desirability of such immortality. We can consider these questions without losing our capacity to live a rooted, dignified, realistic life.

It would be a mistake to suppose that we must always take the constrained perspective; this would lead to an undesirable narrowness of vision. As I pointed out in Chapter Six, if people at the beginning of the twentieth century didn't dream of greater longevity, we would still be stuck with an average lifespan of forty years. Now it is eighty! It would also be a mistake to think that we should always take the unconstrained perspective; this would eliminate our ability to accept our limitations with grace and wisdom, and to live accordingly. Here again I would encourage a middle path. We are concrete organisms but also reflective beings, and thus we can take a perspective appropriate to the context. We can gracefully accept our limitations, but also think seriously and creatively about our path forward. We can live rich, rooted lives, fully

---

11. Nuland, *How We Die*, 84.

present to others and ourselves, without giving up the ambition to push the frontiers of human life ever outward.[12]

The Epicureans tried to convince us that death itself, the state of being dead, cannot be a bad thing for the individual who dies. We know, however, that dying can be a bad thing. In particular, our modern way of extending life can issue in sterility and loneliness, when we most need loving companionship. I have suggested that the story told by NDEs includes travel to the unknown, guided by a loving parent. What is crucial in this story is *not* a supernatural destination or beings. It is loving companionship in the voyage into the unknown. We do not need to believe in the literal reality of supernatural realms or beings in order to understand the story of NDEs and to learn from it. NDEs highlight and deepen the insights of Nuland, Gawande, Warraich, Cave, and so many others: we need not travel to the boundary of the unknown *alone*.[13]

As philosophers from Aristotle to the present have emphasized, human beings are social animals.[14] We sometimes want solitude— no doubt. But even notorious lone wolves have beloved families and

---

12. The distinction between the unconstrained and constrained perspectives is similar to that between the zoom-out and zoom-in perspectives discussed in Chapter One. Note that the zoom-out perspective is more extreme than the unconstrained perspective; from the latter we can still see the details of human life. Here, as in our previous discussions of meaning and autonomy, it is important to see that we, unlike (other) animals, have the capacity to take various different perspectives on life (and the world).

13. In his article in *The Los Angeles Times*, Bill Plashke describes the "No One Dies Alone Program," a nationwide service that offers companionship to dying patients: Bill Plashke, "The End Tone," *The Los Angeles Times* (August 12, 2018): D1, D8. The volunteers in this program are always "on call." When they are called, they rush to the hospital to be there with dying patients until their families, loved ones, or friends can arrive. The article describes the participation of a famous sports broadcaster in Southern California. A family arrived at the hospital to see him holding the hand of a member of their family, and saying to her, "It's OK . . . I'm right here . . . You're not alone" (D1). He also described himself as a "guide" in the individual's continued path forward.

14. We are social animals, but not "supersocial" animals, such as ants, bees, and termites. Our social nature implies that meaning in life is enhanced by social activities and relationships. But autonomy is also necessary for meaning in life—for writing our own story. That we have autonomy implies that we are not supersocial. It also explains why we can't easily relate to science fiction portrayals of future "hive selves": John Martin Fischer and Ruth Curl, "Philosophical Models of Immortality in Science Fiction," in George Slusser, Gary Westfahl, and Eric S. Rabkin, eds., *Immortal Engines: Life Extension and Immortality in Science Fiction* (Athens: University of Georgia Press, 1996): 3–12; reprinted in Fischer, *Our Stories*, 93–101.

friends: Henry David Thoreau had Ralph Waldo Emerson. (Wolves travel in packs!) Our treatment of the elderly increasingly recognizes the fact that we don't want to die alone. NDEs are profound in part because they metaphorically capture this idea. NDEs are transformative because they make us more "prosocial." Perhaps one of the specific ways in which NDEs can point us to a better future is by encouraging the development of more humane care as we approach the end of our lives.

NDEs do not *just* represent (in their explicit content) a portal to the afterlife—a glimpse into what it will be like when we are dead (i.e., in the state of being dead). We noted in Chapter Two that "death" can either refer to the state of being dead or the process of dying. If we interpret the stories of NDEs in the way I have suggested—as a journey guided by a loving parental figure—then we can also see NDEs as giving us a glimpse of *dying*.

As such, they teach us the importance of loving companionship. This should be further impetus to continue to change our sterile practices of extending life in hospitals and other institutions, away from family and loved ones. NDEs are fascinating and multifaceted phenomena, and this interpretation connects them to end-of-life care in an illuminating way. There was wisdom in the traditional practice of dying surrounded by family and loved ones. Companionship, solidarity in the face of the unknown, and love should surround us in the final chapter.

Annotated Suggestions for Further Reading

Some important explorations of contemporary ways of treating older people, including living arrangements for "seniors," nursing homes, and end-of-life care are found in Sherwin Nuland, MD, *How We Die: Reflections on Life's Final Chapter* (New York: Alfred A. Knopf, 1994); Atul Gawande, MD, *Being Mortal: Medicine and What Matters in the End* (New York: Metropolitan Books, 2014); Haider Warraich, MD, *Modern Death: How Medicine Changed the End of Life* (New York: St. Martin's Press, 2017); and Stephen Cave, *Immortality: The Quest to Live Forever and How It Drives Civilization* (New York: Crown, 2012). In light of the prospects of the infirmities and deterioration of old age, and our current practices of extending life in sterile institutional settings, Ezekial J. Immanuel expresses the hope that he will not live past seventy-five years of age: "Why I Hope to Die at 75," The Atlantic 2014; available at TheAtlantic.com.

Three moving memoirs about dying are Christopher Hitchens, *Mortality* (New York: Twelve, 2012); Paul Kalinithi, MD, *When Breath Becomes Air* (New York: Random House, 2016); and Cory Taylor, *Dying: A Memoir*

(Edinburgh, UK: Cannongate Books, 2017). Such memoirs tell us what the authors value about life, as well as how they approach dying (and death). Kate Boller's book about confronting death, and the lessons for living life, is insightful and even amusing: *Everything Happens for a Reason: And Other Lies I've Loved* (New York: Random House, 2018). She is still alive and thriving, despite a diagnosis of stage-four cancer. (She has benefitted from an experimental therapy.)

Roger Rosenblatt writes about the aftermath of losing his daughter to cancer in *Making Toast* (New York: HarperCollins, 2010). The philosopher of religion Nicholas Wolterstorff struggles with the loss of his son in a rock-climbing accident in *Lament for a Son* (Grand Rapids, MI: William B. Eerdmans, 1987). Joshua Glasgow provides a humane and illuminating analysis of the value status of death in the context of the imminent death of his mother in *The Solace* (forthcoming, Oxford University Press).

An early analysis of the funeral industry in the United States is found in Jessica Mitford, *The American Way of Death* (New York: Simon and Schuster, 1963). Mary Roach, in *Stiff: The Curious Lives of Human Cadavers* (New York: W.W. Norton and Company, 2003), discusses our ways of dealing with dead bodies. In a more recent discussion, Bess Lovejoy, *Rest in Pieces: The Curious Lives of Famous Corpses* (New York: Simon and Schuster, 2016), begins by writing: "A corpse is always a problem, both for the living and for the dead."

A nascent movement among funeral directors and others associated with funerals, memorial services, and the treatment of the body after death, encourages us to explore less "sterile" and "institutionalized" forms of memorializing the dead. One salient group proposes "green burials," in which the family cleans and prepares the body for burial in an environmentally friendly way. This would be a way in which we would be coming home, very literally. We have seen that birth and death are "bookends" to our lives, and Lucretius recommended a certain symmetry in our attitudes pertaining to the time before birth and after death. The increasing interest in green burials and natural childbirths ("home-births") brings out a way in which our attitudes toward birth and death are in important ways symmetric. Green burials are the mirror images of home-births.

For an interesting "travelogue" of sorts highlighting different funeral practices throughout the world, see Caitlin Doughty, *From Here to Eternity: Traveling the World to Find the Good Death* (New York: W.W. Norton, 2017). This is helpful on green and "alternative" burials. Doughty is a "death-positive" mortician, and she has a series on YouTube ("Ask the Mortician"). She's also prominent in the Order of the Good Death (http://www.orderofthegooddeath.com/), a death-positive advocacy group. The death-positive view emphasizes the possibility of a good death—dying well—as opposed to the sterile and institutionalized deaths of the contemporary world.

End Game, a 2018 documentary film directed by Rob Epstein and Jeffrey Friedman, discusses the Zen Hospice Project (associated with the University of California, San Francisco Medical School). The Zen Hospice Guest House—a peaceful and inviting place—is a model of humane end-of-life treatment.

"Death cafés" have also helped to "humanize death"; these are informal "salons" that have sprung up all over the United States and Europe: Jack Fong, *The Death Café Movement: Exploring the Horizons of Mortality* (Basingstoke, UK: Palgrave Macmillan, 2017). The first chapter of this book is called "Death and Coffee." One can look at all of these "alternative burial" practices as bringing death "down to earth"—sorry! This is similar to much of the humor about death. The idea is that as death becomes more "familiar"—a topic of coffee conversation—it becomes less frightening.

For an alternative approach to memorializing the dead, see Candi K. Cann, *Virtual Afterlives: Grieving the Dead in the Twenty-First Century* (Lexington: University Press of Kentucky, 2015). Cann charts out many of the online ways of maintaining a presence after one has died, including archives, videos, avatars, and so forth. In the future, one's avatar might be able to "give advice" to one's grand- or great-grandchildren. Already various cemeteries, including the (in)famous Hollywood Forever have video archives you can visit. It is interesting that approaches to memorializing the dead divide (like strategies for achieving immortality) into a biological ("meat-puppet) and cybernetic ("robo-cop") model.

The Institute for Death and Society at the University of Bath, United Kingdom, is pursuing a broad range of issues about death, dying, and society. The DeathLab at Columbia University is exploring memorialization practices in urban contexts, where space is limited. The philosopher Michael Cholbi is the founding president of the International Association for the Philosophy of Death and Dying, which hosts a biennial conference in which philosophers present papers on these topics.

Readers who have got this far—congratulations!—may be ready to tackle some more challenging material: Jeff McMahan, *The Ethics of Killing: Problems at the Margins of Life* (New York: Oxford University Press, 2002); F.M. Kamm, *Morality, Mortality Volume I: Death and Whom to Save from It* (New York: Oxford University Press, 1998); and *Morality, Mortality Volume II: Rights, Duties, and Status* (New York: Oxford University Press, 2001) and *Creation and Abortion: A Study in Moral and Legal Philosophy* (New York: Oxford University Press, 1992); and Ronald Dworkin, *Life's Dominion: An Argument about Abortion, Euthanasia, and Individual Freedom* (New York: Vintage, 2013). These important works exhibit the connections between complex metaphysical and ethical issues pertaining to death.

INDEX

....

Twain, Mark, 132n20, 135
Tyndale House (publisher), 147n8

Van Lommel, Pim, 144

Wagner, Richard, 110
Walton, Gregory M., 11n15
Warraich, Haider, 189–190,
    190n10, 193
Warren, James, 45n26
Warren, Rick, 8–9, 8n11
weak experience requirement, 52–59
Weiner, Jonathan, 88–89, 90

Whitney, Helen, 106n9
Williams, Bernard, 25, 81–82, 96–97,
    97n36, 102–103, 118, 121–123, 130
wisdom, 190–191
Wolf, Susan, 4, 7, 12–15, 21, 23,
    183–184
Wolpe, David, 40n17
Wordplay (film), 14n20
Wrathall, Mark, 102n2

Yalom, Irving, 42n20

zoom-out argument, 17, 184, 193n12